Walking Washington, D.C.

WALKING WASHINGTON, D.C.

30 treks to the newly revitalized capital's cultural icons, natural spectacles, urban treasures, and hidden gems

Barbara J. Saffir

Walking Washington, D.C.: 30 treks to the newly revitalized capital's cultural icons, natural spectacles, urban treasures, and hidden gems

Project editor: Holly Cross; proofreader: Emily Beaumont; indexer: Ann Cassar
Cover and interior photos: copyright © by Barbara J. Saffir, except where noted
Author photo: copyright © by Steve Heap
Cartographer: Steve Jones
Original cover and interior design: Larry B. Van Dyke and Lisa Pletka

Library of Congress Cataloging-in-Publication Data

Saffir, Barbara J.
Walking Washington, D.C. : 30 treks to the newly revitalized capital's cultural icons, natural spectacles, urban treasures, and hidden gems / Barbara J. Saffir.
pages cm
Includes index.
ISBN 978-0-89997-765-2—ISBN 0-89997-765-0—ISBN 978-0-89997-766-9 (eISBN)
1. Washington (D.C.)—Guidebooks. 2. Walking—Washington (D.C.)—Guidebooks. I. Title.
F192.3.S228 2015
917.5304'44—dc23
2015008838

Manufactured in the United States of America

Published by: **WILDERNESS PRESS**
An imprint of Keen Communications, LLC
2204 First Avenue South, Suite 102
Birmingham, AL 35233
800-443-7227; fax 205-326-1012
wildernesspress.com

Distributed by Publishers Group West

Cover photos: *Front, clockwise from top left:* Blue crabs at seafood market on Southwest Waterfront, The White House from Lafayette Park, Library of Congress, U.S. Capitol, Washington National Cathedral, Franciscan Monastery, aerial view of The National Mall. *Back, top to bottom:* Yards Park bridge, giant panda at Smithsonian National Zoological Park, Japanese stone lantern and cherry trees at Tidal Basin.

Frontispiece: Supreme Court (see Walk 23, Capitol Hill)

SAFETY NOTICE Although Wilderness Press and the author have made every attempt to ensure that the information in this book is accurate at press time, they are not responsible for any loss, damage, injury, or inconvenience that may occur to anyone while using this book. You are responsible for your own safety and health while following the walking trips described here. Always check local conditions, know your own limitations, and consult a map.

Dedication

To the late and great David Broder. As "Dean of the Washington Press Corps" and my former boss at *The Washington Post*, he inspired me with his old-fashioned "shoe-leather" reporting and journalistic integrity.

Acknowledgments

Since I aimed to create a holistic guidebook rather than an ordinary tourist book—with a schmear of nature; a spattering of architecture; and a sprinkling of politics, pop culture, and spies—I especially appreciated all the diverse folks who shared their time and expertise. A special thanks to everyone at Wilderness Press and Keen Communications, including Holly Cross, Susan Haynes, Tim W. Jackson, Steve Jones, Scott McGrew, Molly Merkle, Liliane Opsomer, Bob Sehlinger, and Tanya Sylvan. Thanks to Jeannette, Anne, Becky, and Laura for their support; Sharon and Art for their insiders' tours; the District of Columbia Public Library's Jerry McCoy; Destination DC; Cultural Tourism DC; the Historical Society of Washington, D.C.; Kenilworth Park & Aquatic Gardens' Douglas Rowley and Robert Steele; geologists Callan Bentley, David Prowell, Elizabeth O. Doyle, and Tony Fleming; the District Department of the Environment's Daniel Rauch; the OSS Society's Charles Pinck; the National Security Agency's Louis J. Leto and Jennifer Wilcox; surveyor Joe Snider; historians Michael R. Harrison and David Rotenstein; Architect of the Capitol Curator Barbara Wolanin; and the region's volunteer hike leaders (including fellow author Paul Elliott), who lead group treks to encourage healthy and happy walking.

Author's Note

I devised these routes to entice newcomers as well as the most jaded Washingtonians. Hopefully the lesser-known "fun facts" I discovered will help convert our sometimes cold capital from a mere acquaintance into a warm friend.

Numbers on this locator map correspond to Walk numbers.

Table of Contents

INTRODUCTION

Welcome to your kinetic capital. Washington, D.C., is every American's—and every freedom lover's—home away from home. To feel more at home, please lace up your most comfortable walking shoes (it makes a huge difference); open your eyes, your heart, and your mind; and have a ball discovering or rediscovering the District, which keeps growing and getting better. Just since I arrived in the mid-1980s, Washington has transformed. It used to be a staid, government-centric "company town" with a monolithic beige, white, and gray cityscape; many crime-plagued neighborhoods; and only a handful of yummy restaurants. Now it's a diverse, high-tech foodie's paradise, with more eye-popping neighborhoods and safer streets.

Since D.C. is a compact city with terrific public transportation, it's easy to explore both its high-profile side and its less famous persona. After walking a few miles, you might fall in love. But even love stories are imperfect. Be careful; like all big cities, D.C. still has crime and other irritations. And books are sometimes imperfect, too, especially in a city that's constantly on the move. Call destinations before you go. If you find any updates needed for our next edition, please email barbarawalkingdcbook@gmail.com.

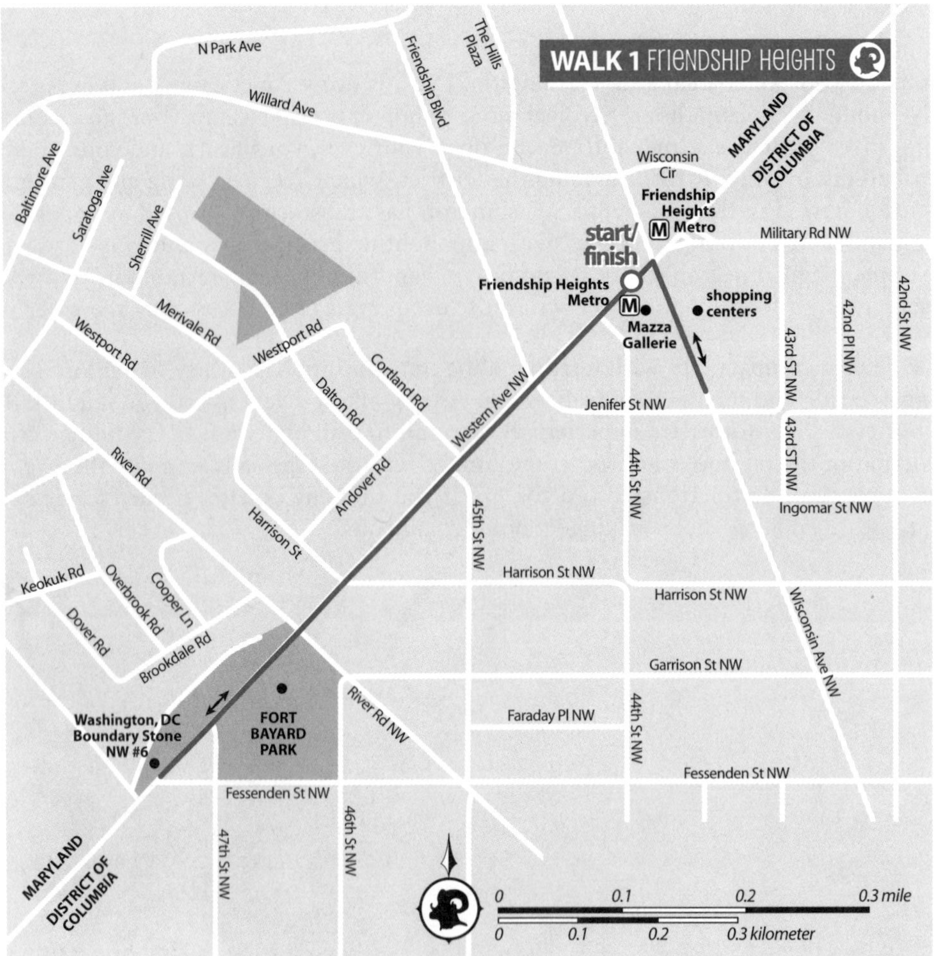
WALK 1 Friendship Heights
N Park Ave
Willard Ave
Friendship Blvd
The Hills Plaza
Baltimore Ave
Saratoga Ave
Sherrill Ave
Merivale Rd
Westport Rd
Westport Rd
Dalton Rd
Cortland Rd
Western Ave NW
Wisconsin Cir
MARYLAND
DISTRICT OF COLUMBIA
Friendship Heights Metro
start/ finish
Military Rd NW
Friendship Heights Metro
Mazza Gallerie
shopping centers
43rd ST NW
42nd Pl NW
42nd St NW
Jenifer St NW
River Rd
Andover Rd
Harrison St
45th St NW
44th St NW
43rd ST NW
Ingomar St NW
Harrison St NW
Harrison St NW
Keokuk Rd
Overbrook Rd
Cooper Ln
Dover Rd
Brookdale Rd
Wisconsin Ave NW
Garrison St NW
Washington, DC Boundary Stone NW #6
FORT BAYARD PARK
River Rd NW
Faraday Pl NW
44th St NW
Fessenden St NW
Fessenden St NW
47th St NW
46th St NW
MARYLAND
DISTRICT OF COLUMBIA
0
0.1
0.2
0.3 mile
0
0.1
0.2
0.3 kilometer

1 Friendship Heights: Baubles and Boundaries

BOUNDARIES: Western Avenue NW, Wisconsin Avenue NW, Jenifer Street NW, and Fessenden Street NW
DISTANCE: 1.5 miles
DIFFICULTY: Easy
PARKING: Limited free and metered street parking, multiple parking garages
PUBLIC TRANSIT: Friendship Heights Metro Station is served by numerous buses.

Tourists don't typically flock to Friendship Heights, but they might if they knew about its disparate trove of treasures. They can buy a bauble or a beaded evening gown and then saunter down a tree-lined road to sample the capital's slowly disappearing history: D.C.'s original boundary markers and a Civil War fort. Most of Washington's boundary stones are still around, but they're typically inaccessible and are slowly disintegrating in the rain, snow, and pollution. But this stone is easy to ogle in a public park. Practically across the street is Fort Bayard. Although no visible remnants remain of this Civil War fort, it's still a green oasis with towering persimmon trees and chirping birds—and it makes one heck of a sledding hill. A whole ring of similar forts once circled the city, modeled after European fortifications of the 17th and 18th centuries. Washington had one lone fort when the Civil War commenced in the spring of 1861. By the war's end four years later, that number had skyrocketed to 68. These days there are more than 68 shops and restaurants around the junction of Wisconsin and Western Avenues.

- **Start at the Metro station on the southwestern side of Western Avenue NW. Unlike most stations, it sports a cool circular foyer with a vaulted ceiling, and "the most important spy you've never heard of" plied her tradecraft there, according to FBI documents and *The Washington Post*. In June 2001, FBI agents tracked Cuban spy Ann Belen Montes when she drove her red Toyota to Friendship Heights. The Defense Intelligence Agency analyst walked to the Metro station to call her handlers on a pay phone. She was arrested September 21 and pled guilty to espionage in 2002 in exchange for a 25-year sentence.**

- **Walk southwest on Western Avenue NW to the Boundary Park Neighborhood Conservation Area. To the right, in a pint-size park, one of Washington's original 40 boundary stones is ensconced in an iron-barred cage. A Maryland historical marker proclaims**

Boundary Stones: From Dust to Dust?

Dying. Washington's oldest federal monuments are dying—of neglect. Forty boundary stones were erected in 1791 and 1792 to mark the original 100-square-mile boundary of the new federal capital. Now all the sandstone monuments still embedded in the ground are decomposing, and several are just little nubs, missing entirely, or have been moved from their original locations. These lesser-known landmarks will be lost forever, unless the government steps in to preserve them permanently.

For the past century, volunteers and other advocates have fought to protect them. In 1915, the Daughters of the American Revolution (DAR) began erecting iron-barred cages around the markers. But at least three fences are missing, one from an inaccessible stone and two on private property, according to the volunteer website, boundarystones.org.

The 40 stones were laid at 1-mile intervals along a 10-mile diamond by surveyor Maj. Andrew Ellicott after the District was selected for the capital by President George Washington. Maryland and Virginia ceded land to form the new capital, but in 1846 Virginia took back its land and its 14 boundary stones along with it.

The DAR still helps individually, and now also as part of a volunteer coalition called the Nation's Capital Boundary Stones Committee. The coalition includes more than two dozen groups, such as the National Park Service, the American Society of Civil Engineers (ASCE), the District Department of Transportation, and the D.C. Surveyor's office. Co-chairman Stephen Powers of ASCE organizes biannual cleanups and is attempting to get the orphan stones recognized as a Historic Civil Engineering Landmark.

When the stones were laid, each was typically 1 foot wide and 4 feet long, except for the 5-foot-long cornerstones, according to a U.S. Geological Survey report. The same Aquia Creek sandstone that the survey stones are made of was also used to build the Capitol and the White House. It was dug from a quarry roughly 40 miles south of D.C. in Stafford County, Virginia. That rock pit is now part of "Government Island," and it's protected as a public park.

that it was erected in 1792. It's called NW #6 because it's 6 miles from the western cornerstone. It marks the dividing line between D.C. and Maryland.

- Reverse direction to walk northeast on Western Avenue NW for Fort Bayard Park on the right. It was named for Brig. Gen. George Dashiell Bayard of the First Pennsylvania Cavalry. The soldiers who lived in its troop barracks defended the important River Road entrance into the city with four 20-pounder Parrott rifles and two 12-pounder field howitzers, the National Park Service says.

- Continue northeast on Western Avenue NW. Just before Wisconsin Avenue NW, turn right into Mazza Gallerie, a keystone of consumerism since 1978. Shoppers can snag a pair of $1,000 boots at Neiman Marcus or pay $100 for a complete outfit at discounter T.J. Maxx.

- Exit Mazza Gallerie and turn right to walk southeast on Wisconsin Avenue NW to the traffic light at Jenifer Street NW. Cross Wisconsin Avenue NW for designer deals on the right at the Nordstrom Rack outlet, Marshalls, and DSW Designer Shoe Warehouse. Inside 5335 Wisconsin Avenue NW is Range, one of several restaurants in the corral of James Beard Foundation Award finalist and TV's *Top Chef* alum Bryan Voltaggio. It serves such delicacies as Muscovy duck rillettes and sweetbreads.

- Continue northwest on Wisconsin Avenue NW to the Metro—or shoppers with Champagne tastes can amble a couple of blocks farther to Chevy Chase, Maryland, to pick up some trinkets at Tiffany & Co., Cartier, Gucci, and other posh stores.

Points of Interest

Friendship Heights Metro Station 5337 Wisconsin Ave. NW, 202-637-7000, wmata.com/rail/station_detail.cfm?station_id=11

Washington, D.C., Boundary Stone NW6 in Boundary Park Neighborhood Conservation Area 5000 Western Ave., Chevy Chase, MD; montgomeryparks.org/parks_facilities_directory/boundarypnca.shtm

Fort Bayard Western Avenue NW and River Road NW, nps.gov/cwdw/historyculture/fort-bayard.htm

Mazza Gallerie 5300 Wisconsin Ave. NW, 202-966-6114, mazzagallerie.com

Shopping Centers 5333 and 5335 Wisconsin Ave. NW

route summary

1. Exit the Metro station at Western and Wisconsin Avenues.
2. Walk southwest on Western Avenue NW.
3. Turn right into Boundary Park Neighborhood Conservation Area.
4. Reverse direction.
5. Turn right into Fort Bayard park.
6. Walk northeast on Western Avenue NW.
7. Turn right just before Wisconsin Avenue NW into Mazza Gallerie.
8. Exit Mazza Gallerie onto Wisconsin Avenue NW.
9. Turn right to continue southeast on Wisconsin Avenue NW for one block.
10. Turn left to cross Wisconsin Avenue NW at Jenifer Street NW.
11. Turn left to head back northwest on Wisconsin Avenue NW.

Shoppers' paradise at Friendship Heights Metro

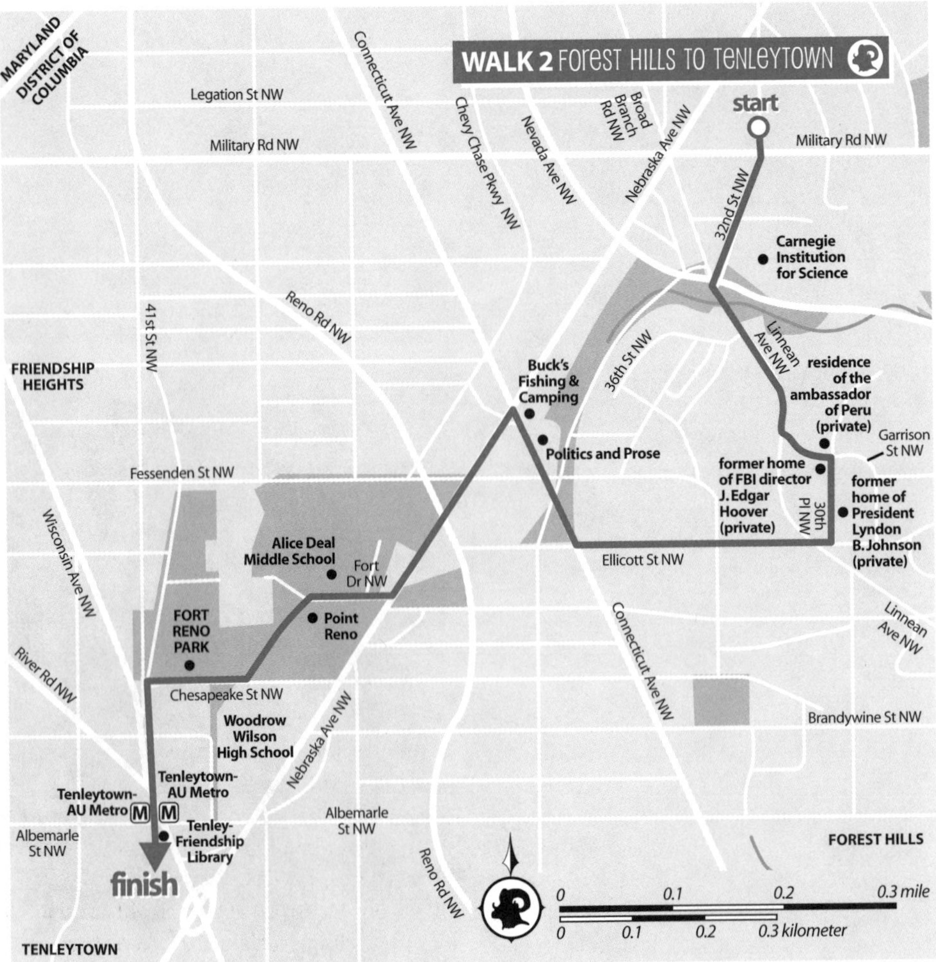

WALK 2 FOREST HILLS TO TENLEYTOWN
MARYLAND
DISTRICT OF COLUMBIA
start
finish
Legation St NW
Military Rd NW
Connecticut Ave NW
Chevy Chase Pkwy NW
Nevada Ave NW
Broad Branch Rd NW
Nebraska Ave NW
32nd St NW
Carnegie Institution for Science
Reno Rd NW
41st St NW
FRIENDSHIP HEIGHTS
36th St NW
Linnean Ave NW
residence of the ambassador of Peru (private)
Buck's Fishing & Camping
Politics and Prose
Garrison St NW
former home of FBI director J. Edgar Hoover (private)
former home of President Lyndon B. Johnson (private)
30th Pl NW
Fessenden St NW
Wisconsin Ave NW
Alice Deal Middle School
Fort Dr NW
Ellicott St NW
FORT RENO PARK
Point Reno
River Rd NW
Chesapeake St NW
Woodrow Wilson High School
Brandywine St NW
Tenleytown-AU Metro
Tenleytown-AU Metro
Tenley-Friendship Library
Albemarle St NW
Albemarle St NW
FOREST HILLS
TENLEYTOWN
0
0.1
0.2
0.3 mile
0.3 kilometer

2 Forest Hills to Tenleytown: Take Me Higher

BOUNDARIES: Military Road NW, 30th Place NW, Albemarle Street NW, and Wisconsin Avenue NW
DISTANCE: 2.3 miles
DIFFICULTY: Easy
PARKING: 2- to 4-hour free street parking along the route, 4-hour meters at Fort Reno
PUBLIC TRANSIT: At start: Metrobuses E2, 3, and 4 (Military Road–Crosstown Line) stop at Military Road NW and 32nd Street NW, connecting the Friendship Heights and Fort Totten Metro stations. At finish: Tenleytown-AU Metro.

It's no Mount Everest. D.C.'s highest natural point is 409 feet, just a tad below Everest's 29,028 feet, the world's highest peak above sea level. But lest anyone rush too soon to explore this natural wonder off busy Wisconsin Avenue NW, begin instead in a ritzy residential corner of D.C. known as Forest Hills. That's where some of the nation's top scientists are studying something much higher: the stars. (The closest star, our sun, orbits about 491 billion feet above our heads.) These scholars work for the renowned Carnegie Institution for Science. Carnegie's Forest Hills campus lies near the sprawling estate of the ambassador of Peru, a country known for its bucket-list hike to 7,970-foot-high Machu Picchu. Along the route are the former home of the country's most powerful FBI director, haunts of novelists and newshounds, a Cold War bunker, and an underground arrest.

- **Start at Military Road NW and 32nd Street NW. Walk south one block on 32nd Street NW under six-story-high willow oak trees for the broad lawn, tan-brick mansion, and observatory of the private Carnegie Institution for Science on the left. Since 1903, the institute has been dedicated to scientific discovery to improve mankind and is one of 23 organizations created by industrialist Andrew Carnegie. Its headquarters is downtown. This 7-acre campus is called the Department of Terrestrial Magnetism. Originally tasked with studying Earth's magnetic field, now its astronomers, astrophysicists, and other scientists are working to discover planets, determine the age and structure of the universe, and investigate the causes of earthquakes and volcanoes. Carnegie's website says its famous researchers have included Edwin Hubble, "who revolutionized astronomy with his discovery that the universe is expanding and that there are galaxies other than our own Milky Way," and Vera Rubin, who confirmed the existence of dark matter in the universe. Carnegie hosts occasional public lectures at both campuses.**

- With Carnegie to the left, continue south on 32nd Street across Broad Branch Road NW, and turn left onto Linnean Avenue NW. Walk uphill and turn left on Garrison Street NW. On the left, the private three-story manor house where Peru's ambassador lives isn't visible from the street, but the gate hints at the history of this 25-acre compound on Rock Creek Park. Two gold coats of arms decorate the gate's black metal bars. The emblem depicts Peru's national animal, a llama-like *vincuña*, a cinchona tree (used to make the antimalarial treatment quinine), and a cornucopia stuffed with coins. On the left stone entrance post, it says "Battery Terrill" for the Civil War fort that once stood there. The ambassador's 16-room colonial revival home was designed in 1928 for Charles and Lida Tompkins, the contractors who built many D.C. landmarks, including the east and west wings of the White House. Peru bought the site in 1944. Incidentally, a U.S. senator put Peru's Machu Picchu on the map. Sen. Hiram Bingham, who lived in Georgetown and "bears a resemblance to the fictional Indiana Jones," discovered the Incan ruins with a team of seven explorers in 1911, the Senate website says.

- Turn right on 30th Place NW, where at least two famous feds once lived. On the right at 4936 is the two-story brick home of Washingtonian J. (for John) Edgar Hoover, who headed the FBI from 1924 until his death in 1972. This lifelong bachelor bequeathed his home to FBI associate director and fellow bachelor Clyde A. Tolson. They are buried near each other at Congressional Cemetery. On the left at 4921 is a similar house, where President Lyndon Baines Johnson lived when he was senator, says the "Forest Hills" guidebook. Immediately after President Kennedy was assassinated, then Vice President Johnson phoned his former neighbor. According to taped conversations posted by Southern California Public Radio, LBJ asked Hoover if any of the three bullets was fired at him. "No," Hoover assured him. LBJ later asked the legendary G-man if he should have a bulletproof limousine. Hoover, who was chauffeured around in one himself, replied, "You most certainly should."

- Turn right on Ellicott Street NW, past more elaborate-looking homes, and then turn right onto a commercial strip of Connecticut Avenue NW. On the right is the purple awning that marks Politics and Prose bookstore and coffeehouse. Started in 1984 by Carla Cohen and Barbara Meade, it seems like every novelist, politician, and journalist who has ever penned a newsworthy tome has conducted a book signing there. The shop is owned by two former *Washington Post* reporters, Bradley Graham and Lissa Muscatine. Muscatine was Hillary Clinton's speechwriter and a spokesperson at the White House and at the State Department. Some of the couple's news colleagues live in the neighborhood. It was also home to muckraker Isidor "Izzy" Feinstein Stone, who wrote an exposé of Hoover's FBI in the 1940s, the *Forest Hills Connection* newsletter says.

- A few doors down on the right is Buck's Fishing & Camping restaurant. Some of the world's most powerful people have dined there, such as (according to the *Post*) Supreme Court justices Elena Kagan and Sonia Sotomayor.

- Turn left on Nebraska Avenue NW. Walk three blocks and turn right on Fort Drive NW. Fort Reno Park is on the left, and Alice Deal Middle School is on the right. Multibillionaire Warren Buffett, a Nebraska native and the fourth-richest person in the world (in 2014), graduated from Deal and Woodrow Wilson High School. He lived in D.C. during his father's six years in the U.S. House of Representatives.

Washingtonians know Fort Reno Park chiefly for its tennis courts, soccer fields, and summer concerts. But it is also a reservoir, with fortifications that have long protected the capital, and it's the apex of Washington. After years of controversy over D.C.'s highest *natural* point due to decades of construction and artificial berming on the hill, the summit was officially declared in 2007. GPS users can reach Point Reno with these coordinates from the Highpointers Club and the District of Columbia Association of Land Surveyors: 38.95198 North and 77.075922 West. Non-techies can start at Fort Drive NW, facing uphill toward the water towers, with the southwestern edge of the school on the right. Turn left onto the gravel trail and walk to the end of the tree line on the left. Make a U-turn and walk back along the opposite side of the trees

The Peruvian coat of arms announces the ambassador's compound.

Fort Reno Park: It's Not Always What It Seems

The castle towers and Tudor-style home that perch atop Fort Reno Park *appear* to be a vestige of America's British roots. But, as the saying goes in our spy-crazed capital, things are not always as they seem. These structures surrounded by a fence are part of the District of Columbia Water and Sewer Authority's water pumping station and reservoirs. The two Norman-style stone water towers were built in 1929, and the flat-top brick water tower in 1903, says Judith Beck Helm's book, *Tenleytown, D.C.* However, the modern-looking brick tower in the adjacent fenced compound conceals a Cold War relic and some 21st-century secrets. The John F. Kennedy Presidential Library says this once top-secret White House Army Signal Agency structure was code-named "Cartwheel." At least part of it was built from 1961 to 1962, when the country was on the brink of a nuclear disaster during the Cuban Missile Crisis, according to the library's online photos. "This was one of several Presidential Emergency Facilities scattered throughout the mid-Atlantic to provide a quick and safe refuge in the event of nuclear war," says historian David S. Rotenstein. Like similar hideaways at Camp David and Mount Weather, this 24/7 bunker provided "communications equipment to handle the continuity of government." Today a sign declares it a communications site for the Federal Aviation Administration, which joined the newly formed Department of Homeland Security after 9/11. During the Civil War, the city's highest point served as a fort. Originally called Fort Pennsylvania, it was built in 1861, but no *apparent* remnants exist.

for roughly 50 steps. Turn right and walk about 16 steps to the small, round, metal survey disk embedded in the middle of a grassy field. When you reach the 409-foot marker, a huge oak tree will be alone downhill to the right.

- **Return to the gravel trail and follow it left to the sidewalk on Chesapeake Street NW. Turn right on Chesapeake; turn left on 41st Street NW, which merges with Wisconsin Avenue NW. Walk south two blocks on Wisconsin to the Tenley-Friendship branch of the DC Public Library on the right. Pop in to learn more about the U.S. capital, including the D.C. adventurers who first reached the top of the world—the North Pole. District**

residents Capt. Robert Peary and his African American assistant, Matthew Henson, are credited as the first men to reach the pole in 1909. Frances "Fran" Phipps, of Ottawa (Canada's capital), was the first woman there in 1971.

- **Exit the library and cross Wisconsin Avenue NW to descend into the Tenleytown-AU Metro. Stay to the right on Metro escalators so Type A Washingtonians can zip past. Don't even think about eating or drinking on the subway. Washingtonians learned the hard way. On Oct. 23, 2000, a 12-year-old girl was handcuffed and arrested there for eating a French fry. In 2004, then U.S. Court of Appeals Judge John G. Roberts wrote in the court's ruling that no one was happy that a plainclothes Metro Transit Police officer arrested a "frightened, embarrassed and crying" Alice Deal Middle School student, but Metro acted within its constitutional rights. Metro has changed its policy, Roberts noted. Roberts has changed his robe. Now he's the Chief Justice of the Supreme Court—America's *highest* tribunal.**

Points of Interest

Carnegie Institution for Science 5241 Broad Branch Road NW, 202-387-6400, dtm.carnegiescience.edu

(Private) residence of Peru's ambassador 3001 Garrison St. NW, 202-833-9860 (embassy), embassyofperu.org

(Private) former home of FBI Director J. Edgar Hoover 4936 30th Place NW

(Private) former home of President Lyndon B. Johnson 4921 30th Place NW

Politics and Prose 5015 Connecticut Ave. NW, 202-364-1919, politics-prose.com

Buck's Fishing & Camping 5031 Connecticut Ave. NW, 202-364-0777, bucksfishingandcamping.com

Alice Deal Middle School 3815 Fort Dr. NW, 202-939-2010, alicedeal.org

Fort Reno Park Chesapeake Street NW and Nebraska Avenue NW, 202-895-6000, nps.gov/cwdw/historyculture/fort-reno.htm

Tenley-Friendship Neighborhood Library 4450 Wisconsin Ave. NW, 202-727-1488, dclibrary.org/tenley

Tenleytown-AU Metro 4501 Wisconsin Ave. NW, 202-637-7000, wmata.com/rail/station_detail.cfm?station_id=10

route summary

1. Start at Military Road NW and 32nd Street NW.
2. Walk south on 32nd Street NW.
3. Turn left on Linnean Avenue NW.
4. Turn left on Garrison Street NW.
5. Turn right on 30th Place NW.
6. Turn right on Ellicott Street NW.
7. Turn right on Connecticut Avenue NW.
8. Turn left on Nebraska Avenue NW.
9. Turn right on Fort Drive NW.
10. Turn left on a gravel path.
11. Turn right on Chesapeake Street NW.
12. Turn left on 41st Street NW.
13. Turn left on Wisconsin Avenue NW.
14. Exit the library and cross Wisconsin Avenue NW for the Metro.

CONNECTING THE WALKS

For Walk 4 (Foxhall and Beyond), continue south on Wisconsin Avenue NW and turn right on Nebraska Avenue NW.

DC Water and Sewer Authority's stately towers

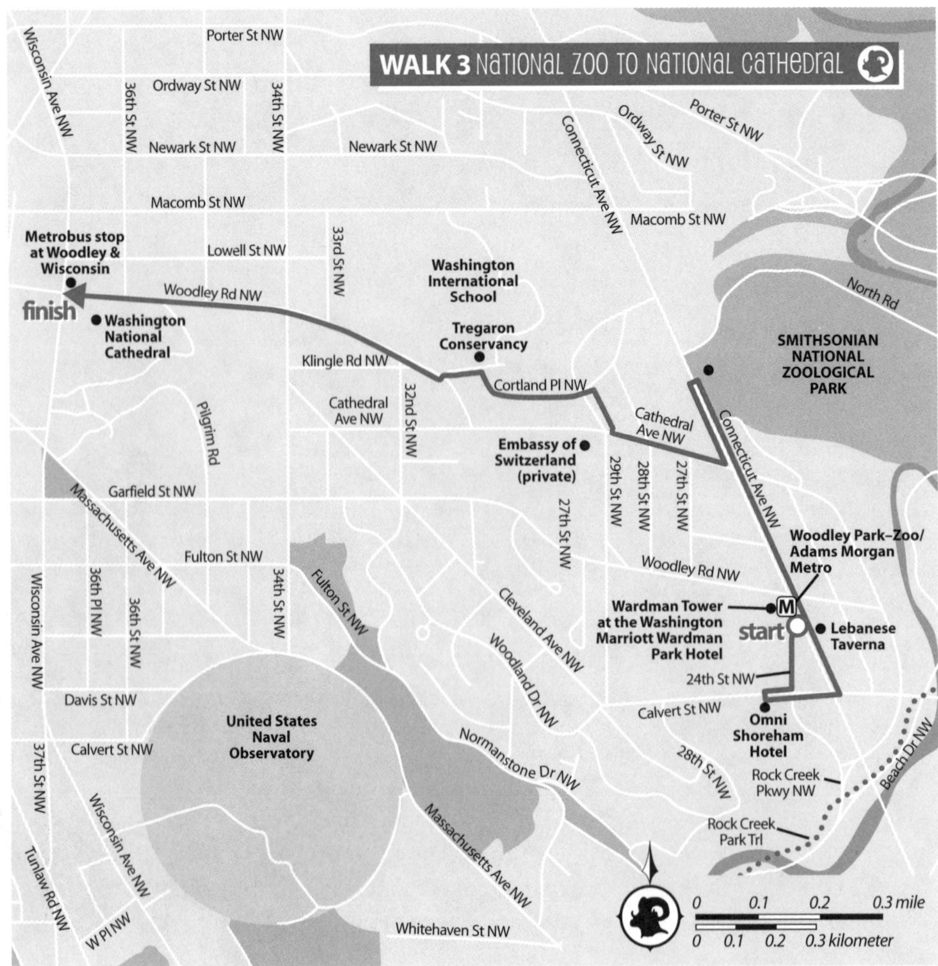
WALK 3 National Zoo to National Cathedral
Porter St NW
Ordway St NW
Newark St NW
Macomb St NW
Lowell St NW
Woodley Rd NW
Klingle Rd NW
Cortland Pl NW
Cathedral Ave NW
Garfield St NW
Fulton St NW
Davis St NW
Calvert St NW
Whitehaven St NW
W Pl NW
Wisconsin Ave NW
36th St NW
34th St NW
33rd St NW
32nd St NW
29th St NW
28th St NW
27th St NW
24th St NW
36th Pl NW
37th St NW
Tunlaw Rd NW
Pilgrim Rd
Massachusetts Ave NW
Connecticut Ave NW
Cleveland Ave NW
Woodland Dr NW
Normanstone Dr NW
28th St NW
North Rd
Beach Dr NW
Rock Creek Pkwy NW
Rock Creek Park Trl
Metrobus stop at Woodley & Wisconsin
finish
Washington National Cathedral
Washington International School
Tregaron Conservancy
Embassy of Switzerland (private)
SMITHSONIAN NATIONAL ZOOLOGICAL PARK
Woodley Park–Zoo/ Adams Morgan Metro
Wardman Tower at the Washington Marriott Wardman Park Hotel
start
Lebanese Taverna
Omni Shoreham Hotel
United States Naval Observatory
0 0.1 0.2 0.3 mile
0 0.1 0.2 0.3 kilometer

3 National Zoo to National Cathedral: Homes Sweet Homes

BOUNDARIES: Woodley Road NW, Connecticut Avenue NW, Calvert Street NW, and Wisconsin Avenue NW
DISTANCE: 2 miles (excluding the zoo's multiple paths)
DIFFICULTY: Easy, excluding the zoo; moderate to strenuous if taking an optional trek through the hilly zoo
PARKING: 2-hour limited street parking; parking lots at Omni Shoreham, National Zoo, and National Cathedral; Metro recommended
PUBLIC TRANSIT: Woodley Park–Zoo/Adams Morgan Metro. Metrobuses 96, 97, and X3 link the Woodley Park Metro to the cathedral.

Everyone loves pandas. The National Zoo's übercute cub, Bao Bao, even scored a birthday tweet from First Lady Michelle Obama. Although the Giant Panda "palace" is enough of a reason to trek to the zoo, 1,800 other cute critters also reside within the 163-acre oasis. After schlepping around the animals' hillside homes, it's only a short walk past fashionable human homes and hotels to one of the city's most elaborate houses of God—the Washington National Cathedral, which is the sixth-largest cathedral in the world. Along the way are the Swiss ambassador's ultra-edgy residence and a newly public garden by the Post cereal heir's former mansion.

- **Start at the Woodley Park–Zoo/Adams Morgan Metro station at Connecticut Avenue NW and 24th Street NW. Walk south on 24th Street NW past apartments and eateries, and turn right on Calvert Street NW for the Omni Shoreham Hotel on the left. This elegant hotel overlooks verdant Rock Creek Park and its hiker-biker trail. A famous fixture since 1930 (it was even a Kennedy hangout), these days it's best known for hosting families and conventions. In 1964, its fame went viral when the Beatles called it home during their first American concert (see Walk 24, NoMa and Union Market). They spent a few hours performing at the Washington Coliseum, but they spent a few days in Suite 625, the hotel says. A plaque on the door proclaims it the "Beatles Suite."**

- **After the hotel, reverse direction on Calvert Street NW to head east. Turn left on Connecticut Avenue NW for Lebanese Taverna restaurant on the right. This family-owned,**

Arlington-based company has been pleasing palates with its hummus, tabouleh, and other yummy specialties from their homeland since 1979. It's one of the Abi-Najm family's 11 Lebanese Taverna eateries.

- Continue north on Connecticut Avenue NW for Wardman Tower on the left. Once home to luminaries such as Presidents Herbert Hoover, Dwight Eisenhower, and Lyndon Johnson; vice presidents; members of Congress; two Supreme Court chief justices; and Hollywood legend Marlene Dietrich, it has been part of the Washington Marriott Wardman Park hotel since 1998. Now the 1928 annex is being converted into 32 prestigious, private residences.

- Walk north on Connecticut Avenue NW, past upscale apartments and condos to the (free and must-see) Smithsonian National Zoological Park on the right. Among its roughly 1,800 residents are some rarities, the zoo says, such as a Micronesian kingfisher (one of 129 in the world) and Sumatran tigers (400 live on the planet). The lush green zoo is well known for its many public programs, including "Snore and Roar" sleepovers for adults and kids. What isn't well known is that it's also a "geologist's paradise," says the zoo's history. A fault zone burrows beneath it. The zoo straddles the boundary or fall line between two major geographic provinces: the Piedmont (hilly with ancient, hard igneous and metamorphic rocks) and the Coastal Plain (flat with younger, softer gravel, sand, and clay). The lone visible fault is at the southeastern edge of the zoo across Rock Creek Parkway. (See Walk 9, Adams Morgan.)

- After the zoo, reverse direction on Connecticut Avenue NW. Turn right on Cathedral Avenue NW. On the left at 29th Street NW is the private Embassy of Switzerland. The ambassador's avant-garde home on the compound opened in 2006. Designed by a team of American and Swiss architects, its black and white façades (charcoal-colored concrete and sand-blasted structural glass planks) were inspired by the rugged, snow-covered Swiss Alps, the embassy says. The Swiss sponsor movies, concerts, and other cultural events at their embassy and around the city.

- Turn right on 29th Street NW to head north past some of the gracious historic houses that typify the surrounding Woodley Park and Cleveland Park neighborhoods. Turn left on Cortland Place NW, which dead-ends at the pedestrian entrance to the Tregaron Conservancy park at the Washington International School. Trails loop through the lush

D.C.'S OWN (SQUIRRELY) PLYMOUTH ROCK

The year 1902 might be remembered elsewhere as the date the first Automat opened, but in Washington it marks a memorable if not momentous event in mammal history. That's when the National Zoo released eight "Pilgrim" black squirrels along the rocky, northwestern edge of the zoo by its Connecticut Avenue NW entrance. The glossy black mammals were imported as part of a squirrel exchange with Canada. After a second release of 10 more in 1906, today the descendants of these unusual squirrels scurry all over the city. They're the same Eastern gray squirrels (*Sciurus carolinensis*) as their more common gray-colored cousins, but they have a mutant color gene. D.C. is also home to some less common white squirrels (leucistic or partially lacking color) and rarer albinos (white with pink eyes). All four colors hang out on the National Mall. They're smart critters. Once a squirrel near the White House waited by a crosswalk and didn't cross until humans began walking across the street, said Richard W. Thorington Jr., curator of mammals at the Smithsonian's National Museum of Natural History and co-author of *Squirrels of the World*. Thorington said it "may have been accidental but gray squirrels are bright enough that this may have been a conscious strategy."

valley below the hilltop school. Marjorie Merriweather Post's brick mansion atop the hill is now part of the private school. The Post cereal heir and her husband, Ambassador Joseph E. Davies, lived at this 20-acre enclave until they divorced and she moved to her Hillwood Estate (now a museum) in 1955. The nonprofit conservancy opened Tregaron to the public in 2006. Just outside the garden to the west is the 26-room Twin Oaks mansion, built by National Geographic Society founder Gardiner Hubbard in 1888. Now his wooden home on 18 acres of that estate is a private cultural center owned by the Taiwan government. To the east is long-closed Klingle Road NW. Construction began in July 2015 to transform it into the Klingle Valley hiker-biker trail.

- Exit Tregaron and turn right to head west on Klingle Road NW. Turn right on Woodley Road NW for the Washington National Cathedral's side entrance on the left. This

Gothic cathedral was a work in progress from 1907 to 1990. Construction had to begin anew in 2011 to fix damages caused by a rare earthquake. The Indiana limestone landmark is the tallest man-made point in Washington. Its website says it rises 676 feet above sea level: the central tower is 301 feet 3 inches high, and it was built on Mount St. Albans, which is about 375 feet above sea level. Helen Keller is buried there, along with President Woodrow Wilson. The cathedral has hosted 11 presidential funerals and memorials. Visitors can attend services or drop a dime on an insider's tour to view the 231 stained glass windows, 112 gargoyles, and other historic architectural details, including a modern-day oddity: a Darth Vader sculpture. It was added in the 1980s during a children's sculpture competition. The pedestrian-friendly grounds are home to Olmsted Woods, "one of the few old growth forests still standing in the nation's capital," the church says; the private National Cathedral School for girls; and the private St. Albans School for boys. Vice President Al Gore was a junior there when he attended the 1964 Beatles concert. Gore isn't the only one with swell memories of those days, *The Washington Post* reported in 2010. "The trip to Washington is a very romantic time in my memory," said Beatle Paul McCartney.

POINTS OF INTEREST

Woodley Park–Zoo/Adams Morgan Metro Station Connecticut Avenue NW and 24th Street NW, 202-637-7000, wmata.com/rail/station_detail.cfm?station_id=7

Omni Shoreham Hotel 2500 Calvert St. NW, 202-234-0700, omnihotels.com

Lebanese Taverna 2641 Connecticut Ave. NW, 202-265-8681, lebanesetaverna.com

Wardman Tower 2660 Woodley Rd. NW (southwest corner of Connecticut Avenue NW and Woodley Road NW, part of the Washington Marriott Wardman Park Hotel), 202-328-2000, wardmantowerdc.com

Smithsonian National Zoological Park 3001 Connecticut Ave. NW, 202-633-4888, nationalzoo.si.edu

Embassy of Switzerland 2900 Cathedral Ave. NW, 202-745-7900, www.eda.admin.ch/washington

Tregaron Conservancy Klingle Road NW and Cortland Place NW, tregaronconservancy.org

Washington National Cathedral 3101 Wisconsin Ave. NW, 202-537-6200, nationalcathedral.org

route summary

1. Start at the Woodley Park–Zoo/Adams Morgan Metro station, Connecticut Avenue NW and 24th Street NW.
2. Walk south on 24th Street NW.
3. Turn right on Calvert Street NW.
4. After the Omni Shoreham Hotel, reverse direction on Calvert Street NW.
5. Turn left on Connecticut Avenue NW.
6. After the zoo, reverse direction on Connecticut Avenue NW to head south.
7. Turn right on Cathedral Avenue NW.
8. Turn right on 29th Street NW.
9. Turn left on Cortland Place NW.
10. Exit Tregaron and turn right to head west on Klingle Road NW.
11. Turn right on Woodley Road NW.
12. Turn left into the National Cathedral's side entrance at 36th Street NW.

connecting the walks

For Walk 8 (Embassy Row), walk south four blocks on Wisconsin Avenue NW to the Embassy of the Russian Federation on the right.

Panda-monium at Smithsonian's National Zoo

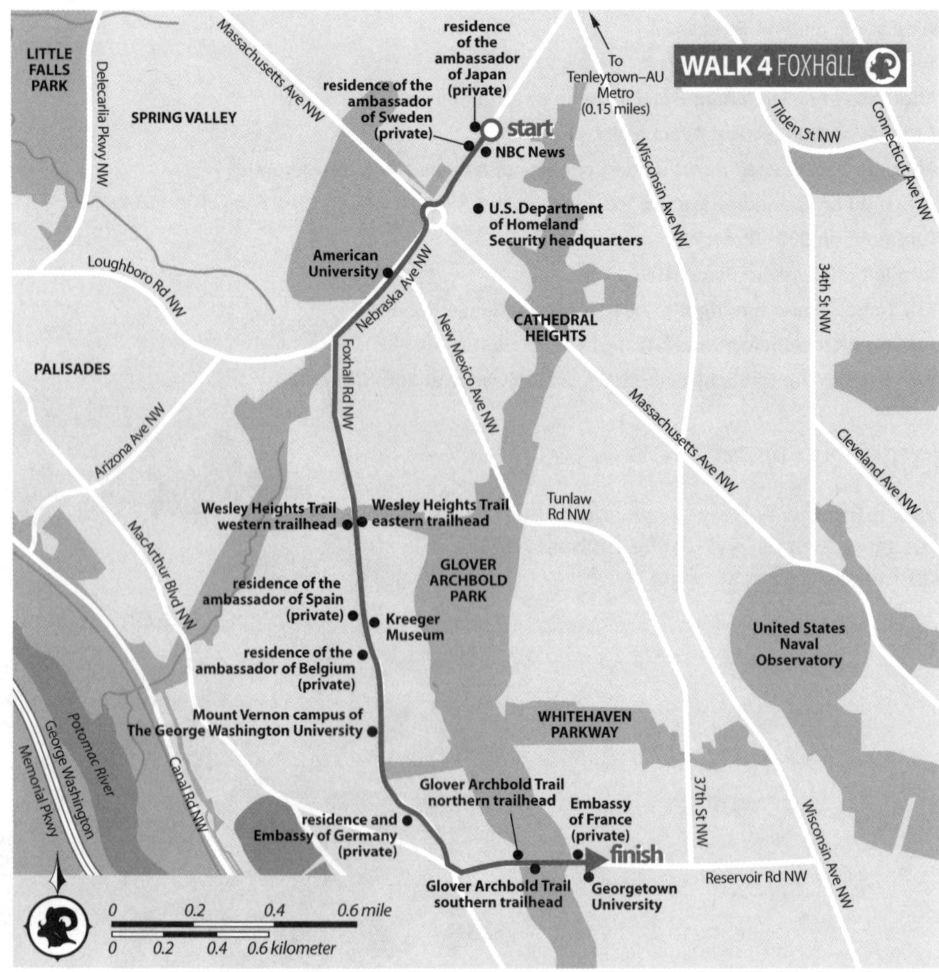

WALK 4 FOXHALL
start
finish
LITTLE FALLS PARK
SPRING VALLEY
PALISADES
CATHEDRAL HEIGHTS
GLOVER ARCHBOLD PARK
WHITEHAVEN PARKWAY
United States Naval Observatory
residence of the ambassador of Japan (private)
residence of the ambassador of Sweden (private)
NBC News
U.S. Department of Homeland Security headquarters
American University
Wesley Heights Trail western trailhead
Wesley Heights Trail eastern trailhead
residence of the ambassador of Spain (private)
Kreeger Museum
residence of the ambassador of Belgium (private)
Mount Vernon campus of The George Washington University
residence and Embassy of Germany (private)
Glover Archbold Trail northern trailhead
Glover Archbold Trail southern trailhead
Embassy of France (private)
Georgetown University
To Tenleytown–AU Metro (0.15 miles)
Massachusetts Ave NW
Delecarlia Pkwy NW
Loughboro Rd NW
Nebraska Ave NW
Foxhall Rd NW
New Mexico Ave NW
Arizona Ave NW
MacArthur Blvd NW
Canal Rd NW
Potomac River
George Washington Memorial Pkwy
Wisconsin Ave NW
Tilden St NW
Connecticut Ave NW
34th St NW
Cleveland Ave NW
Tunlaw Rd NW
37th St NW
Reservoir Rd NW
0 0.2 0.4 0.6 mile
0 0.2 0.4 0.6 kilometer

4 FOXHALL AND BEYOND: THE HIGH LIFE, HIGHER ED, AND U-BOATS

BOUNDARIES: **Nebraska Avenue NW, 42nd Street NW, Reservoir Road NW, and Foxhall Road NW**
DISTANCE: **About 2.7 miles**
DIFFICULTY: **Easy**
PARKING: **2-hour free and metered street parking along the route; Metro recommended**
PUBLIC TRANSIT: **At start: Metrobus M4 runs from the Tenleytown-AU Metro Station to Nebraska Avenue NW. At end: Metrobus D6 runs along Reservoir Road NW to the Dupont Circle Metro Station.**

What an eyeful. This beautiful stroll, most of it along gardenlike Foxhall Road NW, rolls downhill past the homes of diplomats and other bigwigs. One of the honchos who used to live there was David Lloyd Kreeger, a former chairman of Government Employees Insurance Company. Luckily for art and architecture lovers, his modern-style mansion, about midway through this trek, is now a museum. The walk starts near American University (D.C. native Goldie Hawn's alma mater), passes The George Washington University's lesser-known Mount Vernon Campus (Boston Celtics coach Arnold "Red" Auerbach is a GW alum), and winds up at Georgetown University (President Bill Clinton is its most famous grad). The most private stop is the most historic: the building that now houses the headquarters of the U.S. Department of Homeland Security is where the U.S. Navy broke secret codes during World War II.

- **Start at 4000 Nebraska Avenue NW, the private residence of the ambassador of Japan since 1977. Behind the taupe fence surrounding this 12-acre estate is a flat-roofed concrete and stone home with picture windows. It overlooks a traditional Japanese garden and a teahouse that seems to float on a pond.**

- **Next door at 3900 is the ambassador of Sweden's 1923 Spanish-style home. The Nordic diplomat and his Asian neighbor both have tennis courts.**

- **Across the street at 4001 Nebraska Avenue NW are the NBC television studios. The public can't visit, but it's cool to see where *Meet the Press* is taped. It's the longest-running TV show in history. NBC is also where the *Muppets'* Kermit the Frog debuted and where the second of the four Nixon-Kennedy debates was held. They were the nation's first televised presidential debates.**

- NBC's next-door neighbor at 3801 is the U.S. Department of Homeland Security. DHS was created from 22 diverse federal departments and agencies in 2002. It chose a very historic home: the Mount Vernon Seminary, the first school of higher education open to women in D.C. The school moved there in 1917. In 1942, the U.S. Navy took over its Georgian Revival dorms and classrooms, so the school moved to Foxhall Road NW. By the end of World War II, more than 5,000 civilians and soldiers worked at the Navy's communications security section (OP-20-G) breaking Japanese and German codes, according to the National Security Agency (NSA).

- Across Massachusetts Avenue NW is American University, which was chartered by Congress in 1893. Alice Paul is a three-time graduate of American University and the Washington College of Law, the school says. Paul wrote the original Equal Rights Amendment, founded the National Women's Party, and played a key role in securing women's right to vote. These days the school is home to WAMU, American University Radio, a member of National Public Radio.

- At the end of American University, turn left onto Foxhall Road NW. Walk past tall oak trees and vintage brick, Tudor, and fieldstone homes for six blocks. On both sides of the road at Edmunds Street NW are entrances descending to the Wesley Heights Trail. Managed by Rock Creek Park, this ivy-covered stream-valley trail links Battery Kemble and Glover Archbold parks.

- A bit farther down this shady, two-lane road on the right is the walled residence of Spain's ambassador. This contemporary-style brick building was built in 2003 by Pritzker prize–winning architect José Rafael Moneo.

- Across the street is the Kreeger Museum. David and Carmen Kreeger jointly amassed their modern and African art collection, which includes works by Monet, Picasso, and Van Gogh, the museum says. "I never bought art as an investment," said David, GEICO's former chairman. "I bought it for love, and I was lucky." Washington is lucky that the Kreegers chose Philip Johnson to design their modern, travertine home. When he was awarded the Pritzker Architecture Prize, the group called him "one of architecture's most potent forces." He designed the home in 1963, and it became a museum in 1994.

- Downhill on the right is the wooded estate of Belgium's ambassador. While mansions are almost commonplace here, "few can compete with this one for sheer, Gatsbyesque opulence," says the *AIA Guide to the Architecture of Washington, D.C.* The statuesque stone mansion was modeled after the Hôtel de Rothelin-Charolais in Paris. Ann Thompson Dodge, heir to the Dodge automobile fortune, commissioned it in 1931 as a wedding present for her daughter. Dodge died in 1970 at age 103, the same age as D.C. arts patron Rachel "Bunny" Mellon. They were two of the world's wealthiest women.

- Across W Street NW on the right is the 25-acre Mount Vernon campus of The George Washington University, whose main digs are downtown. When it was Mount Vernon Seminary, its famous grads included Ada Louise Comstock, a president of Radcliffe College, and the daughters and granddaughters of telephone inventor Alexander Graham Bell. The seminary morphed into Mount Vernon College and became part of GW in 1999. The campus hosts an annual French film festival and other public events.
- On the next block to the right is the Embassy of Germany and ambassador's residence. Designed in 1994 by Oswald Mathias "O.M." Ungers, the stone residence uses patterns of squares "throughout the complex, with the windows, doorway and artwork—even the furniture and fireplaces—all demonstrating this harmony of design," says Germany's website. Visitors can catch a glimpse from the outside, and they typically are invited inside the compound during the European Union's spring embassy tour.
- Turn left on Reservoir Road NW. On both sides of the road by 44th Street NW is the Glover Archbold Trail, part of a network of wooded trails that crisscrosses D.C. It's named for the parkland's donors, banker Charles Carroll Glover and Anne Archbold, a Standard Oil heir, whose 1922 Tuscan-inspired villa lies northeast of the trailhead in the private, gated Hillandale community.
- Just after the park on the left is the 8-acre Embassy of France, which was also part of Archbold's 78-acre estate.

Philip Johnson–designed Kreeger Museum

Code Breakers: Sinking German Subs

America's future looked dreary during those first few months after Pearl Harbor was bombed. From January to March 1942, German U-boats sank 216 American ships off the East Coast, according to the NSA's National Cryptologic Museum in Annapolis Junction, Maryland. But the tides turned after the workers at the Navy's Nebraska Avenue complex broke the submarines' Enigma-created ciphers. "We were able to sink or capture 95 German U-boats based on this type of information," says the NSA's Jennifer Wilcox. The U.S. Navy focused on the subs' encrypted messages, while the U.S. Army, the British, and others worked on solving the Enigma ciphers of the German Army and Air Force, the NSA says. (A cipher changes individual letters, and a code changes entire words or phrases.) On Nebraska Avenue, roughly 3,000 of the 5,000 workers were WAVES, or Women Accepted for Volunteer Emergency Service. They worked 24/7 using 121 massive Bombe machines that replicated the typewriter-like Enigma enciphering machines used by the Germans. Some of the cryptanalysts also focused on Japanese codes. One of them was Agnes Meyer Driscoll, also known as Miss Aggie or Madame X. This pioneer cryptanalyst "broke a multitude of Japanese naval systems, as well as [being] a developer of early machine systems," the NSA said when it inducted her into its Hall of Honor in 2000. Driscoll moved from the Navy to the NSA when it took over some of the military's cryptologic duties. She's buried in Arlington National Cemetery.

Behind the metal-barred gate, the French sponsor wine tastings, movies, concerts, art exhibits, a Bastille Day celebration, and more. Its modern, white-marble campus was built in 1984.

- **Georgetown University starts across the street. Its medical school and hospital front Reservoir Road NW. Behind that, the rest of its camera-worthy campus stretches roughly a half mile.**

Points of Interest

(Private) residence of the ambassador of Japan 4000 Nebraska Ave. NW, 202-238-6900, us.emb-japan.go.jp/jicc/index.html

NBC4 Washington and NBC News 4001 Nebraska Ave. NW, 202-885-4000, nbcwashington.com and nbcnews.com/meet-the-press

(Private) residence of the ambassador of Sweden 3900 Nebraska Ave. NW, 202-467-2600, swedenabroad.com

Department of Homeland Security 3801 Nebraska Ave. NW, 202-282-8000, dhs.gov

American University 4400 Massachusetts Ave. NW, 202-885-1000, american.edu

National Park Service's Wesley Heights Trail Foxhall Road NW at Edmunds Street NW, 202-895-6000, nps.gov/rocr/index.htm

Kreeger Museum 2401 Foxhall Rd. NW, 202-337-3050, kreegermuseum.org

(Private) residence of the ambassador of Spain 2350 Foxhall Rd. NW, 202-452-0100, spainemb.org

(Private) residence of the ambassador of Belgium 2300 Foxhall Rd. NW, 202-333-6900, countries.diplomatie.belgium.be/en/united_states

Mount Vernon Campus of The George Washington University Foxhall Road NW and Whitehaven Parkway NW, 202-994-1000, gwu.edu/mount-vernon-campus

(Private) Embassy of Germany and residence of the ambassador 1800 Foxhall Rd. NW, 202-298-4000, germany.info/embassy

National Park Service's Glover-Archbold Trail Reservoir Road NW at 44th Street NW, 202-895-6000, nps.gov/rocr/index.htm

(Private) Embassy of France 4101 Reservoir Rd. NW, 202-944-6000, ambafrance-us.org

Georgetown University Reservoir Road NW to Prospect Street NW (main entrance: 3700 O St. NW), 202-687-0100, georgetown.edu

route summary

1. **Start at 4001 Nebraska Avenue NW.**
2. **Turn left on Foxhall Road NW.**
3. **Turn left on Reservoir Road NW.**

connecting the walks

For Walk 2 (Forest Hills to Tenleytown), take the M4 bus on Nebraska Avenue NW about ½ mile to the Tenleytown-AU Metro station. For Walk 5 (Georgetown North), continue east on Reservoir Road NW to Wisconsin Avenue NW.

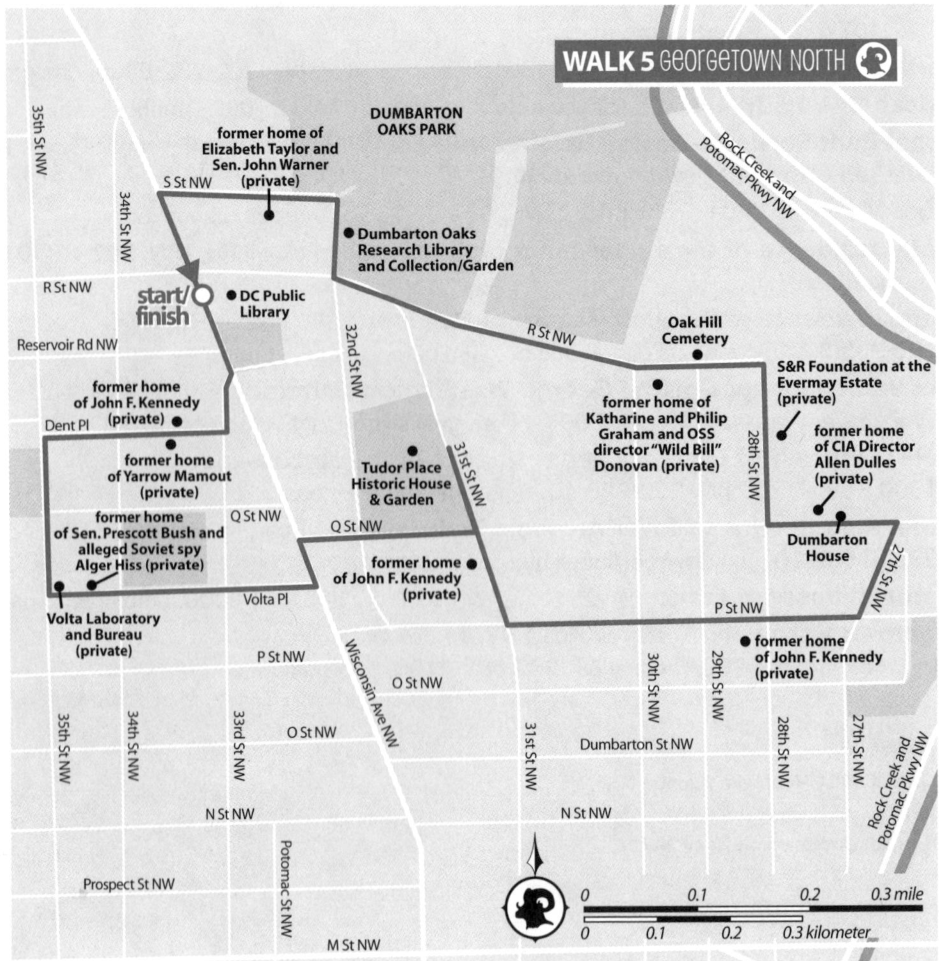
WALK 5 Georgetown North
DUMBARTON OAKS PARK
former home of Elizabeth Taylor and Sen. John Warner (private)
Dumbarton Oaks Research Library and Collection/Garden
Rock Creek and Potomac Pkwy NW
start/finish
DC Public Library
Oak Hill Cemetery
S&R Foundation at the Evermay Estate (private)
former home of John F. Kennedy (private)
former home of Katharine and Philip Graham and OSS director "Wild Bill" Donovan (private)
former home of Yarrow Mamout (private)
Tudor Place Historic House & Garden
former home of CIA Director Allen Dulles (private)
former home of Sen. Prescott Bush and alleged Soviet spy Alger Hiss (private)
Dumbarton House
former home of John F. Kennedy (private)
Volta Laboratory and Bureau (private)
former home of John F. Kennedy (private)
35th St NW
34th St NW
33rd St NW
32nd St NW
31st St NW
30th St NW
29th St NW
28th St NW
27th St NW
S St NW
R St NW
Reservoir Rd NW
Dent Pl
Q St NW
Volta Pl
P St NW
O St NW
Dumbarton St NW
N St NW
Prospect St NW
Potomac St NW
M St NW
Wisconsin Ave NW
0
0.1
0.2
0.3 mile
0.3 kilometer

5 Georgetown North: Silver Spoons and Spies

BOUNDARIES: **S Street NW, 27th Street NW, P Street NW, and 35th Street NW**
DISTANCE: **2.5 miles**
DIFFICULTY: **Easy, except optional hilly cemetery walk**
PARKING: **Free Sunday street parking throughout D.C. unless otherwise marked; 4-hour meters by the library; and limited 2-hour free and metered spaces elsewhere; parking garages on Wisconsin Avenue NW**
PUBLIC TRANSIT: **Circulator bus and Metrobus 31 run along Wisconsin Avenue NW to several Metro stations.**

Camelot lives. With its storybook row houses and mansions, narrow streets, and brick sidewalks, the historic district of Georgetown seems as magical now as it was when John F. Kennedy and his glamorous colleagues gravitated there in the 1950s. Now D.C.'s oldest neighborhood is home to 21st-century jet-setters, such as Secretary of State John Kerry, Washington Nationals part-owner Mark Lerner, and Under Armour founder Kevin Plank. Their residential architecture grabs center stage each winter after the scarlet dogwood, orange-red sweetgum, and yellow gingko trees drop their festive curtain of leaves.

- **Start at the Georgetown branch of the DC Public Library, 3260 R Street NW. The stately brick building, which was renovated after a 2007 fire, is a lending library, and it preserves a Georgetown history collection. Its crown jewel is a rare 1822 oil painting of freed slave Yarrow Mamout. The library also hosts public events, such as talks by the neighborhood's own celebrity biographer Kitty Kelley, who is penning a book on Georgetown. With the library to the left, walk to the corner and turn left on Wisconsin Avenue NW.**

- **Turn right on 33rd Street NW and right on Dent Place NW. Then Massachusetts Senator John F. Kennedy leased this narrow three-story brick duplex at 3321 in December 1953 after he married Jacqueline Bouvier in September, says the John F. Kennedy Presidential Library and Museum. Across the street at 3324 is the empty lot where freed slave Yarrow Mamout once lived. Originally from Guinea, West Africa, Mamout grew wealthy after gaining his freedom in 1807, says Cultural Tourism DC's *African American Heritage Trail* brochure.**

- Continue on Dent Place and turn left on 35th Street NW to walk past more elaborate row houses. On the left at Volta Place NW is the templelike Volta Laboratory and Bureau. Telephone inventor Alexander Graham Bell built this neoclassic yellow-brick structure in 1893 as a center of information for the hearing-impaired. He started the bureau at his dad's four-story gray house across the street.

- Turn left on Volta Place. Next door to the lab is the suspected spy den where President George H. W. Bush once slept, says Pamela Kessler's *Undercover Washington.* Bush stayed there when it was the home of his father, Connecticut Sen. Prescott S. Bush. Before that, the brick and clapboard house was one of three Georgetown homes that State Department aide and alleged Soviet spy Alger Hiss rented. Georgetown "has a rich history of espionage and intrigue," adds Carol S. Bessette, the retired Air Force officer who leads the popular Spies of Washington Tour that she founded.

- Continue east on Volta Place, past Volta Park, where the Kennedy clan played touch football. Turn left on Wisconsin Avenue NW and turn right onto Q Street NW. Turn left on 31st Street NW to walk uphill to Tudor Place Historic House & Garden on the left. The neoclassic mansion was built in 1816 by William Thornton, architect of the first U.S. Capitol. Since 1988, it has welcomed the public to its 5.5-acre landmark home and garden. It was built by Georgetown's first mayor and his wife, a granddaughter of First Lady Martha Washington.

- Reverse direction on 31st Street NW for another former Kennedy home on the right at 1528. Kennedy rented this three-story, flat-roofed, brick home from 1946 to 1949 after his election to Congress. He lived with his younger sister, Eunice; an aide; a cook; and a butler, says WETA public television's local history blog.

- Continue south on 31st Street NW and turn left on P Street NW for the two-story dark gray brick rowhouse on the right at 2808, which the Kennedys rented from January to February 1957.

- Continue east on P Street NW and turn left on 27th Street NW. Turn left on Q Street NW for the Dumbarton House on the right. Visitors can tour this elegant brick Federal-style home built around 1800. It's the headquarters of The National Society of The Colonial Dames of America.

- Dumbarton's next-door neighbor is a private three-story brick house with a gray balustrade where spymaster Allen Dulles lived. In 1953, President Dwight Eisenhower appointed Allen as director of the CIA and his brother, John Foster Dulles (the namesake of Washington Dulles International Airport), who lived nearby, as Secretary of State. Allen served from 1953 to 1961, the golden age for the spy agency—as its own history states, "a time of derring-do, when the public viewed the CIA as a patriotic organization of people fighting our Cold War enemies."

- Turn right on 28th Street NW to pass the rear of Herman Hollerith's former estate on the left (see cemetery below) and the beveled brick wall surrounding the landmark Evermay estate on the right. Its grand Federal-style brick home, with 12 fireplaces and a killer view downhill toward the Washington Monument, was built in 1801. In 2011, Sachiko Kuno and Ryuji Ueno bought the 3.5-acre estate. Now it's the headquarters of their S&R Foundation, which "offers promising artists and scientists a place to perform and be inspired."

- Continue north on 28th Street NW and turn left on R Street NW for the Oak Hill Cemetery on the right, which sweeps downhill to Rock Creek. Its Gothic chapel was designed by James Renwick Jr., who also created the Smithsonian's Castle and its Renwick Gallery. The gray and red stone chapel sits next to the plain gray gravestones of the *Washington Post*'s former publishers, Katharine "Kay" Graham and her husband, Philip, who shot himself in 1963. Stark gray stones also mark the grave of Herman Hollerith, whose company morphed into IBM. (See Walk 7, Georgetown Southeast.) Some other notable graves belong to architect Adolph Cluss, who designed the Eastern Market, and Confederate

Oak Hill Cemetery's Renwick-designed chapel

spies Lillie Mackall and Bettie Duval. Banker William Wilson Corcoran is buried in a white marble pavilion with eight columns. He founded the cemetery in 1849.

- Across the street is the Grahams' former three-story house on the left with a big green lawn. Kay bought the cream-colored brick home from "Wild Bill" Donovan, the head of the Office of Strategic Services (OSS), the CIA's predecessor. Her home was a bipartisan hub. "In the life of Washington, [she] played a vital role: she was a convener," Vernon Jordan told *Newsweek* magazine when she died in 2001. "She invited to her table people of vastly different views, men and women who otherwise would never have had a reason to sit in the same room." In 2002, Washington Kastles tennis team owner Mark Ein bought the landmark.

- Walk west on R Street NW, past walker-friendly Montrose and Dumbarton Oaks parks to the Georgian-style brick mansion of Dumbarton Oaks Research Library and Collection/Garden on the right. National Geographic named its formal, terraced garden as one of the top 10 on the planet. Beatrix Jones Farrand, one of America's first landscape architects, designed its garden rooms and rich architectural details with Mildred Barnes Bliss, heir to the Fletcher's Castoria laxative fortune, after she and her husband, diplomat Robert Woods Bliss, bought the estate in 1920. Now it's a Harvard University institute. Its free museum showcases Byzantine, pre-Columbian, and European art, and its Renaissance-style music room hosts public lectures and concerts. In 1959, celebrated architect Philip Johnson began concocting a masterpiece to display the Blisses' gold, ceramic, and other pre-Columbian treasures. Johnson's nearly transparent pavilion is composed of eight domed, circular, glass galleries supported by marble-clad, cylindrical columns surrounding a fountain-filled atrium.

- Turn right on 32nd Street NW and left on S Street NW for the private, two-story brick home on the left, where film legend Elizabeth Taylor lived with her sixth husband, D.C.-born John Warner. She and the Virginia senator lived next door to his first wife, Catherine Conover, the granddaughter of billionaire financier and National Gallery of Art founder Andrew Mellon. In 1976, Taylor, adorned in a fox-trimmed coat, and Warner, in a coat and tie, married in a cow-filled pasture at his roughly 2,600-acre estate near Middleburg, Virginia. Warner said he bought the S Street property after finding it in a three-line newspaper ad. Back then it had a small stone house and an active horse barn. Warner, a civil engineer, lawyer, and former Secretary of the Navy, built his

family home in 1962 with concrete and steel. It had a greenhouse and an art gallery. "We were very happy there," he reminisced on the last day of 2014. Now Dumbarton's director lives in the Harvard-owned residence. Continue west on S Street NW and turn left on Wisconsin Avenue NW for the library on the left.

POINTS OF INTEREST

DC Public Library 3260 R St. NW, 202-727-0232, dclibrary.org/georgetown

(Private) former home of John F. Kennedy 3321 Dent Place NW

(Private) former home of Yarrow Mamout 3324 Dent Place NW

(Private) Volta Laboratory and Bureau (now the Alexander Graham Bell Association for the Deaf and Hard of Hearing) 1537 35th St., 202-337-5220, listeningandspokenlanguage.org

(Private) former home of Sen. Prescott Bush and Soviet spy Alger Hiss 3415 Volta Place NW

Tudor Place Historic House & Garden 1644 31st St. NW, 202-965-0400, tudorplace.org

(Private) former home of John F. Kennedy 1528 31st St. NW

(Private) former home of John F. Kennedy 2808 P St. NW

Dumbarton House 2715 Q St. NW, 202-337-2288, dumbartonhouse.org

(Private) former home of Allen Dulles 2723 Q St. NW

(Private) S&R Foundation 1623 28th St. NW, 202-298-6007, evermayestate.org

Oak Hill Cemetery 3001 R St. NW, 202-337-2835, nps.gov/nr/travel/wash/dc9.htm

(Private) former home of Katharine and Philip Graham 2920 R St. NW

Dumbarton Oaks Research Library and Collection/Garden 1703 32nd St. NW, 202-339-6401, doaks.org

(Private) former home of Sen. John Warner 3240 S St. NW

route summary

1. Start at the DC Public Library, 3260 R Street NW.
2. With the library to the left, walk to the corner and turn left on Wisconsin Avenue NW.
3. Turn right on 33rd Street NW.
4. Turn right on Dent Place NW.
5. Turn left on 35th Street NW.
6. Turn left on Volta Place NW.
7. Turn left on Wisconsin Avenue NW.
8. Turn right on Q Street NW.
9. Turn left on 31st Street NW.
10. Reverse direction on 31st Street NW.
11. Turn left on P Street NW.
12. Turn left on 27th Street NW.
13. Turn left on Q Street NW.
14. Turn right on 28th Street NW.
15. Turn left on R Street NW.
16. Turn right on 32nd Street NW.
17. Turn left on S Street NW.
18. Turn left on Wisconsin Avenue NW.

CONNECTING THE WALKS

For companion Walk 6 (Georgetown Southwest), continue south on Wisconsin Avenue NW.

William Wilson Corcoran's distinguished final resting place

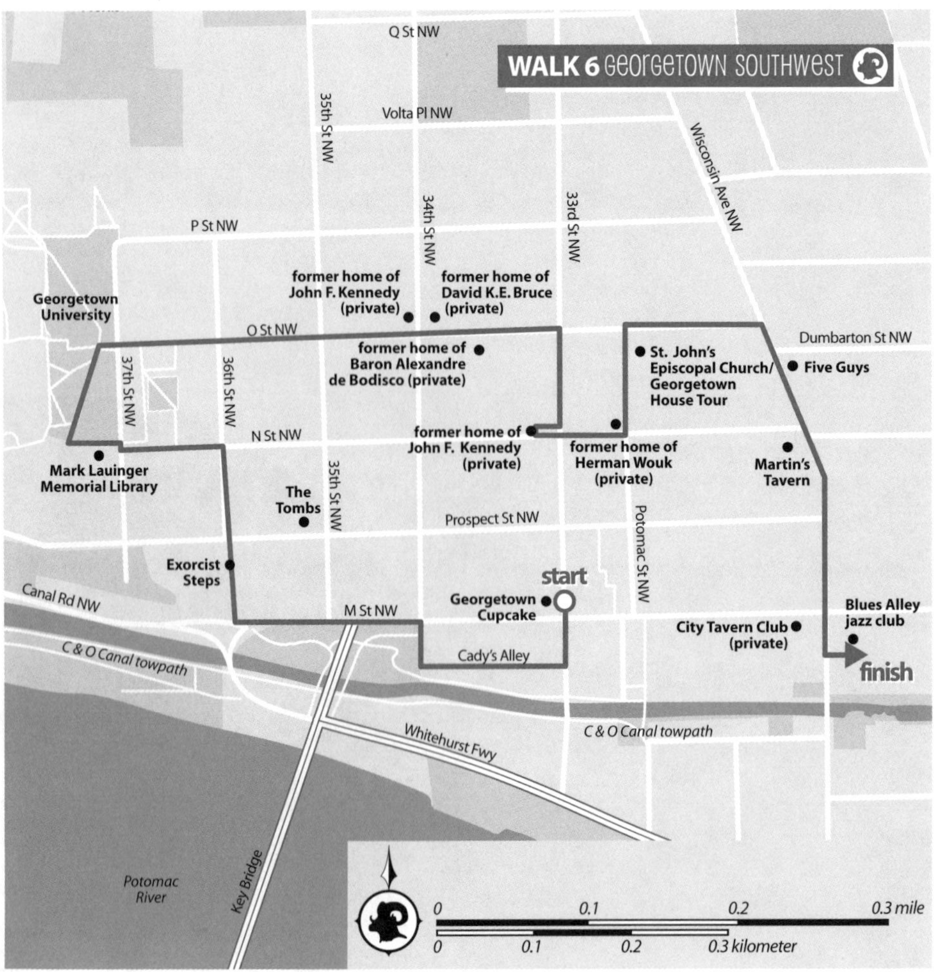

WALK 6 Georgetown Southwest
Q St NW
Volta Pl NW
35th St NW
34th St NW
33rd St NW
Wisconsin Ave NW
P St NW
former home of John F. Kennedy (private)
former home of David K.E. Bruce (private)
Georgetown University
O St NW
former home of Baron Alexandre de Bodisco (private)
Dumbarton St NW
St. John's Episcopal Church/ Georgetown House Tour
Five Guys
37th St NW
36th St NW
N St NW
former home of John F. Kennedy (private)
former home of Herman Wouk (private)
Martin's Tavern
Mark Lauinger Memorial Library
The Tombs
35th St NW
Prospect St NW
Potomac St NW
Exorcist Steps
start
Canal Rd NW
Georgetown Cupcake
M St NW
Blues Alley jazz club
City Tavern Club (private)
Cady's Alley
C & O Canal towpath
finish
Whitehurst Fwy
C & O Canal towpath
Potomac River
Key Bridge
0
0.1
0.2
0.3 mile
0
0.1
0.2
0.3 kilometer

6 Georgetown Southwest: Covert Cupcakes

BOUNDARIES: O Street NW, just east of Wisconsin Avenue NW, Blues Alley, and just west of 37th Street NW
DISTANCE: 1.5 miles
DIFFICULTY: Moderate due to stairs
PARKING: Limited street parking; parking garages on M Street NW, K Street NW, and elsewhere
PUBLIC TRANSIT: D.C.'s Circulator bus and Metrobus D5 run along M Street NW to several Metro stations.

New money, old money, little money. Everyone flocks to Georgetown. The main difference is that some can afford to stay longer and exploit more of its many riches. But the best thing about Georgetown is free: its gorgeous, walkable streets. The entire neighborhood of Georgetown, with its Federal-style brick row houses and mash-up of mansions, became a protected historic district in 1950. Even though visitors won't find many meaningful historical markers on the buildings, history thrives on every scenic street. If you squint your eyes and ignore the pricey electric Tesla automobiles (D.C.'s sole remaining new-car showroom), most streets almost look like they did in the 1800s—back when cupcakes first became popular.

- **Start at Georgetown Cupcake, 3301 M Street NW, to beat the line that sometimes forms there for the gooey-sweet goodies. The stars of TLC's *DC Cupcakes* TV show, sisters Katherine Kallinis Berman and Sophie Kallinis LaMontagne, founded it in 2008.**

- **Walk south on 33rd Street NW and turn right onto the brick and granite cobblestones of Cady's Alley, where you'll find food, furniture, and fashion boutiques in reinvented industrial buildings.**

- **Turn right on 34th Street NW and then left on M Street NW, Georgetown's main drag, with oodles of restaurants, bars, and retail therapy in historic row homes and commercial buildings. Turn right past Georgetown University's Car Barn building to climb the 75 Exorcist Steps. This steep outdoor staircase became famous in the 1973 horror flick *The Exorcist* when Father Karras tumbled down it. The Exorcist's author and screenwriter is Georgetown alumnus William Peter Blatty.**

- Follow the steps to 36th Street NW. Pass the Tombs restaurant and bar on the left, the Georgetown University hangout that inspired the movie *St. Elmo's Fire.* Turn left on N Street NW and follow it across 37th Street NW to climb 48 stairs into Georgetown University, the nation's oldest Catholic and Jesuit university. At the top, turn left into the Mark Lauinger Memorial Library. The granite-flecked concrete structure was designed in 1970 by John Carl Warnecke, who also designed President Kennedy's grave at Arlington National Cemetery. The library's vast collections, which are accessible to researchers, include the Russell J. Bowen Collection on Intelligence, Security and Covert Activities. CIA technical analyst Col. Russell J. Bowen donated most of this unparalleled collection in 1993. CIA directors William E. Colby and Richard Helms, who both lived in Georgetown, later donated papers. Exit the library and stay right on the diagonal brick sidewalk toward the O Street exit gate. On the left is Georgetown's flagship building, Healy Hall. The massive granite building with a steeple-like clock tower was built in 1877.

- Walk east on O Street NW to 34th Street NW. On the northwest corner is the four-story brick house where then-Congressman John F. Kennedy lived with his sister, Eunice, from 1949 to 1951, says Paul Kelsey Williams' book, *The Historic Homes of J.F.K.* Henry Addison also lived there. He was mayor of Georgetown before it became part of Washington, D.C. On the northeast corner is the rambling, two-story brick mansion that Under Armour sports clothing founder Kevin Plank bought in 2013, *Washingtonian* magazine says. In 1996, Plank started his Baltimore-based company a block away in his grandmother's three-story town house. His "new" eight-bedroom house, with a 34-foot ballroom and a heated lap pool, was also home to longtime ambassador David K. E. Bruce, who once worked for the OSS, America's first modern-day spy agency.

- Continue walking east on the cobblestone street with metal tracks from the defunct DC Transit streetcar system, which stopped running in 1962. On the right is the Bodisco House, famous as a federal period brick home and because Baron Alexandre de Bodisco, the 54-year-old Russian ambassador who owned it, married a 16-year-old, the Library of Congress says. Now it's home to Secretary of State and former Democratic presidential candidate John Kerry and his Mozambique-born wife, Maria Teresa Thierstein Simões-Ferreira Heinz Kerry, heir to the ketchup fortune of her late husband, Republican Sen. Henry John Heinz III.

- Turn right on 33rd Street NW and right again on N Street NW for the Kennedys' former home one door down on the right. They lived in this three-story brick home with green shutters with Caroline and little "John-John" right before moving into the White House. (JFK's pal Ben Bradlee moved next door after working as press attaché for the American Embassy in Paris and then for *Newsweek,* says Gregg Herken's 2014 book, *The Georgetown Set.*)

- Reverse direction on N Street NW for a brick town house with a red-orange door on the left at 3255. This is where Herman Wouk "began the narrative writing of *The Winds of War,* and (conducted) extensive research for *War and Remembrance,"* says the author's website. Wouk, who celebrated his 100th birthday in May 2015, wasn't the only hot-shot wordsmith in the neighborhood. Fellow Nobel Prize winner Sinclair Lewis, who wrote *Main Street* and *Arrowsmith,* lived at 3028 Q Street NW in the 1920s. And Pulitzer Prize winner Larry McMurtry taught at American and George Mason universities and owned a bookstore in Georgetown called Booked Up from 1971 to 1993. The author of *Lonesome Dove, The Last Picture Show,* and *Terms of Endearment* still runs the fine and scholarly bookshop—online and in his hometown of Archer City, Texas.

- Turn left on Potomac Street NW and right on O Street NW for the tan and white St. John's Episcopal Church on the right, where President Thomas Jefferson and Francis Scott Key once worshiped. Each spring since 1931, the church has sponsored its popular Georgetown House Tour to help support charities. Tickets include a self-guided tour of 8 to 10 coveted homes and gardens followed by tea sandwiches at the church. In the past, visitors have seen a stable cleverly converted into a home, abodes of current and former politicians, and a media honcho's historic mansion, among others.

St. John's Episcopal Church hosts the annual Georgetown House Tour.

- Continue on O Street NW and turn right on Wisconsin Avenue NW, Georgetown's main north–south shopping street, with stores such as UGG Australia, in rehabbed row houses and commercial structures. Across Wisconsin Avenue NW is Five Guys Burgers and Fries, which was a 24-hour French bistro called Au Pied de Cochon until 2004. A brass wall plaque inside marks the table where Soviet spy Vitaly Yurchenko ordered his "last supper" before skipping out from the CIA in 1985. That same year CIA veteran Aldrich Hazen Ames traded secret documents for cash with the Soviets at Chadwicks, a nearby pub, which closed its K Street location in 2014.

- Walk downhill on Wisconsin Avenue NW for Martin's Tavern on the right. Founded in 1933, the pub often welcomed President Kennedy and hosted every president from Harry S. Truman (Booth 6) to George W. Bush (Table 12).

- Continue down Wisconsin to cross M Street NW. One door down on the right at 3206 is the three-and-a-half-story building called the City Tavern Club. This private social club's brick clubhouse is "a rare surviving example of a federal period tavern," says the National Park Service. Built in 1796, it's also one of D.C.'s oldest buildings. When it was a public inn, the club says it welcomed George Washington and Thomas Jefferson.

- Continue south on Wisconsin Avenue NW and turn left into an alley for Blues Alley in a brick carriage house on the right. It calls itself "the nation's oldest continuing jazz supper club."

POINTS OF INTEREST

Georgetown Cupcake 3301 M St. NW, 202-333-8448, georgetowncupcake.com

Exorcist Steps Between M and Prospect Streets NW at 36th Street NW, maps.georgetown.edu/exorciststeps

Georgetown University: Joseph Mark Lauinger Memorial Library's Russell J. Bowen Collection on Intelligence, Security and Covert Activities 37th and N Streets NW, 202-687-7607, library.georgetown.edu/libraries/lauinger

(Private) former home of John F. Kennedy 1400 34th St. NW

(Private) former home of David K. E. Bruce 1405 34th St. NW

(Private) former home of Baron Alexandre de Bodisco 3322 O St. NW, loc.gov/pictures/item/dc0422 and lcweb2.loc.gov/master/pnp/habshaer/dc/dc0400/dc0422/data/dc0422data.pdf

(Private) former home of John F. Kennedy 3307 N St. NW

(Private) former home of Herman Wouk 3255 N St. NW

St. John's Episcopal Church 3240 O St. NW, 202-338-1796, stjohnsgeorgetown.org and facebook.com/thegeorgetownhousetour

Five Guys Burgers and Fries 1335 Wisconsin Ave. NW, 202-337-0400, fiveguys.com

Martin's Tavern 1264 Wisconsin Ave. NW, 202-333-7370, martinstavern.com

(Private) City Tavern Club 3206 M St. NW, 202-337-8770, citytavernclubdc.org

Blues Alley 1073 Wisconsin Ave. NW, 202-337-4141, bluesalley.com

route summary

1. Start at Georgetown Cupcake, 3301 M Street NW.
2. Walk south on 33rd Street NW.
3. Turn right into Cady's Alley.
4. Turn right on 34th Street NW.
5. Turn left on M Street NW.
6. Walk about 1.5 blocks. After passing the Car Barn on the right, turn right to walk up the Exorcist Steps leading to 36th Street NW.
7. Turn left on N Street NW.
8. Continue across 37th Street NW to walk up the steps into Georgetown University.
9. At the top of the stairs, turn left into the Lauinger Library.
10. After exiting, stay right on the diagonal brick sidewalk to the O Street exit gate.
11. Walk east on O Street NW.
12. Turn right on 33rd Street NW.
13. Turn right on N Street NW and then reverse direction.
14. Turn left on Potomac Street NW.
15. Turn right on O Street NW.
16. Turn right on Wisconsin Avenue NW.
17. Turn left into Blues Alley.

connecting the walks

To reach three companion walks from Blues Alley: Head north on Wisconsin Avenue for Walk 5 (Georgetown North); head south on Wisconsin Avenue NW to the Potomac River for Walk 13 (Potomac River Panorama and Watergates); and head east on Blues Alley to 31st Street NW for Walk 7 (Georgetown Southeast).

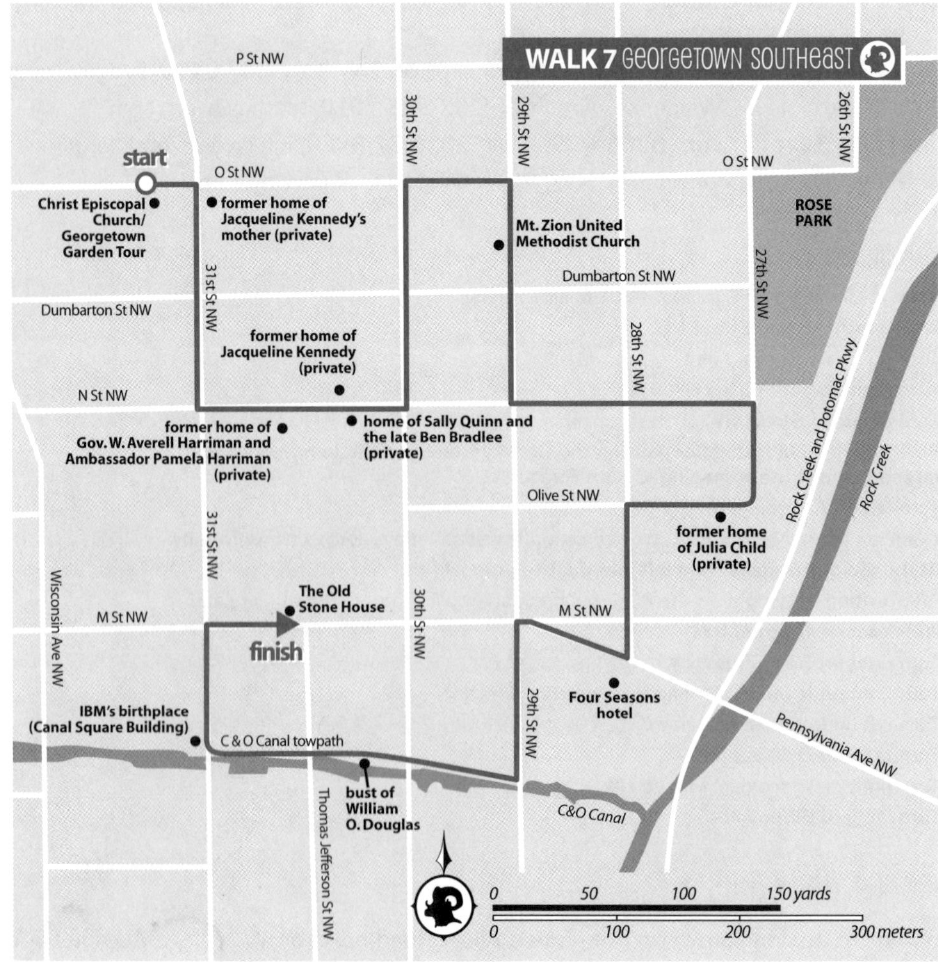
WALK 7 Georgetown Southeast
P St NW
O St NW
start
Christ Episcopal Church/ Georgetown Garden Tour
former home of Jacqueline Kennedy's mother (private)
30th St NW
29th St NW
26th St NW
Mt. Zion United Methodist Church
ROSE PARK
Dumbarton St NW
31st St NW
27th St NW
28th St NW
former home of Jacqueline Kennedy (private)
N St NW
former home of Gov. W. Averell Harriman and Ambassador Pamela Harriman (private)
home of Sally Quinn and the late Ben Bradlee (private)
Olive St NW
Rock Creek and Potomac Pkwy
Rock Creek
former home of Julia Child (private)
Wisconsin Ave NW
The Old Stone House
M St NW
finish
Four Seasons hotel
IBM's birthplace (Canal Square Building)
C & O Canal towpath
Pennsylvania Ave NW
bust of William O. Douglas
Thomas Jefferson St NW
C&O Canal
0 50 100 150 yards
0 100 200 300 meters

7 GEORGETOWN SOUTHEAST: LEGENDS AND GARDENS

BOUNDARIES: O Street NW, 27th Street NW, C&O Canal, and 31st Street NW
DISTANCE: 1.3 miles
DIFFICULTY: Easy
PARKING: Limited street parking; parking garages on M Street NW, K Street NW, and elsewhere
PUBLIC TRANSIT: The DC Circulator bus and Metrobus D5 run along M Street NW to several Metro stations.

Sure, size matters. But a Renoir is a Renoir whether it's large or small. And the same holds for Georgetown's exquisite gardens, from pocket-size gems behind skinny row houses to magnum masterpieces at lavish mansions. A few of the gardens take to the public stage each spring at Georgetown's Garden Tour. Some belong (or once belonged) to movers and shakers and spies. Georgetown has attracted legends since the bustling tobacco port formally became a city in 1751, named George Town, Maryland, likely after England's King George II. Later Georgetown was absorbed into the newly minted city of Washington, D.C. and was forced to change virtually all of its street names. But it never lost its identity or its allure. It attracted Julia Child in the 1940s. Way before Child became "The French Chef," she lived in a petite row house when she worked at America's World War II spy agency. In the 1980s, *The Washington Post*'s Ben Bradlee bought an estate as big as the larger-than-life executive editor himself. Even computer giant IBM got its start here.

- **Begin at Christ Church Georgetown, a brick Episcopal church with Gothic arches, on the southwest corner of 31st and O Streets NW. This 1818 church is home base for the annual Georgetown Garden Tour, run by the Georgetown Garden Club. Founded in 1924, the nonprofit club invites visitors each spring to tiptoe near the tulips of about eight masterfully designed gardens to help fund its beautification projects. Tickets include afternoon tea at the church. There's no winter tour, but some Georgetown gardens even light up in January with sunny-yellow winter jasmine vines and little white snowdrops pushing up through the crackled dirt and snow.**

- **On the southeast corner is the private Queen Anne–style mansion from 1870 where Jacqueline Kennedy's mom, Janet, and her stepdad, Hugh Auchincloss, lived. When "new" owners Jennifer and Laughlin Phillips, of the Phillips Collection museum, put it** on the market in 2000, Hillary Rodham Clinton toured the nine-bedroom, 12-fireplace, three-car-garage mansion for more than an hour, *The Washington Post* reported. She and hubby Bill wound up choosing a more secluded home on a dead-end street.

- Turn right to walk south on 31st Street NW and turn left on storied N Street NW, with its brick herringbone sidewalk. On the right at 3038 is the split-level brick house of former New York governor and Under Secretary of State William Averell Harriman and his second wife, Marie. After her death, he married British-born Pamela Beryl Digby Churchill Hayward, who became a big Democratic fundraiser and then an ambassador to France. A few doors down at 3014 is the 1700s estate with a tennis court, where *The Washington Post*'s Sally Quinn lives. Her late husband, Ben Bradlee, the *Post*'s executive editor during the Watergate era and beyond, bought it in 1983, the *Post* says. President Abraham Lincoln's son, Robert, lived there in the early 1900s. Across the street at 3017 is the 1794 three-story brick house, with its four-columned white porch, where Jacqueline Kennedy dwelled for almost a year after JFK's assassination. She also lived briefly at the Harriman's mansion before she bought this house in 1964 for $175,000, news reports show.

- Continue east on N Street NW and turn left on 30th Street NW. Turn right on O Street NW and right again on 29th Street NW for Mt. Zion United Methodist Church on the right. Founded in 1816, it's D.C.'s oldest African American congregation, says Cultural Tourism DC's *African American Heritage Trail* brochure. This 15-block Herring Hill neighborhood, from 29th and P Streets to Rock Creek Park, was once the center of Georgetown's black community. Now blacks are a minority in Georgetown.

- Continue south on 29th Street NW and turn left on N Street NW. Turn right on 27th Street NW to walk past the tail end of Rose Park, a flat stretch of green overlooking Rock Creek Parkway's profusion of spring daffodils below. Turn right on Olive Street NW for the small, daffodil-yellow row house on the left, where cooking guru and one-time spy Julia Child lived. Julia "and her new husband, Paul, first moved to Olive Street in 1948, after they'd met in Ceylon, where both were posted for the Office of Strategic Services (OSS)," says *Washingtonian* magazine. After a stint in France, they returned in 1956. For more than a year in the 1950s, Julia ran a cooking class for her powerful neighbors, including Kay Graham and Polly Wisner, wife of deputy CIA director Frank Wisner, says C. David Heymann's book, *The Georgetown Ladies' Social Club.*

- Continue west on Olive Street NW and turn left on 28th Street NW. Cross Pennsylvania Avenue NW for the Four Seasons hotel. It may not be *1600* Pennsylvania Avenue, but its White House–connected power players and celebrities sometimes luxuriate at this modern, brick hotel. Visitors don't have to stay there to enjoy its quiet elegance, plush spa, and restaurants alongside Lock 1 of the C&O Canal.

- With the hotel to the rear, turn left to walk west on Pennsylvania Avenue NW and turn left on 29th Street NW. Turn right on the brick towpath along the canal, which was completed in 1850 as a shipping corridor along the sometimes unnavigable Potomac River. Walk 1.5 blocks to Lock 3 for a bust of William O. Douglas in a brick plaza. In 1954, the Supreme Court Justice, then 55 years old, hiked from Cumberland, Maryland, to Georgetown on the 184.5-mile-long dirt towpath to help prevent it from becoming a highway.

- Continue on the towpath across Thomas Jefferson Street NW for an Amsterdam-like block with a canal lock and colorful row houses. Turn right on 31st Street NW. On the left corner facing the canal is the brick building where IBM started. Herman Hollerith ran his Tabulating Machine Company there in the 1890s. It "was consolidated into the Computing-Tabulating-Recording Co. in 1911, and CTR . . . was renamed IBM 13 years later," says IBM. This "father of modern automatic computation" built the first punched-card tabulating and sorting machines and the first key punch. His ideas sprang from his stint as a statistician for the federal government's Census Office, which hand-counted its census in 1880. Census put Hollerith's new tabulating "machine to work on the 1890 census. It did the job in two years" (instead of seven to eight) and "saved the government $5 million," says IBM and the United States Census Bureau. The Census used modified versions of his technology until computers took over in the 1950s, says the agency. His wife, Lucia Beverly Talcott Hollerith, who co-founded the Georgetown Garden Club, might be pleased with her hubbie's old factory. Now it's part of Canal Square, an award-winning rehab project by architect Arthur Cotton Moore. Part of it is the Sea Catch Restaurant & Raw Bar, which has a canal-side patio and a gardenlike view.

- Continue north on 31st Street NW and turn right on M Street NW for the Old Stone House. Visitors can tromp up the narrow stairs in this rustic granite home to see how working families lived in the 18th century, with their big stone cooking fireplace and compact, Spartan sleeping quarters. The National Park Service says this 1765 house

is D.C.'s oldest structure on its original foundation. When the government bought it in 1953, it was a used-car lot.

Points of Interest

Christ Church/Georgetown Garden Tour 31st and O Streets NW, 202-333-6677, christchurchgeorgetown.org

(Private) former home of Jacqueline Kennedy's mother 3044 O St. NW

Private homes on N Street NW W. Averell and Pamela Harriman, 3038; Ben Bradlee and Sally Quinn, 3014; and Jacqueline Kennedy, 3017

Mt. Zion United Methodist Church 1334 29th St. NW, 202-234-0148, mtzionumcdc.org

(Private) former home of Julia Child 2706 Olive St. NW

Four Seasons hotel 2800 Pennsylvania Ave. NW, 202-342-0444, fourseasons.com/washington

Bust of William O. Douglas Chesapeake & Ohio Canal between Thomas Jefferson and 30th Streets NW, 301-767-3714, nps.gov/choh/planyourvisit/georgetownvisitorcenter.htm

IBM's birthplace (Canal Square Building) 1054 31st St. NW, www-03.ibm.com/ibm/history/exhibits/vintage/vintage_4506VV2027.html

The Old Stone House 3051 M St. NW, 202-895-6070, nps.gov/olst/index.htm

Route Summary

1. Start at Christ Church Georgetown, 3116 O Street NW.
2. Turn right on 31st Street NW.
3. Turn left on N Street NW.
4. Turn left on 30th Street NW.
5. Turn right on O Street NW.
6. Turn right on 29th Street NW.
7. Turn left on N Street NW.
8. Turn right on 27th Street NW.
9. Turn right on Olive Street NW.

10. Turn left on 28th Street NW.
11. Cross Pennsylvania Avenue NW.
12. Facing the hotel, turn right to walk west on Pennsylvania Avenue NW.
13. Turn left on 29th Street NW.
14. Turn right on the C&O Canal's brick towpath.
15. Turn right on 31st Street NW.
16. Turn right on M Street NW.

CONNECTING THE WALKS

For companion Walk 6 (Georgetown Southwest), turn left instead of right on M Street NW. For Walk 13 (Potomac River Panorama and Watergates), follow 31st Street NW south to the Potomac River.

One of Georgetown's five C&O Canal locks

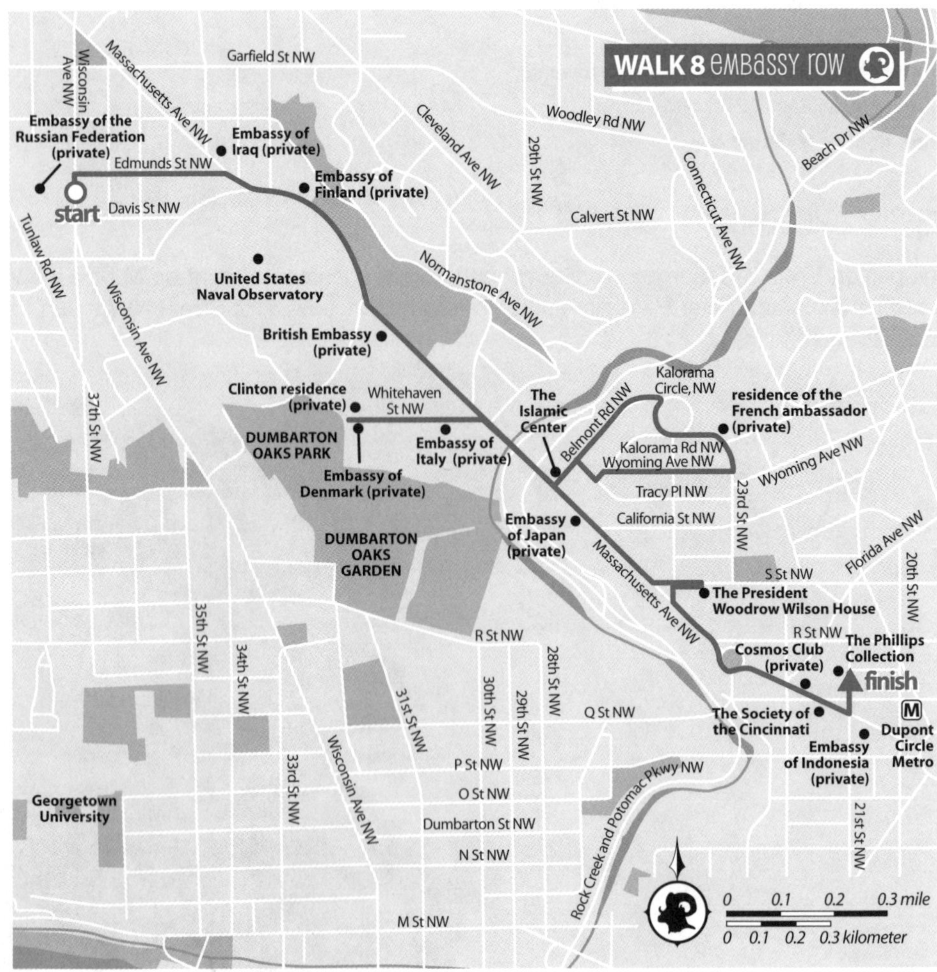
WALK 8 embassy row
Garfield St NW
Wisconsin Ave NW
Massachusetts Ave NW
Embassy of the Russian Federation (private)
Embassy of Iraq (private)
Edmunds St NW
Embassy of Finland (private)
start
Davis St NW
Cleveland Ave NW
29th St NW
Woodley Rd NW
Connecticut Ave NW
Beach Dr NW
Calvert St NW
Tunlaw Rd NW
United States Naval Observatory
Normanstone Ave NW
Wisconsin Ave NW
British Embassy (private)
37th St NW
Clinton residence (private)
Whitehaven St NW
DUMBARTON OAKS PARK
Embassy of Italy (private)
Embassy of Denmark (private)
The Islamic Center
Belmont Rd NW
Kalorama Circle, NW
residence of the French ambassador (private)
Kalorama Rd NW
Wyoming Ave NW
Wyoming Ave NW
Tracy Pl NW
23rd St NW
California St NW
Embassy of Japan (private)
DUMBARTON OAKS GARDEN
Massachusetts Ave NW
S St NW
Florida Ave NW
20th St NW
The President Woodrow Wilson House
R St NW
R St NW
Cosmos Club (private)
The Phillips Collection
finish
35th St NW
34th St NW
31st St NW
30th St NW
29th St NW
28th St NW
Q St NW
The Society of the Cincinnati
M
Dupont Circle Metro
Embassy of Indonesia (private)
33rd St NW
Wisconsin Ave NW
P St NW
O St NW
Rock Creek and Potomac Pkwy NW
Georgetown University
Dumbarton St NW
N St NW
21st St NW
M St NW
0 0.1 0.2 0.3 mile
0 0.1 0.2 0.3 kilometer

8 Embassy Row: From Siberia to the Seine

BOUNDARIES: **Wisconsin Avenue NW, Edmunds Street NW, Massachusetts Avenue NW, and 21st Street NW**
DISTANCE: **3.6 miles**
DIFFICULTY: **Moderate**
PARKING: **Limited 2-hour free street parking; parking garages south on Wisconsin Avenue NW; Metro recommended**
PUBLIC TRANSIT: **Metrobus 31 runs along Wisconsin Avenue NW to several Metro stations. Metrobuses N2, N3, N4, and N6 run along Massachusetts Avenue NW to Dupont Circle Metro and other stations.**

Pack a lunch. There's *so* much to see on this journey from Siberia (the Russian Embassy) to the Seine River (the French ambassador's "palace" and a museum with a famous Seine painting). At least it's virtually all downhill on Massachusetts Avenue NW, also called Embassy Row. Since no tour can explore all its treasures, this focuses on several private embassies and three public museums. It also rolls past America's master clock and a former president's private home.

- **Start at the Russian Federation's Embassy, 2650 Wisconsin Avenue NW. Its massive white building was designed by Soviet architect Michael Posokhin, who designed the State Kremlin Palace. Somewhere beneath Wisconsin Avenue NW is (or was) a secret tunnel that the FBI and the National Security Agency used to eavesdrop on the Soviets, wrote Pulitzer Prize–winning author David A. Vise in *The Bureau and the Mole.* FBI counterintelligence agent Robert Philip Hanssen warned the Soviets about the tunnel and a nearby house where the Feds monitored them before he was arrested for spying in 2001. An FBI spokesperson still says it "has never confirmed nor denied such a story."**

- **With the embassy to the left, walk north on Wisconsin Avenue NW and turn right on Edmunds Street NW. When it dead-ends at Massachusetts Avenue NW, the Embassy of the Republic of Iraq is across the street to the left in a Tudor-style brick building. Turn right to pass the dignified stone homes of the Royal Norwegian Embassy and the Holy**

See's equivalent, called an Apostolic Nunciature, on the left. On the right is the fenced campus of the United States Naval Observatory and the vice president's home. It's impossible to miss the red-numbered digital clock out front or the 2,000-foot-diameter Observatory Circle on a map. The Navy needed that buffer to protect its clocks from the vibrations of horse carriage traffic when it moved to the then "dark-sky" outpost in 1893, said spokesman Geoff Chester. Today's traffic doesn't faze its Master Clock, a bank of 100 atomic clocks that keeps precise time for the military, one of the observatory's chief functions. (The National Institute of Standards and Technology is America's *civilian* timekeeper.) Visitors can register online to peer through a telescope and explore the round rare-book library designed by Richard Morris Hunt (who designed North Carolina's famous Biltmore estate) *if* they can snag one of the extremely limited post-9/11 astronomy tours. They won't see the vice president's three-story Queen Anne house, which was built for the superintendent in 1893.

- Across the street is the Embassy of Finland, built in 1994, with its copper-clad walls and ivy-covered trellis. Its interior also blends the Machine Age and nature with blonde-wood floors, a wooden sauna, and a rear two-story window wall framing towering tulip poplars and other trees along Normanstone Parkway. Finland regularly hosts exhibitions, and it invites visitors to register online for a monthly tour of its green building, one of two platinum LEED-certified embassies in the world, the embassy says.

- Just past the Naval Observatory is the British Embassy on the right. Queen Elizabeth might wince if she saw the hundreds of commoners pouring into the ambassador's staid brick country house, designed by Sir Edwin Lutyens, and traipsing through the formal gardens during the unusual access throughout the annual EU Open House. But Anglophiles can't get seem to get enough of the royal compound, even without cherubs from the nearby British School serenading them or the goodies from Union Jack's Pub. After all, it is America's motherland.

- Pass the neoclassical Embassy of South Africa on the left and the cantilevered modern Embassy of Brazil on the right. Turn right on Whitehaven Street NW for the massive Embassy of Italy on the corner. The sculptural structure with its small punctuated windows is an "abstract rendition of a Tuscan palazzo," the American Institute of Architects says. It also expresses D.C.'s original map, with two right triangles (Virginia and Maryland) separated by an atrium (the Potomac River). Italy hosts gobs of public events.

- At the end of Whitehaven is a private embassy on the left, a trailhead to Dumbarton Oaks Park in the middle, and a former president's private residence on the right. President William "Bill" Jefferson Clinton, the first president with an email address, and Hillary Rodham Clinton, who hopes to become America's first female president, bought the brick Georgian-style house in 2001. Across the street is Denmark's 1960 glass and Greenland marble embassy.

- Return to Massachusetts Avenue NW and continue south for the Islamic Center on the left, with its 160-foot minaret. The center welcomes visitors to its bookstore and its eye-popping gilded mosque with blue Turkish tiles and Moroccan stained glass. While it's not an embassy—Egypt, Pakistan, Saudi Arabia, and other countries built it in 1957—the mosque independently runs a bazaar with homemade food and crafts during Passport DC.

- Turn left on shady Belmont Road NW and right on Kalorama Circle. Each Goldilocks-size stone or brick mansion seems more luscious than the last in this early 1900s residential enclave. Turn left on Kalorama Road NW for the private, park-side estate of the French ambassador on the left. French-born Jules Henri de Sibour created this 23,000-square-foot manor house in 1911 for lead-paint manufacturer William Watson Lawrence. The French government bought the brick and stone showplace in 1936. Katy Perry and Kevin Spacey are just two of the droves of celebs who have partied there. They attended the *Vanity Fair*–Bloomberg blowout after the 2013 White House Correspondents' Association Dinner.

- Stay right for 23rd Street NW and turn right on Wyoming Avenue NW to pass several embassies. Turn left on

Hindu goddess Saraswati at the Embassy of Indonesia

Getting Inside Embassy Gates

Even if you aren't a VIP or your job isn't listed in the Plum Book (of presidentially appointed positions), you can still find ways to venture inside some embassies. First, tap their websites. Some countries encourage visitors to subscribe to their mailing lists for movies, tango lessons, wine tastings, and other cultural events. Check out groups that offer entrée onto the embassies' foreign soil, including alumni associations, work-related groups, The Embassy Series concerts, international clubs, and even online Meetups. D.C. also hosts two free embassy festivals each spring. Passport DC's Around the World tour features more than 50 embassies. Cultural Tourism DC started it in 2008 because "it's fun," said Executive Director Steven Shulman. "Where else can you go in the world and capture the culture of different countries from different continents all in an afternoon?" The European Union began its Open House day for its 28 member states in 2007. It's similar to the EU's Europe Day open houses abroad to celebrate peace and unity. Before that, the main way ordinary Washingtonians could visit a slew of embassies was on the annual Goodwill embassy tour. The nonprofit began its famous fundraisers on April 26, 1958, and halted them for security reasons after the September 11, 2001, terrorist attacks. For the most current diplomatic list of the 171 embassies on Embassy Row, the International Chancery Center, and elsewhere, visit the State Department's website at **state.gov/s/cpr/rls/dpl.**

Kalorama Road NW; turn right on Tracy Place NW; turn left on Belmont Road NW; and turn left on Massachusetts Avenue NW for the Embassy of Japan on the right. Behind the Georgian Revival mansion that Japan built in 1931 is its Ippakutei teahouse, which the embassy calls "the greatest of its kind outside of Japan."

- **Continue south and turn left on S Street NW for The President Woodrow Wilson House on the right. Thomas, the 28th president's first name, and his wife, Edith, lived there after he left the White House in 1921. The Georgian Revival brick house is virtually untouched from the days the Wilsons lived there, with their Steinway piano and wall-size Gobelin tapestry from France.**

- Reverse direction on S Street NW and turn left on Massachusetts Avenue NW, past a nearly continuous stream of embassies in former mansions from D.C.'s Gilded Age around the turn of the 20th century. On the right, at Sheridan Circle and 23rd Street NW, is the residence of the ambassador of Turkey. Edward Hamlin Everett, inventor of the fluted bottle cap, built the White House–esque mansion in 1915. On the left at Florida Avenue NW is the prestigious Cosmos Club. Its ornate Indiana limestone façade was "inspired by the style of Louis XVI," the club's history says. The three-and-a-half-story main building flanked by two-story wings was designed in 1904 for railroad heir Mary Scott Townsend. Formed in 1878 "by men distinguished in science, literature and the arts," the club voted to admit female members in 1988, after the D.C. Office of Human Rights ruled that it may have violated the city's antidiscrimination law and the Supreme Court broadened "the power of cities and states to ban discrimination against women and minorities," the Associated Press wrote at the time. "Until 1973, women guests were required to enter the club through a side door."

- Across the street is The Society of the Cincinnati's museum and headquarters in a monumental mansion with arched gates and a semicircular portico. It was founded in 1783 by officers of the Continental Army and their French counterparts who served in the American Revolution. Member and diplomat Larz Anderson and his author wife, Isabel, built the 50-room villa with a tennis court and three-story carriage house as a winter home in 1904.

- One door down at 21st Street NW is the Embassy of Indonesia, the regal mansion where the last private owner of the Hope Diamond lived. Socialite Evalyn Walsh McLean didn't let the 45.52-carat blue beauty surrounded by 16 white diamonds gather dust in her jewelry box. Now it's one of the hottest draws at the Smithsonian National Museum of Natural History.

- Turn left on 21st Street NW for The Phillips Collection on the left. More than 3,000 impressionist and modern works of art by Rothko, van Gogh, and other artists grace this private museum. It opened in 1921 and was expanded in 2006. The museum says its best-known artwork is Pierre-Auguste Renoir's *Luncheon of the Boating Party,* a painting of friends sharing food and wine on a balcony overlooking the Seine River.

POINTS OF INTEREST

(Private) Embassy of the Russian Federation 2650 Wisconsin Ave. NW, 202-298-5700, russianembassy.org

(Private) United States Naval Observatory and vice president's private residence 3450 Massachusetts Ave. NW, 202-762-1467, www.usno.navy.mil/USNO

(Private) Embassy of Finland 3301 Massachusetts Ave. NW, 202-298-5800, finland.org

(Private) British Embassy 3100 Massachusetts Ave. NW, 202-588-6500, gov.uk/government/world/organisations/british-embassy-washington

(Private) Embassy of Italy 3000 Whitehaven St. NW, 202-612-4400, www.ambwashingtondc.esteri.it/Ambasciata_Washington

(Private) Embassy of Denmark 3200 Whitehaven St. NW, 202-234-4300, usa.um.dk

(Private) home of former President William Jefferson Clinton 3067 Whitehaven St. NW

The Islamic Center 2551 Massachusetts Ave. NW, 202-332-8343, islamiccenterdc.com

(Private) residence of the French ambassador 2221 Kalorama Rd. NW, 202-944-6000, ambafrance-us.org

(Private) Embassy of Japan 2520 Massachusetts Ave. NW, 202-238-6700, www.us.emb-japan.go.jp/english/html

The President Woodrow Wilson House 2340 S St. NW, 202-387-4062, woodrowwilsonhouse.org

(Private) Cosmos Club 2121 Massachusetts Ave. NW, 202-387-7783, cosmosclub.org

The Society of the Cincinnati 2118 Massachusetts Ave. NW, 202-785-2040, societyofthecincinnati.org

(Private) Embassy of Indonesia 2020 Massachusetts Ave. NW, 202-775-5200, embassyofindonesia.org

The Phillips Collection 1600 21st St. NW, 202-387-2151, phillipscollection.org

route summary

1. Start at the Embassy of the Russian Federation, 2650 Wisconsin Avenue NW.
2. With the embassy to the left, walk north on Wisconsin Avenue NW.
3. Turn right on Edmunds Street NW.
4. Turn right on Massachusetts Avenue NW.
5. Turn right on Whitehaven Street NW and reverse direction.
6. Turn right on Massachusetts Avenue NW.
7. Turn left on Belmont Road NW.
8. Turn right on Kalorama Circle NW.
9. Turn left on Kalorama Road NW.
10. Stay to the right for 23rd Street NW.
11. Turn right on Wyoming Avenue NW.
12. Turn left on Kalorama Road NW.
13. Turn right on Tracy Place NW.
14. Turn left on Belmont Road NW.
15. Turn left on Massachusetts Avenue NW.
16. Turn left on S Street NW and reverse direction.
17. Turn left on Massachusetts Avenue NW.
18. Turn left on 21st Street NW.

connecting the walks

For Walk 3 (National Zoo to National Cathedral), continue north on Wisconsin Avenue NW, and for Walk 5 (Georgetown North), head south. Walk 12 (Dupont Circle) starts two blocks from the end at the Dupont Circle Metro.

The Islamic Center welcomes visitors.

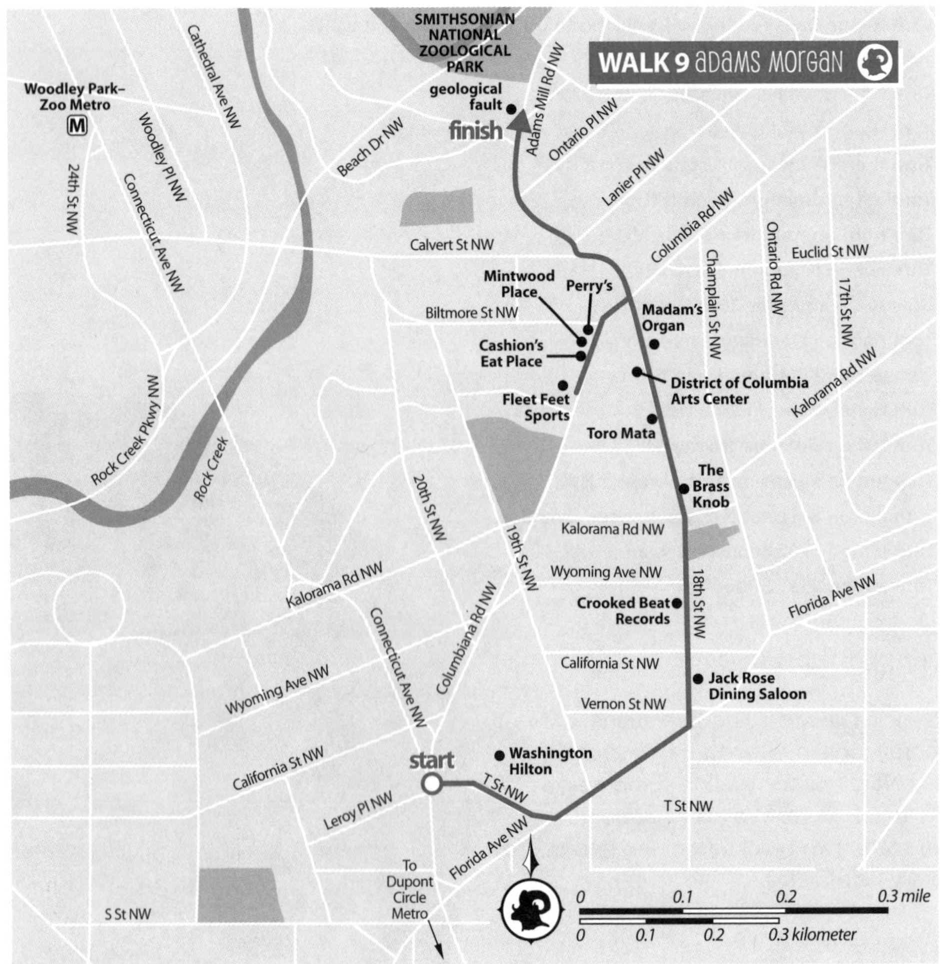
WALK 9 adams morgan
SMITHSONIAN NATIONAL ZOOLOGICAL PARK
geological fault
finish
Woodley Park–Zoo Metro
M
Cathedral Ave NW
Woodley Pl NW
24th St NW
Connecticut Ave NW
Beach Dr NW
Adams Mill Rd NW
Ontario Pl NW
Lanier Pl NW
Columbia Rd NW
Calvert St NW
Euclid St NW
Ontario Rd NW
Champlain St NW
17th St NW
Mintwood Place
Perry's
Madam's Organ
Biltmore St NW
Cashion's Eat Place
District of Columbia Arts Center
Fleet Feet Sports
Toro Mata
Kalorama Rd NW
Rock Creek Pkwy NW
Rock Creek
20th St NW
The Brass Knob
Kalorama Rd NW
19th St NW
Wyoming Ave NW
Kalorama Rd NW
18th St NW
Crooked Beat Records
Florida Ave NW
Connecticut Ave NW
Columbiana Rd NW
California St NW
Wyoming Ave NW
Jack Rose Dining Saloon
Vernon St NW
start
Washington Hilton
California St NW
T St NW
T St NW
Leroy Pl NW
Florida Ave NW
To Dupont Circle Metro
S St NW
0
0.1
0.2
0.3 mile
0
0.1
0.2
0.3 kilometer

9 ADAMS MORGAN: STILL ROCKING D.C.

BOUNDARIES: **Connecticut Avenue NW, T Street NW, 18th Street NW, and Clydesdale Place NW**
DISTANCE: **1.3 miles**
DIFFICULTY: **Easy**
PARKING: **Limited street parking; parking garages on 18th and Champlain Streets NW and at the Washington Hilton**
PUBLIC TRANSIT: **The Dupont Circle Metro is a half mile south of the start on Connecticut Avenue NW. The Woodley Park-Zoo/Adams Morgan Metro station is a half mile from the end of the walk on Connecticut Avenue NW. Metrobuses L1 and L2 link the two stations. At the finish at 18th and Calvert Streets NW, the DC Circulator bus runs to the Woodley Park Metro, and Metrobuses 90 and 93 connect to the U Street Metro.**

Way back in the 1980s and 1990s, when tightly wound Washington was the farthest thing from cool, Adams Morgan was arguably its hippest hangout. Adams Morgan is still cool—even after rocketing rents and renaissance shooed away some of its hipsters and their art and nightlife. It's just more settled now, if not more mature. Its Adams Morgan Day festival is approaching midlife, and it's still hanging on. And the dozens of restaurants, shops, and (sometimes rowdy) bars in this multicultural neighborhood still pack allure. Adams Morgan is anchored to the southwest by a landmark for an event that rocked D.C.'s recent past and to the north by some rocks that shook its ancient history and might rattle its future.

- **Start at the Washington Hilton, a 1,070-room hotel at 1919 Connecticut Avenue NW. The T Street entrance to this curvy, concrete building is where John W. Hinckley Jr. tried to assassinate then-President Ronald Reagan in 1981. White House Press Secretary Jim Brady, who suffered severe injuries, died in 2014. Hinckley resides in D.C.'s St. Elizabeth's psychiatric hospital.**

- **With the hotel entrance to the rear, turn left to walk east on T Street NW. Turn left on Florida Avenue NW and turn left on 18th Street NW for Adams Morgan's main drag. Cafés, bars, and stores fill the color-splashed Victorian row houses along the nine-block strip.**

- At the bottom of 18th Street NW on the right is Jack Rose Dining Saloon. Diners can choose from more than 1,800 bottles of bourbon, Scotch, and rye whiskeys at Jack's, "one of the largest retailers of whiskey in the Western Hemisphere," *The Washington Post* says.

- One block on the left is Crooked Beat Records, a basement store stocked with thousands of new and used vinyl records from the rock-and-roll era and beyond.

- A couple of blocks uphill on the right is the purple and pink home of The Brass Knob Architectural Antiques. It has been supplying savvy decorators with brass, glass, crystal, and bronze doorknobs, hardware, lighting, and other vintage treasures since 1981.

- One block farther on the left is Toro Mata. The decade-old shop sells art, jewelry, alpaca clothing, and home decorations handcrafted by Peruvian artisans, such as yellow butterfly wings encased in sterling silver pendants and a colorful collection of retablos (religious-themed folk-art figurines in shadowboxes). It's one of several shops and cafés that reflect the Latin immigrants who live nearby.

- Also on the left is the District of Columbia Arts Center. At the top of a creaky wooden staircase is the center's 800-square-foot art gallery and 46-seat theater. The nonprofit began in 1989 as an alternative arts haven. Alternative lifestyles have a history in the neighborhood: Adams Morgan was home to the "radical" Black Panthers and Students for a Democratic Society in the 1960s and 1970s.

- Across the street on the right is Madam's Organ. The blues bar is known for the two-story-high mural of a chesty redhead on the side of its town house and as one of Adams Morgan's oldest bars and music venues. It's also the site of the first Toys R Us store. Native son Charles P. Lazarus opened his Children's Bargain Town baby furniture store in his dad's bike shop in 1948, and it grew into an international chain with more than 1,700 stores, says Cultural Tourism DC's *Adams Morgan Heritage Trail* brochure and the company.

- Continue on 18th Street NW and turn left on Columbia Road NW for a trio of palate-pleasing restaurants on the right.

- First up is Perry's restaurant, a people-pleaser for about 30 years, known for its sushi, Sunday drag queen brunch, and rooftop terrace.

Best Time to Visit D.C.

There is no bad time to visit Washington.

Fall is a fabulous time for a stroll under canopies of red oak, orange maple, and yellow sycamore trees that brighten the streets and parks; a new Supreme Court session; the start of Washington Wizards basketball; and a new season of plays, concerts, and festivals, such as Adams Morgan Day.

Winter is a wonderful time for a trek by the Washington Monument when it rises from a sheet of snow; plummeting hotel prices; holiday shopping at crowd-free museums; and leafless trees that offer clear views of bald eagles (our national emblem) fishing to feed their babies, which typically hatch in January or February.

Spring is a spectacular time for sauntering under fluffy cherry blossoms around the Tidal Basin; the White House Easter Egg Roll; Capitol Hill and Georgetown home and garden tours; and an around-the-world spree at Passport DC's and the European Union's embassy open houses.

Summer is a superb time for ambling along the National Mall; sampling world cultures at the Smithsonian Folklife Festival; the Mall's less crowded dress rehearsals the day before the televised Memorial Day and Fourth of July concerts; Nationals baseball; and cruising the Potomac and Anacostia Rivers like Captain John Smith did in 1608.

- Next door is a restaurant fit for a president. President Obama and the first lady dined there in 2012. The president ordered a cheeseburger, according to the photo posted on his Instagram page. *Condé Nast Traveler* magazine named Mintwood as one of the best new restaurants in the world in 2013.

- Cashion's Eat Place, next door, has been winning accolades since it opened in 1995. Restaurant founder Ann Cashion is gone, but praises continue for its Mediterranean-infused American dishes, such as spit-roasted goat with caramelized onions. *Washingtonian* magazine pegged Cashion's and Mintwood as two of the top 100 restaurants in the whole DMV. (DMV is "millennial speak" for D.C. and its Maryland and Virginia suburbs.)

- **Also on the right is Fleet Feet Sports. This shoe store for runners, walkers, and other fitness buffs has been run by the family of former D.C. Mayor (and triathlete) Adrian Fenty since 1984.**

- **Reverse direction on Columbia Road NW. Turn left on Adams Mill Road NW and walk about four blocks to Clydesdale Place NW. Just past the employee entrance to the National Zoo on the left is a geological fault cordoned off by a chain-link fence, concrete, and stone cage. This is the sole visible fault of a fault zone beneath the zoo, says the zoo's geological history. Geologist N. H. Darton fenced it in during the 1920s to protect it from vandalism, but he didn't keep out the decades-old beech tree, whose roots poke through it. "Faults are abundant in the bedrock around Washington but they are generally old, 'dead' [inactive] faults associated with tectonic events that occurred hundreds of millions of years ago," said professional geologist Tony Fleming, author of the geologic map of this part of D.C. "This one, however, cuts a much younger gravel deposit and is probably less than a million years old. Anything that recent is potentially still active."**

- **After the fault, reverse direction on Adams Mill Road NW. At Calvert Street NW, catch the DC Circulator Bus to the Woodley Park-Zoo/Adams Morgan Metro.**

POINTS OF INTEREST

Washington Hilton 1919 Connecticut Ave. NW, 202-483-3000, thewashingtonhilton.com

Jack Rose Dining Saloon 2007 18th St. NW, 202-588-7388, jackrosediningsaloon.com

Crooked Beat Records 2116 18th St. NW, 202-483-2328, crookedbeat.com

The Brass Knob Architectural Antiques 2311 18th St. NW, 202-332-3370, thebrassknob.com

Toro Mata 2410 18th St. NW, 202-232-3890, toromata.com

District of Columbia Arts Center 2438 18th St. NW, 202-462-7833, dcartscenter.org

Madam's Organ 2461 18th St. NW, 202-667-5370, madamsorgan.com

Perry's 1811 Columbia Rd. NW, 202-234-6218, perrysadamsmorgan.com

Mintwood Place 1813 Columbia Rd. NW, 202-234-6732, mintwoodplace.com

Cashion's Eat Place 1819 Columbia Rd. NW, 202-797-1819, cashionseatplace.com

Fleet Feet Sports 1841 Columbia Rd. NW, 202-387-3888, fleetfeetdc.com

Geological fault Northwest side of Adams Mill Road NW at Clydesdale Place NW, nationalzoo.si.edu/AboutUs/History/beneathitall.cfm

route summary

1. **Start at the Washington Hilton hotel, 1919 Connecticut Avenue NW.**
2. **With the hotel's entrance to the rear, turn left to walk east on T Street NW.**
3. **Turn left on Florida Avenue NW.**
4. **Turn left on 18th Street NW.**
5. **Turn left on Columbia Road NW.**
6. **Reverse direction on Columbia Road NW.**
7. **Turn left on Adams Mill Road NW (stay right when it forks at Calvert Street NW).**
8. **After Clydesdale Place NW, reverse direction on Adams Mill Road NW.**

connecting the walks

For Walk 11 (16th Street NW), from the Washington Hilton, continue east on T Street NW to 16th Street NW.

Toro Mata's intriguing retablos

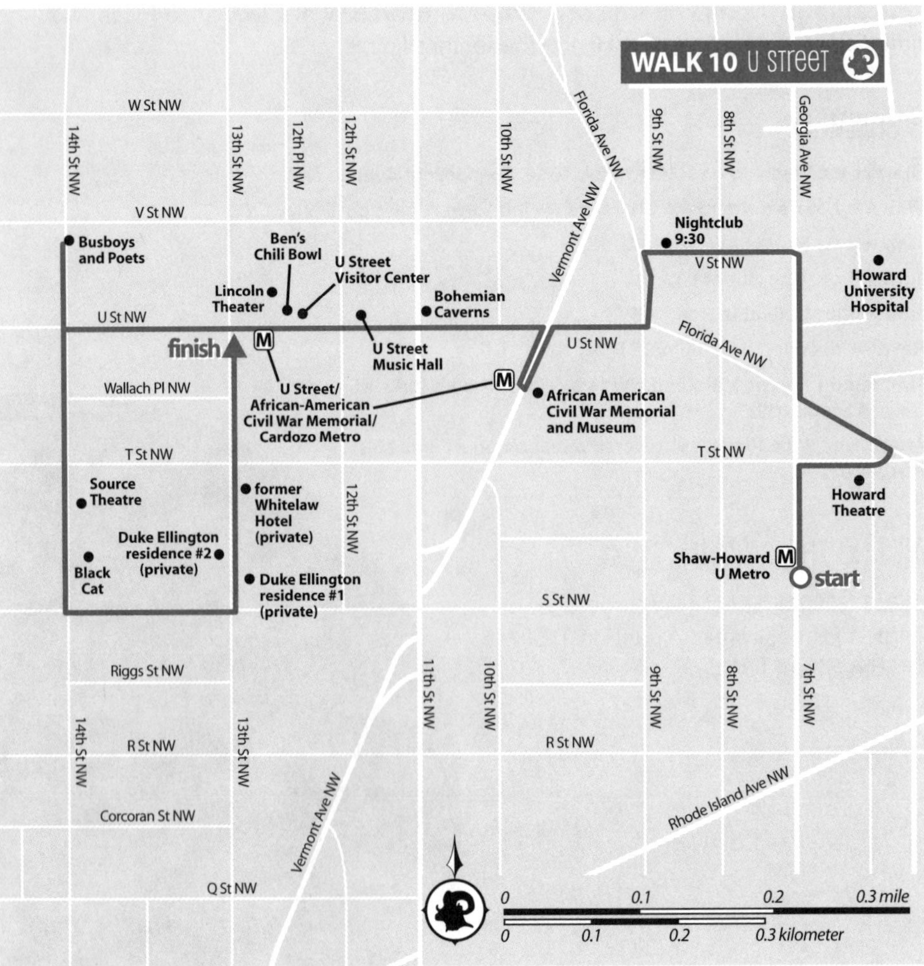

WALK 10 U STREET
W St NW
14th St NW
13th St NW
12th Pl NW
12th St NW
10th St NW
Florida Ave NW
9th St NW
8th St NW
Georgia Ave NW
V St NW
Vermont Ave NW
Nightclub 9:30
Busboys and Poets
Ben's Chili Bowl
U Street Visitor Center
V St NW
Howard University Hospital
Lincoln Theater
Bohemian Caverns
U St NW
Florida Ave NW
U St NW
finish
U Street Music Hall
Wallach Pl NW
U Street/ African-American Civil War Memorial/ Cardozo Metro
African American Civil War Memorial and Museum
T St NW
T St NW
Source Theatre
former Whitelaw Hotel (private)
12th St NW
Howard Theatre
Duke Ellington residence #2 (private)
Black Cat
Shaw-Howard U Metro
start
Duke Ellington residence #1 (private)
S St NW
Riggs St NW
11th St NW
10th St NW
9th St NW
8th St NW
7th St NW
14th St NW
R St NW
13th St NW
R St NW
Rhode Island Ave NW
Corcoran St NW
Vermont Ave NW
Q St NW
0
0.1
0.2
0.3 mile
0
0.1
0.2
0.3 kilometer

10 U Street: Music and Mirth

BOUNDARIES: V Street NW, Wiltberger Street NW, and S Street NW, and 14th Street NW
DISTANCE: 1.7 miles
DIFFICULTY: Easy
PARKING: Extremely limited 2-hour street parking; Metro highly recommended
PUBLIC TRANSIT: Shaw and U Street Metro stations; Metrobus 52 and the DC Circulator bus run down 14th Street, connecting several Metro stations.

U Street was once known as Black Broadway. Duke Ellington lived there. Pearl Bailey, Cab Calloway, and other legends played at its thriving clubs and theaters and stayed in its hotels during the days of racial segregation. Then, like some other parts of D.C., it sank into despair following the 1968 race riots. But now it's a haven for fun again. Today's action largely centers around U and 14th Streets. The shops, cafés, theaters, and clubs spill south on 14th Street NW until they collide with the fringes of the Dupont and Logan Circles neighborhoods. Luckily, D.C.'s African American history wasn't completely obliterated during its (ongoing) economic and cultural metamorphosis.

- **Start at the Shaw-Howard U Metro station at Seventh and S Streets NW. Walk north on Seventh Street NW and turn right on T Street NW for the Howard Theatre on the right. Built in 1910 as the first major theater for African Americans, it was restored, after decades of neglect, in 2012. Now it hosts concerts and other performances. Duke Ellington, Louis Armstrong, Billie Holliday, Marvin Gaye, Aretha Franklin, and The Supremes performed there.**

- **Turn left on Florida Avenue NW and right onto Georgia Avenue NW. Historically black Howard University, which was founded in 1867, begins here. On the right at V Street NW is Howard University Hospital. Its former chief of surgery, Charles R. Drew, is considered the Father of the Blood Bank. Griffith Stadium stood there from 1911 to 1965. The stadium was home to the Washington Senators baseball team and the Washington Redskins football team. Pennsylvania's Negro League team, the Homestead Grays, also played there sometimes. Home plate is now the site of the building's main lobby elevators, the hospital says.**

- Turn left on V Street NW for Nightclub 9:30 on the right. One of D.C.'s oldest music venues, the 930 Club, as it is also known, moved from 930 F Street NW to this edgier neighborhood in 1995. The club enforces a very strict dress code: its website says, "We only insist that you be dressed and wear shoes."

- Turn left on Ninth Street NW, right on U Street NW, and left on Vermont Avenue NW. The African American Civil War Memorial & Museum is on the left, and a Civil War sculpture is in the plaza on the right. Since 1999, the museum says, it has been telling the tales of "the largely unknown role" of the United States Colored Troops "who fought for freedom from slavery during the Civil War."

- Reverse direction on Vermont Avenue NW and turn left on U Street NW. The Bohemian Caverns supper club is on the right. A jazz bastion since 1926, the club was originally called the Crystal Caverns and then Club Caverns. John Coltrane, Miles Davis, and other legends performed there, says Cultural Tourism DC's *Greater U Street Heritage Trail* booklet.

- On the next block on the right is the U Street Music Hall, which opened in 2010. This 500-person dance club and music venue was tapped by *Rolling Stone* magazine as one of the top 10 dance clubs in America in 2013.

- Also on the right on the next block is Ben's Chili Bowl and the U Street Visitor Center. Just before Ben's beaming red, white, and orange building, a narrow stairway leads up to the restaurant's gift shop and the small visitor center. A D.C. landmark since 1958, Ben's has served its famous Chili Half-Smoke sausage to everyone from janitors to presidents. The building was constructed in 1910 as a silent movie house called the Minnehaha Theater.

- Next door is the restored Lincoln Theatre. Built in 1922, its reserved, buff-colored brick shell belies its glamorous, gilded interior and plush seats. It was a cultural hub showcasing performers such as Louis Armstrong during U Street's heyday. In 2013, it was reincarnated as a music and performance hot spot.

- Turn right on 14th Street NW for the flagship location of Busboys and Poets on the right. It's not just a yummy restaurant. It's also a space for art, culture, and politics. Owner Anas "Andy" Shallal, an Iraqi-American artist, activist, and former mayoral candidate, named it for American poet James Mercer Langston Hughes. Hughes, the son of a lawyer, worked as a busboy at the ritzy Wardman Park Hotel in 1925 before he gained his fame. Shallal opened this restaurant in 2005, and several others after that.

- Reverse direction on 14th Street NW. Just after T Street NW on the left is the 100-seat Source Theatre. It's owned by the arts group, CulturalDC. This nonprofit stages a three-week Source festival each summer with new plays. The rest of the year, the Washington Improv Theater, the Constellation Theatre Company, and the In Series stage their own comedies, plays, and operas there. (Cultural Tourism DC is a different nonprofit that sponsors hundreds of year-round events and the embassy tour.)

- A block farther on the right is the Black Cat Cafe. A haven for live, independent music since 1993, its stage has hosted performers such as Echo & the Bunnymen and John Entwhistle.

- Turn left on S Street NW and left on 13th Street NW for the two town houses where native Washingtonian Edward Kennedy "Duke" Ellington lived from age 11 to 18, according to the heritage trail brochure. On the right at 1805 is his former two-story brick town house. Across the street at 1816 is his fancier three-story town house with a classic pediment and curved corners. Ellington gained national fame when he played Harlem's famous "Cotton Club," but he also continued to play in his hometown. PBS calls him "the most prolific composer of the twentieth century in terms of both number of compositions and variety of forms."

- Farther down the street on the right is the Whitelaw Hotel. When it opened in 1919, it gave African Americans their first chance to stay in a first-class hotel in segregated D.C. The brick building is now affordable housing—an oasis surrounded by sky-high rents and mortgages.

- Continue on 13th Street NW for the Metro station one door down on the right, on U Street NW.

POINTS OF INTEREST

Shaw-Howard U Metro Seventh and S Streets NW, 202-637-7000, wmata.com/rail/station_detail.cfm?station_id=72

The Howard Theater 620 T Street NW, 202-803-2899, thehowardtheatre.com

Howard University 2041 Georgia Ave. NW, 202-865-6100, howard.edu

Nightclub 9:30 815 V St. NW, 202-265-0930, 930.com

African American Civil War Memorial & Museum 1925 Vermont Ave. NW, 202-667-2667, afroamcivilwar.org

Bohemian Caverns 2001 11th St. NW, 202-299-0800, bohemiancaverns.com

U Street Music Hall 1115 U St. NW, 202-588-1889, ustreetmusichall.com

U Street Visitor Center 1211 U St. NW, culturaltourismdc.org

Ben's Chili Bowl 1213 U St. NW, 202-667-0909, benschilibowl.com

Lincoln Theatre 1215 U St. NW, 202-888-0050, thelincolndc.com

Busboys and Poets 2021 14th St. NW, 202-387-7638, busboysandpoets.com

The Source Theatre 1835 14th St. NW, 202-315-1305, culturaldc.org

Black Cat 1811 14th St. NW, 202-667-4490, blackcatdc.com

(Private) former residence of Duke Ellington 1805 13th St. NW

(Private) former residence of Duke Ellington 1816 13th St. NW

(Private) apartment building, formerly the Whitelaw Hotel 1839 13th St. NW

U Street/African-American Civil War Memorial/Cardozo Metro 1240 U Street NW, 202-637-7000, wmata.com/rail/station_detail.cfm?station_id=73

route summary

1. Start at the Shaw-Howard U Metro.
2. Walk north on Seventh Street NW.
3. Turn right on T Street NW.
4. Turn left on Florida Avenue NW.
5. Turn right on Georgia Avenue NW.
6. Turn left on V Street NW.
7. Turn left on Ninth Street NW.
8. Turn right on U Street NW.
9. Turn left on Vermont Avenue NW.
10. Reverse direction on Vermont Avenue NW.
11. Turn left on U Street NW.
12. Turn right on 14th Street NW.
13. Reverse direction on 14th Street NW.
14. Turn left on S Street NW.
15. Turn left on 13th Street NW.
16. Continue on 13th Street NW for the Metro station one door down on the right at U Street NW.

connecting the walks

For Walk 11 (16th Street NW), walk west on U Street two blocks to 16th Street. For Walk 9 (Adams Morgan), walk west on U Street and turn right on 18th Street NW.

Howard Theatre reopened in 2012.

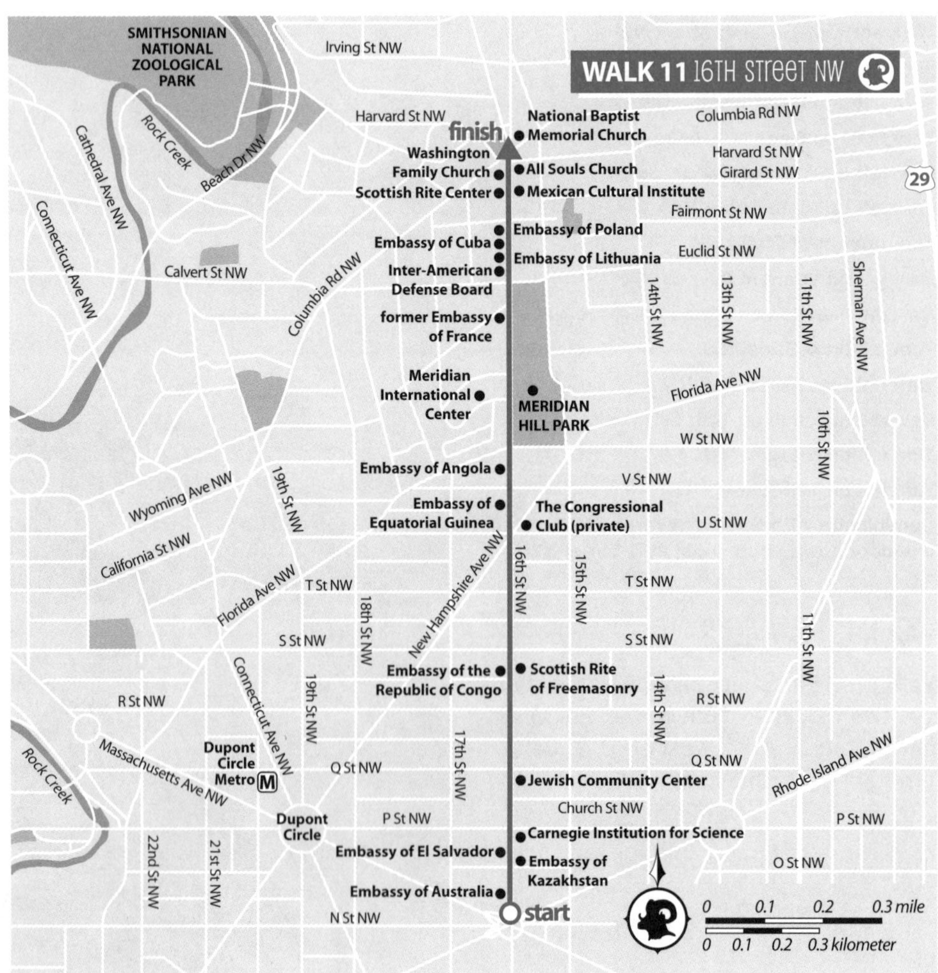
WALK 11 16TH STREET NW
SMITHSONIAN NATIONAL ZOOLOGICAL PARK
Irving St NW
Harvard St NW
Columbia Rd NW
Harvard St NW
Girard St NW
Fairmont St NW
Euclid St NW
Calvert St NW
Rock Creek
Beach Dr NW
Cathedral Ave NW
Connecticut Ave NW
Columbia Rd NW
finish
National Baptist Memorial Church
Washington Family Church
All Souls Church
Scottish Rite Center
Mexican Cultural Institute
Embassy of Poland
Embassy of Cuba
Embassy of Lithuania
Inter-American Defense Board
former Embassy of France
Meridian International Center
MERIDIAN HILL PARK
Florida Ave NW
W St NW
V St NW
U St NW
T St NW
S St NW
R St NW
Q St NW
P St NW
O St NW
N St NW
Church St NW
14th St NW
13th St NW
11th St NW
Sherman Ave NW
10th St NW
29
Embassy of Angola
Embassy of Equatorial Guinea
The Congressional Club (private)
Wyoming Ave NW
California St NW
19th St NW
18th St NW
17th St NW
16th St NW
15th St NW
New Hampshire Ave NW
Florida Ave NW
Embassy of the Republic of Congo
Scottish Rite of Freemasonry
Connecticut Ave NW
Dupont Circle Metro
Massachusetts Ave NW
Rock Creek
Jewish Community Center
Rhode Island Ave NW
Dupont Circle
Carnegie Institution for Science
Embassy of El Salvador
Embassy of Kazakhstan
Embassy of Australia
22nd St NW
21st St NW
start
0 0.1 0.2 0.3 mile
0 0.1 0.2 0.3 kilometer

11 16TH STREET NW: FROM DOWN UNDER TO HEAVEN

BOUNDARIES: **16th Street NW between Massachusetts Avenue NW and Columbia Road NW**
DISTANCE: **1.3 miles**
DIFFICULTY: **Easy**
PARKING: **Limited 2-hour metered and 2-hour free street parking**
PUBLIC TRANSIT: **Dupont Circle and Columbia Heights Metro stations are within walking distance at the start and finish, respectively. Metrobuses S2 and S4 run south along 16th Street NW to the Farragut North Metro station and north to the Silver Spring, Maryland, Metro station.**

Architecture and embassy buffs thrive here. This partially uphill walk along 16th Street—D.C.'s most important north–south numbered street—rises from "the Land Down Under" (the contemporary-style Embassy of Australia) to a trio of heavenly churches. It also passes several vintage embassies and other international hubs, one of America's most unusual buildings, a bastion of science, a renowned publisher's childhood mansion, and a park with a view. Most of the structures are bursting with architectural details. Several of the lavish embassies were built by Mary Foote Henderson and her husband, Missouri Senator John B. Henderson, after he retired from Congress in 1887. She spearheaded the development of Meridian Hill as a prime embassy enclave and even lobbied to move the White House there. Most of her embassies survived. But all that's left of the couple's own Romanesque mansion, dubbed Henderson's Castle, is a turret-topped brownstone wall across from Meridian Hill Park.

- **Start at 16th Street and Massachusetts Avenue NW, where orange, yellow, and earth-tone indigenous paintings grace the embassy of one of America's closest allies. The Commonwealth of Australia welcomes the public to its 1965-era embassy for art exhibits and other events.**

- **Cross 16th Street for the Embassy of the Republic of Kazakhstan. Built in 1888, this three-story, Richardson Romanesque building was home to a vice president and two senators. It also served as syndicated columnist Jack Anderson's office, according to the book *Sixteenth Street Architecture.* Kazakhstan has occupied the brick and stone structure since 1992, the year after it gained independence from the USSR.**

- Next door, the monumental structure with 10 grand Ionic columns is the headquarters for the Carnegie Institution for Science. It was completed in 1909 by architects John Carrére and Thomas Hastings, who also designed the New York Public Library and the Russell Senate and Cannon House office buildings. Industrialist Andrew Carnegie founded the institute in 1901. Carnegie hosts a public lecture series here and at its suburban campus. (See Walk 2, Forest Hills to Tenleytown.)

- Across the street, the Republic of El Salvador's Embassy is tucked away in a modern brick office building.

- Two blocks up on the right at Q Street NW is the monumental Washington DC Jewish Community Center, with its four curlicue-capped columns. Open to all, the JCC hosts film, literary, and music festivals; theater performances; fitness classes; and much more.

- Also on the right is one of the nation's most unique structures: the must-see headquarters of the Supreme Council, 33°, Scottish Rite of Freemasonry, Southern Jurisdiction. This "House of the Temple" mirrors one of the Seven Wonders of the Ancient World, the now destroyed Tomb of Mausolus in Turkey. It was the first monumental D.C. commission of legendary architect John Russell Pope. Designed in 1915, the 130-foot-high limestone temple is topped with a stepped-pyramid roof and surrounded by 33 massive Ionic columns and pilasters and two sphinxes. Its theatrical atrium features four dark-green polished Windsor granite columns and black marble Egyptian statues. Upstairs, the magnificent Temple Room centers around a black-and-gold marble altar under a 100-foot-high skylighted dome. Some building details relate to the Masons' affinity for symbols—such as the 33 individual 33-foot-high columns, which symbolize the 33rd degree or top level that a Mason can achieve—but they chose this ancient-themed design because it was architecturally fashionable at the time, a spokesperson says. Freemasonry began as a stonemasons' guild; now it's a nonsectarian fraternal group. Free tours are available.

- Across the street, the Embassy of the Republic of Congo moved into this dark red brick building in 2011. Supreme Court Justice Henry B. Brown built the 12,000-square-foot mansion in 1894. Two years later, he wrote the opinion in the "separate but equal" Plessy v. Ferguson case, which upheld segregation. His unusual stepped-gable home with horizontal rows of stone is a rare example of Flemish Renaissance architecture in D.C., the American Institute of Architects guide says.

- Four blocks up on the right at U Street NW is the private Congressional Club. Founded in 1909, this Beaux Arts beauty is open to the spouses of current and former members of Congress, Supreme Court justices, and members of the president's cabinet.

- Across the street on the left in a four-story tan-brick row house is the Embassy of Equatorial Guinea, the only Spanish-speaking country in Africa.

- Also on the left is the Embassy of the Republic of Angola in a gray, four-story building with a Spanish tile roof.

- A block north is the original boundary of L'Enfant's City of Washington. Now called Florida Avenue NW, it was Boundary Street until 1893. It's also the start of Meridian Hill and the fall line where the hilly Piedmont collides with the flat Coastal Plain. Designed between 1912 and 1936, Meridian Hill Park exploits the slope with terraced stairs and cascading waterfalls reminiscent of formal Italian gardens. The 12-acre park once hosted concerts by Pearl Bailey, the Von Trapp Family Singers, and other entertainers. By the 1980s, this national landmark, also known as Malcolm X Park, "had the dubious distinction of being known as the 'most violent national park in the region,'" the nonprofit Project for Public Spaces says. Now it's a gem again.

- Across the street is the remnant of Henderson's Castle. One block north is Meridian International Center's walled campus. Since 1960, this

Discoveries abound at the Carnegie Institution for Science.

nonprofit has worked hand in hand with the U.S. State Department and others to promote international understanding with professional and cultural exchange programs." Occasionally it hosts public exhibits. The two main buildings, the regal, French-flavored Meridian House and the brick, Georgian-style White-Meyer House, were designed for two American diplomats by John Russell Pope. *Washington Post* publisher Katharine Graham moved into the White-Meyer house when she was in the seventh grade, she wrote in her Pulitzer Prize–winning memoir *Personal History.* Graham said her two-story hilltop mansion, bedecked with Cézanne and Renoir paintings, was small compared with the family's Mount Kisco, New York, estate.

- One block farther north on the left is a sumptuous limestone mansion with a cylindrical tower punctuated by round windows. This was the French Embassy from 1908 to 1936. Since 1997 it has served as a private office building for the Council for Professional Recognition, following a stint as the Embassy for Ghana and decades as a rooming house.

- On the left between Euclid Street NW and Fuller Street NW is the Cuban Embassy and three landmarks designed by Henderson's hand-picked architect, George Oakley Totten: the Inter-American Defense Board, the Embassy of the Republic of Lithuania, and the Embassy of the Republic of Poland. The defense board, which calls itself the oldest regional defense organization, occupies the Pink Palace, named for its once pink and still ornate Venetian-Gothic palazzo design. Next door, Lithuania's Embassy is a five-story tan villa with arched doors and windows and a sculptural parapet edging its roof. Its neighbor is the limestone embassy with a four-columned porte cochere built for Cuba in 1919. When Cuba and the United States broke off relations in 1961, Cuba left. It returned in 1978, a year after the countries agreed to establish "Interest Sections" on each other's soil. Cuba reopened the lavish building as an official embassy in 2015, when the countries resumed relations. Next door, Poland established its four-story formal embassy topped by a trio of arched dormer windows in 1919, the year after it won independence.

- Across Fuller Street NW is the former Italian Embassy, which was designed in 1924 when dictator Benito Mussolini was in power. Warren & Wetmore, the architectural firm that created D.C.'s Mayflower Hotel and New York City's Grand Central Terminal, designed this quintessential, three-story Renaissance palace. It's slated to become a private residential development.

- Across the street is a Totten-designed Beaux Arts mansion with a huge arched entry and classical balustrades. This was the Embassy of Spain from 1927 until the 1990s. Now it's the Spain-USA Foundation, which hosts exhibits, films, and other public events.

- Next door is the four-story Beaux Arts mansion that served as the Embassy of Mexico from 1921 to 1989. Today it welcomes tourists as the Mexican Cultural Institute.

- Across the street is the private temple of the Washington, D.C., Scottish Rite Center, with its orange sunburst mosaic and two-headed eagle.

- Next door is the Washington Family Church. This Unification Church, known for its mass weddings, was built in 1933 for the Church of Jesus Christ of Latter-day Saints. The Mormons left in 1975. They built the steel-framed church with birdseye limestone (called marble by builders) from Utah, their home state. It's hard to miss the oval and other "birdseye" shaped fossils in the gray stone building, says Christopher J. Barr in his online *Guide to Washington's Accidental Museum of Paleontology.* The Utah Geological Survey says they were formed 58 to 66 million years ago by "algae that grew around snail shells, twigs, or other debris."

- Across the street is the All Souls Church Unitarian, which debuted in 1923. This brick church with a clock atop its steeple is a copy of the St. Martin-in-the-Fields Church, which was built in London in 1726.

- One block north on the right is the National Baptist Memorial Church with a circular, domed steeple. It was built in 1926. At Columbia Road NW, you can catch the bus back to the start.

POINTS OF INTEREST

Embassy of Australia 1601 Massachusetts Ave. NW, 202-797-3000, usa.embassy.gov.au

Embassy of the Republic of Kazakhstan 1401 16th St. NW, 202-232-5488, kazakhembus.com

Carnegie Institution for Science 1530 P St. NW, 202-387-8092, carnegiescience.edu

Embassy of the Republic of El Salvador 1400 16th St. NW, 202-595-7500, elsalvador.org

Washington DC Jewish Community Center 1529 16th St. NW, 202-518-9400, washingtondcjcc.org

Supreme Council, 33°, Scottish Rite of Freemasonry, Southern Jurisdiction headquarters 1733 16th St. NW, 202-232-3579, scottishrite.org

Embassy of the Republic of Congo 1720 16th St. NW, 202-726-5500, ambacongo-us.org

The Congressional Club 2001 New Hampshire Ave. NW, 202-332-1155, thecongressionalclub.com

Embassy of Equatorial Guinea 2020 16th St. NW, 202-518-5700, egembassydc.com

Embassy of the Republic of Angola 2100–2108 16th St. NW, 202-785-1156, angola.org

Meridian Hill Park 16th Street NW to 15th Street NW and from W Street NW to Euclid Street NW, 202-895-6070, nps.gov/mehi/index.htm

Meridian International Center 1630 Crescent Place NW, 202-667-6800, meridian.org

Former French Embassy (now the private Council for Professional Recognition) 2460 16th St. NW

Inter-American Defense Board 2600 16th St. NW, 202-939-6041, iadb.jid.org

Embassy of the Republic of Lithuania 2622 16th St. NW, 202-234-5860, usa.mfa.lt/usa/en

Embassy of Cuba 2630 16th St. NW, 202-797-8518, cubadiplomatica.cu/sicw/EN/Home.aspx

Embassy of the Republic of Poland 2640 16th St. NW, 202-499-1700, polandembassy.org

Former Italian Embassy 2700 16th St. NW (about to become a private residential development)

Mexican Cultural Institute 2829 16th St. NW, 202-728-1628, instituteofmexicodc.org

Scottish Rite of Freemasonry District of Columbia chapter 2800 16th St. NW, 202-232-8155, dcsr.org

Washington Family (Unification) Church 1610 Columbia Road NW, 202-462-5700, unification.net/ucdc

All Souls Church Unitarian 1500 Harvard St. NW, 202-332-5266, all-souls.org

National Baptist Memorial Church 1501 Columbia Road NW, 202-265-1410, nbmchurchdc.org

route summary

1. **Start at the Embassy of Australia, 1601 Massachusetts Avenue NW.**
2. **Walk north on 16th Street NW.**
3. **At Columbia Road NW, catch the bus back to the start.**

connecting the walks

For Walk 9 (Adams Morgan), turn left on U Street NW and walk three blocks west to 18th Street NW. For Walk 10 (U Street), turn right on U Street NW and walk two blocks east to 14th Street NW. For Walk 16 (Downtown: News Junkies West), head south on 16th Street NW from the start.

The Mexican Cultural Institute celebrates Dia de los Muertos.

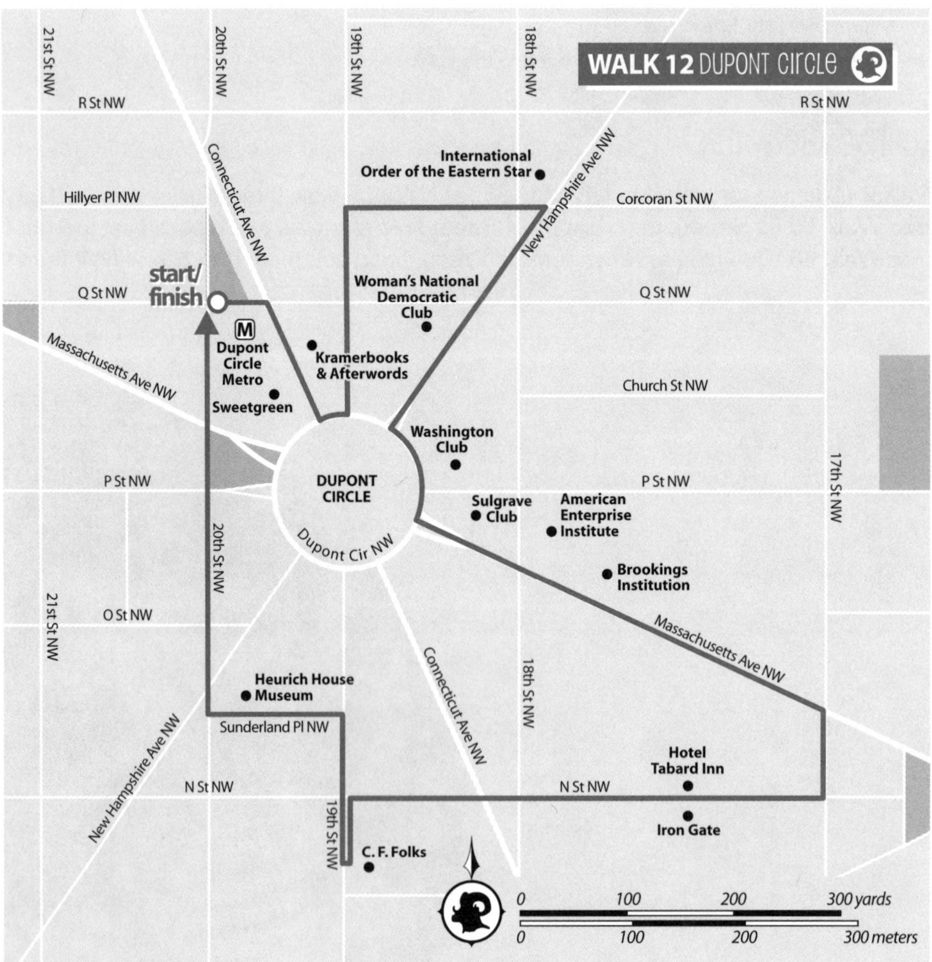
WALK 12 DUPONT CIRCLE
21st St NW
20th St NW
19th St NW
18th St NW
R St NW
R St NW
Connecticut Ave NW
International Order of the Eastern Star
New Hampshire Ave NW
Hillyer Pl NW
Corcoran St NW
start/ finish
Q St NW
Woman's National Democratic Club
Q St NW
Massachusetts Ave NW
Dupont Circle Metro
Kramerbooks & Afterwords
Church St NW
Sweetgreen
Washington Club
DUPONT CIRCLE
P St NW
P St NW
17th St NW
Sulgrave Club
American Enterprise Institute
20th St NW
Dupont Cir NW
Brookings Institution
21st St NW
O St NW
Massachusetts Ave NW
Connecticut Ave NW
18th St NW
Heurich House Museum
Sunderland Pl NW
New Hampshire Ave NW
N St NW
N St NW
Hotel Tabard Inn
19th St NW
Iron Gate
C. F. Folks
0
100
200
300 yards
0
100
200
300 meters

12 DUPONT CIRCLE: OLDIES AND GOODIES

BOUNDARIES: **Corcoran Street NW, 17th Street NW, Jefferson Place NW, and 20th Street NW**
DISTANCE: **1.6 miles**
DIFFICULTY: **Easy**
PARKING: **Limited 2-hour metered and free street parking; Metro recommended; public parking garages in some office buildings**
PUBLIC TRANSIT: **Dupont Circle Metro Station is served by multiple buses.**

If the National Mall is America's Back Yard, Dupont Circle is D.C.'s town square—or town circle. It's a hangout, home, workplace, and historic district flush with vintage embassies and other enviable architecture. Since there are too many embassies to pinpoint here (see Walks 8 and 11 for embassy treks), this focuses on cafés, shops, and other more public buildings on the streets that radiate off the circle. One day soon, even the caverns beneath the circle are expected to spring back to life. The former trolley tunnels are slated to become an arts venue called Dupont Underground. Back in 1871, the Army Corps of Engineers started building Pacific Circle, the National Park Service says. It was later renamed for Rear Admiral Samuel Francis duPont. It centered around a bronze statue of the Civil War hero until 1921, when a white marble fountain replaced it. At the turn of the 20th century this was a fashionable neighborhood for the rich and powerful. In the 1930s, its gay-friendly reputation began, says the bible on D.C.'s neighborhoods, *Washington at Home*. Today, the 2.25-acre park is a humanity magnet: office workers, chess players, dog walkers, and others are drawn to D.C.'s only pedestrian-friendly circle.

- **Start at the Dupont Circle Metro Station, 1525 20th Street NW. Turn right to walk south on this busy commercial leg of Connecticut Avenue NW for Sweetgreen restaurant on the right. Sweetgreen, which specializes in yummy veggies and leafy greens, is a local chain with 31 locations on the East Coast and in Los Angeles. This particular café is also a test kitchen that debuts new dishes. Three Georgetown University grads started the venture in 2007.**

- **Turn left to enter the Dupont Circle traffic circle. Then turn left on 19th Street NW, past a coffee shop on the left and a bar on the right with picture windows facing the circle. A few doors down on the left is the rear "greenhouse" entrance to Kramerbooks &**

Afterwords Cafe & Grill, an old friend to Washingtonians since 1976, where folks drop in for books, booze, munchies, and live tunes.

- After the shop, continue north on 19th Street NW. Turn right on Corcoran Street NW for a massive stone mansion on the left with elaborate arched windows on the second floor. This headquarters of the International Order of the Eastern Star fills up a full (roughly triangular-shaped) block. Designed by a Parisian architect in 1909 as a home for Perry Belmont, the grandson of Commodore Matthew C. Perry, the Eastern Star moved there in 1935. Public tours are available of the lavish structure, which was used only two months of the year for entertaining. The Eastern Star is a Masonic organization that admits women.

- Turn right on New Hampshire Avenue NW to walk past the embassies of Montenegro, Namibia, Zimbabwe, and Argentina to the Woman's National Democratic Club on the right. Designed for opera singer Sarah Adams Whittemore between 1892 and 1894, this house has "the finest Arts and Crafts style exterior in the city," says the book *Buildings of the District of Columbia.* Its narrow Roman bricks in shades of brown and a copper-clad semicircular bay window help make it unique. The club was founded in 1922. It hosts art exhibits and offers tours.

- Continue southwest on New Hampshire Avenue NW for the Dupont Circle traffic circle. Turn left for the grande dame of the circle at P Street NW. This white marble Italianate mansion was home to a private women's club called the Washington Club from 1951 until 2014. Now this four-story landmark is about to become a swanky apartment building. It was designed in 1903 by McKim, Mead & White for Robert Wilson Patterson and Elinor "Nellie" Medill Patterson. Her father, Joseph Meharry Medill, co-owned the *Chicago Tribune* and helped found the Republican party.

- Cross P Street NW for the Sulgrave Club, which also fronts Dupont Circle. This private women's club bought the yellow Roman-brick mansion in 1932. Millionaire gentleman farmer Herbert Wadsworth built it as his winter home in 1902, the club says.

- Turn left on Massachusetts Avenue NW for a limestone-clad Beaux Arts building on the left at 18th Street NW. This four-story building was designed to be "the most luxurious apartment house in Washington," the American Institute of Architects guide says. National Gallery of Art founder Andrew W. Mellon lived there full time from 1922 to 1932 while he was Secretary of the Treasury. Mellon's 11,000-square-foot home on the top floor had six regular bedrooms and five maids' bedrooms, according to the National Register for Historic Places inventory. The six-unit apartment building later served as offices for the National Trust for Historic Preservation and the left-leaning Brookings Institution think tank. The right-leaning American Enterprise Institute think tank is about to make the 1922 landmark its new home.

- One door down on the left is Brookings' modern office building.

- Continue on Massachusetts Avenue NW past the embassies of Uzbekistan, Chile, Trinidad and Tobago, and Peru on the right in converted brick and stone mansions. Turn right on 17th Street NW, and then right again on N Street NW, an architectural candy store of assorted Victorian row houses and the home of two long-treasured restaurants. On the right is the Hotel Tabard Inn, a cozy, European-style boutique hotel stretching across three 1880 row houses. *The Washington Post* tagged its "modern American" restaurant as one of the "best bars and restaurants with fireplaces." Across the street, the equally romantic Iron Gate offers tasting menus in its courtyard garden and carriage house.

- Turn left on 19th Street NW for C.F. Folks restaurant on the left. Open since 1981, this weekday luncheonette "is a 600-square-foot temple of honest cooking and good will," said the James Beard Foundation when it bestowed it with an America's Classics Award in 2013. In the 1960s and 1970s, it was the Jefferson Coffee Shop. Maryland-based crime novelist George Pelecanos worked there when his dad owned it.

- Reverse direction on 19th Street NW. Then turn left on Sunderland Place NW for the Christian Heurich House Museum on the right at 20th Street NW. Dubbed the "Brewmaster's Castle," this brownstone and brick Victorian with a four-story turret was completed in 1894 by this wealthy German brewer. The public can tour its ornate interior, which features hand-carved wood and 15 fireplaces.

- Turn right on 20th Street NW and walk north to Q Street NW for the Dupont Circle Metro on the right.

POINTS OF INTEREST

Dupont Circle Metro Station 1525 20th St. NW, 202-637-7000, wmata.com/rail/station_detail.cfm?station_id=6

Sweetgreen 1512 Connecticut Ave. NW, 202-387-9338, sweetgreen.com

Kramerbooks & Afterwords Cafe & Grill 1517 Connecticut Ave. NW, 202-387-1400, kramers.com/index.html

International Order of the Eastern Star headquarters 1618 New Hampshire Ave. NW, 202-667-4737, oesdistrictofcolumbia.org/chapters-members.html

Woman's National Democratic Club 1526 New Hampshire Ave. NW, 202-232-7363, democraticwoman.org

The Washington Club 15 Dupont Circle

Sulgrave Club 1801 Massachusetts Ave. NW, 202-462-5800, sulgraveclub.org

The American Enterprise Institute 1789 Massachusetts Ave. NW, 202-862-5800, aei.org

The Brookings Institution 1775 Massachusetts Ave. NW, 202-797-6000, brookings.edu

Hotel Tabard Inn 1739 N St. NW, 202-785-1277, tabardinn.com

Iron Gate 1734 N St. NW, 202-524-5202, irongaterestaurantdc.com

C.F. Folks 1225 19th St. NW, 202-293-0162, cffolks.com

Christian Heurich House Museum 1307 New Hampshire Ave. NW, 202-429-1894, heurichhouse.org

ROUTE SUMMARY

1. **Start at the Dupont Circle Metro Station, 1525 20th Street NW.**
2. **Turn right to walk south on Connecticut Avenue NW.**
3. **Turn left to enter the Dupont Circle traffic circle.**
4. **Turn left on 19th Street NW.**
5. **Turn right on Corcoran Street NW.**
6. **Turn right on New Hampshire Avenue NW.**
7. **Turn left to enter the Dupont Circle traffic circle.**
8. **Cross P Street NW.**

9. Turn left on Massachusetts Avenue NW.
10. Turn right on 17th Street NW.
11. Turn right on N Street NW.
12. Turn left on 19th Street NW.
13. Reverse direction to walk north on 19th Street NW.
14. Turn left on Sunderland Place NW.
15. Turn right on 20th Street NW and walk north to Q Street NW for the Metro on the right.

Connecting the Walks

Walk 8 (Embassy Row) ends two blocks from the Dupont Circle Metro. For Walk 9 (Adams Morgan), continue north on Connecticut Avenue NW and turn right on Florida Avenue NW. For Walk 11 (16th Street NW), continue east on Massachusetts Avenue and turn left on 16th Street NW. For Walk 16 (Downtown: News Junkies West), continue south on Connecticut Avenue NW to Desales Street NW.

Dupont Circle Metro's mega escalator

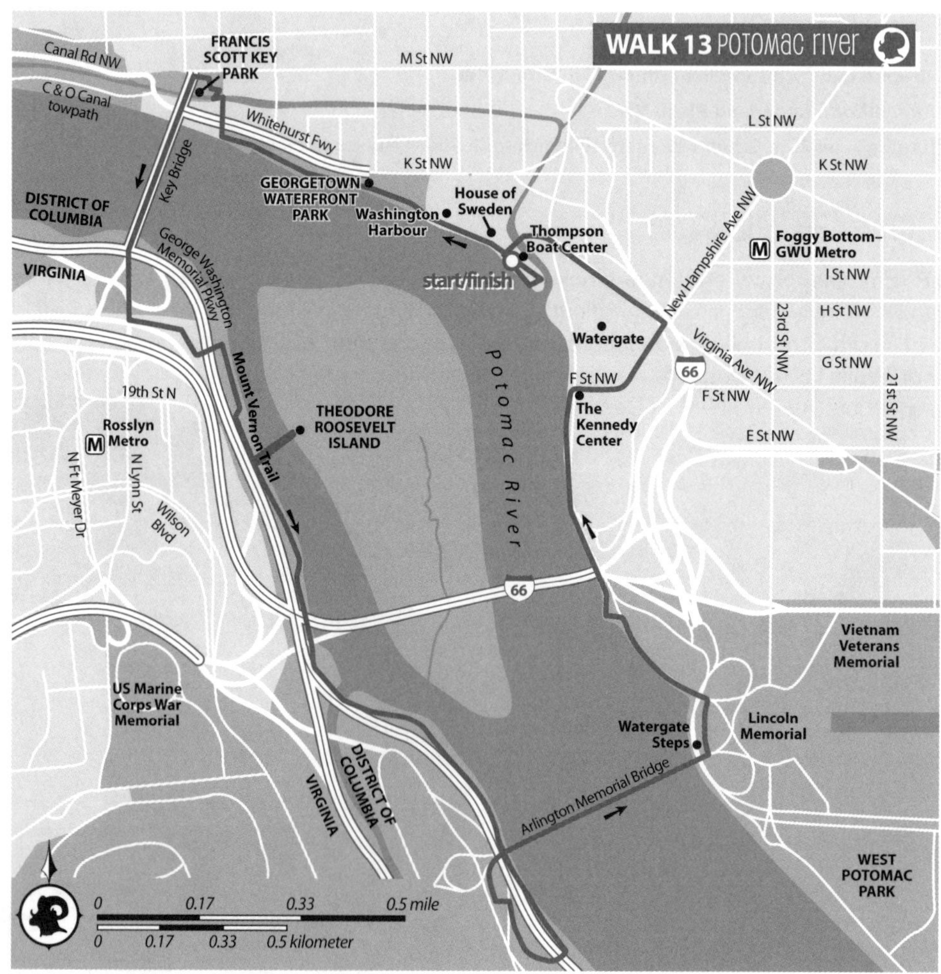
WALK 13 POTOMAC RIVER
Canal Rd NW
FRANCIS SCOTT KEY PARK
M St NW
C & O Canal towpath
Whitehurst Fwy
L St NW
K St NW
K St NW
Key Bridge
GEORGETOWN WATERFRONT PARK
House of Sweden
Washington Harbour
DISTRICT OF COLUMBIA
Thompson Boat Center
New Hampshire Ave NW
Foggy Bottom–GWU Metro
VIRGINIA
George Washington Memorial Pkwy
start/finish
I St NW
H St NW
23rd St NW
Watergate
Potomac River
Virginia Ave NW
G St NW
Mount Vernon Trail
66
F St NW
F St NW
19th St N
THEODORE ROOSEVELT ISLAND
The Kennedy Center
21st St NW
Rosslyn Metro
E St NW
N Ft Meyer Dr
N Lynn St
Wilson Blvd
66
Vietnam Veterans Memorial
US Marine Corps War Memorial
Lincoln Memorial
Watergate Steps
DISTRICT OF COLUMBIA
VIRGINIA
Arlington Memorial Bridge
WEST POTOMAC PARK
0 0.17 0.33 0.5 mile
0 0.17 0.33 0.5 kilometer

13 Potomac River Panorama and Watergates

BOUNDARIES: Waterfront trail along Potomac River, Arlington Memorial Bridge, Mount Vernon Trail, and Key Bridge
DISTANCE: About 5 miles (excluding optional walk on island's dirt trails)
DIFFICULTY: Moderate due to distance; flat except for bridge crossings
PARKING: Metered parking lot at Thompson Boat Center and parking garage at Washington Harbour
PUBLIC TRANSIT: DC Circulator bus stops at 30th and K Streets NW and runs to the Foggy Bottom, Rosslyn, and other Metros.

Runners have a secret. It's this Potomac River loop that's arguably one of the most scenic in D.C. It bestows a panoramic vista of the city, a glimpse of Washington's legendary cherry blossoms, and one of D.C.'s most iconic views of the Lincoln Memorial against the Washington Monument. Other architectural eye candy abounds, including Georgetown University's European-style spires and the bodacious arched bridges themselves. Across the river from the busy Georgetown waterfront, natural Washington thrives, especially on Theodore Roosevelt Island. The nearly 89-acre forested island is a haven for yellow-bellied sapsuckers, long-necked great blue herons, and big bald eagles with their sharp yellow beaks and brawny yellow legs. Although about a mile of this jaunt is in Virginia along the Mount Vernon Trail, many folks don't realize that almost 1.5 miles of the trail crosses D.C.'s own Columbia Island.

- **Start at the Thompson Boat Center, 2900 Virginia Avenue NW. It's the only public boathouse in D.C. that rents rowing shells to the public and offers rowing lessons. It also rents kayaks, canoes, and bikes. Around the southeast side of the building lie the hidden mouth of Rock Creek and the zero mile marker of the C&O Canal towpath.**

- **Continue upriver along the river trail and turn right for the House of Sweden, the first and only embassy directly on the river. The glass-and-concrete marvel, which won Sweden's most prestigious architectural award after its 2006 debut, houses the embassies of the royal Kingdom of Sweden and the constitutional republic of Iceland. Sweden embraces Washingtonians with a slew of public events, including concerts, lectures, art exhibits, and a family-friendly Christmas Bazaar. In March, the embassy teams up with the Washington Area Bicyclist Association (WABA) to host a Vasa bike** ride as an homage to Sweden's Vasaloppet, the world's oldest and biggest cross-country ski race. Cyclists who finish D.C.'s just-for-fun ride in the cheek-chilling cold are rewarded with hot blueberry soup. It might smell odd, but it tastes yummy.

- Next door along the river trail is Washington Harbour, a waterfront complex with an eclectic mix of domes, arches, and columns. It's home to restaurants, bars, luxe condos, offices, an outdoor ice-skating rink (winter only), a tour-boat dock, and waterside bars and restaurants.

- Upriver from the Harbour is Georgetown Waterfront Park. This newest park on the Potomac features a contemplative labyrinth, a kid-friendly fountain, and river steps, which were designed to view regattas.

- When the waterfront trail dead-ends, follow it as it turns right, away from the river. Continue north across Water Street NW and follow 34th Street NW up the hill. Cross the C&O Canal and turn left into Francis Scott Key Park at the Francis Scott Key Bridge. The bridge's namesake was the Georgetown attorney who beheld the bombardment of Baltimore's Fort McHenry in 1814 and then penned "The Star-Spangled Banner," which became America's national anthem in 1931. The reinforced concrete bridge from 1923 soars 72 feet above the river and roughly 1,800 feet across. Architect Nathan C. Wyeth designed it with eight graceful, wide arches topped with a series of tall, narrow Roman arches. He also created the Oval Office in the White House.

- Walk left through the park and turn left to cross the bridge. At the end, turn left to descend to the Mount Vernon Trail, a green-and-asphalt ribbon that leads almost 18 miles to George Washington's estate at Mount Vernon. Political "royalty" and "commoners" jog, walk, and roll on the trail.

- Turn left to cross the pedestrian bridge onto Theodore Roosevelt Island. This wild island with a manicured memorial befits America's 26th president, who championed conservation by protecting roughly 230 million acres of public land. Miles of dirt trails and a boardwalk weave around the planned and planted forest, which was designed to resemble a wilderness. A 17-foot bronze statue of Roosevelt presides over a formal oval plaza. The musky scent of boxwood signals the entrance to the memorial. Once a seasonal fishing village for American Indians, it had multiple names, including Analostan and Mason's Island. Virginia's prominent Mason clan bought it in the early

1700s and ran a ferry to Georgetown. In the 1790s, John Mason built a summer home there and ran a plantation with slaves, Gunston Hall records show. During the Civil War, it became Camp Greene, a training post for African American Union Army troops. During World War II, OSS spies trained there. Today only squirrels and their furry and feathered friends dwell on the enchanting isle.

- Continue downriver and walk underneath the Arlington Memorial Bridge. After roughly a third of a mile, turn right to follow a paved connector trail that cloverleafs to the right up onto the bridge. The 2,163-foot-long structure symbolically links the North and South, essentially connecting the Lincoln (Union) and Robert E. Lee (Confederate) Memorials. This low-profile, arched bridge was designed in 1932 by McKim, Mead & White, the architects who designed New York City's ornate Penn Station.

- At the end of the bridge, turn left and cautiously cross the road to reach the sidewalk that curves left and becomes the Rock Creek Parkway waterfront trail. (If traffic prohibits a safe crossing, turn right at the end of the bridge to cloverleaf back under the bridge.) Turn left for the Watergate Steps. Exercise junkies love racing up and down its 41 steps—including the contestants of the *Biggest Loser* TV show in 2009. Designed as a key ceremonial entry to the capital, it also hosted open-air concerts until the 1970s.

- Continue upriver on the trail and turn right to cross Rock Creek and Potomac Parkway very cautiously to F Street NW (if there is too much traffic, continue to the traffic light) for the Kennedy Center. Take a freebie tour, grab a snack, or enjoy its jaw-dropping river and city views. A living memorial to President John F. Kennedy, this multitheater complex

Frolicking at Georgetown Waterfront Park

WHOOPS! HISTORIC HOME VANISHED

Francis Scott Key and his family lived west of the present-day bridge at 3516–3518 M St. NW (formerly Bridge Street) in a three-and-a-half-story brick home, according to National Park Service (NPS) and other records. His home was directly across the street from Georgetown University's present-day Car Barn, not at Francis Scott Key Park. After living there for about three decades, Key, his wife, Mary, and their 11 children vamoosed to Capitol Hill in the early 1830s, reportedly due to the irksome digging of the Chesapeake and Ohio Canal in their backyard. Key, who also served as Washington's U.S. District Attorney, kept his law office there for a while after he moved. In addition to his main house, which was built in 1795, he also had a coach house, a smokehouse, and other structures on his riverfront property. Key's house later underwent multiple alterations and incarnations (as a hotel, a shoemaker, and more) until the transformed structure—which even lost its residential-style gable roof—was dismantled in 1947 to make way for the Whitehurst Freeway ramp. NPS's plan to reassemble the house or a replica nearby was halted after extended controversies about the project and the fact that the building remnants that the agency stored in various locations had simply vanished.

hosts approximately 3,000 plays, concerts, ballets, operas, and more each year, its website says. The center presents free performances virtually every evening at the Millennium Stage. Two gift shops sell goodies such as replicas of Jackie O.'s blinged-out jewelry and authentic autographed pointe shoes worn by members of the Kennedy Center's Suzanne Farrell Ballet.

- **After exiting the Kennedy Center, turn left to follow New Hampshire Avenue NW to Virginia Avenue NW. Turn left to see the Watergate complex, a symbol of scandals for two presidents. Monica Lewinsky lived briefly in her mom's Watergate South apartment. When the former White House intern hooked up with President William Jefferson Clinton, it led to his impeachment. (He was acquitted.) The Watergate is more famous for leading** to President Nixon's ouster. Five men checked into rooms 214 and 314 of the former Watergate Hotel and were arrested June 17, 1972, for trying to bug the Democratic National Committee's sixth-floor headquarters. No plaque inside the private offices or outside commemorates that history. All five Watergate buildings, however, were listed on the National Register of Historic Places in 2005. In 2013, the National Trust for Historic Preservation moved its headquarters to the Watergate. The newly renovated Watergate Hotel is slated to reopen in November 2015 after an eight-year closure.

Points of Interest

Thompson Boat Center and the zero mile marker of the Chesapeake and Ohio Canal National Historic Park (C&O towpath) 2900 Virginia Ave. NW, 202-333-9543, thompsonboatcenter.com and nps.gov/choh/index.htm

House of Sweden 2900 K St. NW, 202-467-2600, houseofsweden.com/en/House-Of-Sweden

The Washington Harbour and Georgetown Waterfront Park 3000 and 3050 K St. NW, 202-295-5007, thewashingtonharbour.com and georgetownwaterfrontpark.org

Francis Scott Key Bridge and Park M and 35 Streets NW, nps.gov/olst/planyourvisit/keypark.htm

Mount Vernon Trail Along the Potomac River from Key Bridge (D.C.) to Mount Vernon (Virginia), 703-289-2500, nps.gov/pohe/planyourvisit/nova-hike-3.htm

Theodore Roosevelt Island George Washington Memorial Parkway south of Francis Scott Key Bridge, 703-289-2500, nps.gov/this/index.htm

Arlington Memorial Bridge Ohio Drive SW at the Lincoln Memorial, nps.gov/nr/travel/wash/dc69.htm

Watergate Steps Ohio Drive SW between the American Legion Bridge and Rock Creek and Potomac Parkway NW, nps.gov/linc/parkmgmt/upload/LIME_CLR_Chap4_(14).pdf

The Kennedy Center 2700 F St. NW, 202-467-4600, kennedy-center.org/index.cfm

The Watergate Hotel 2650 Virginia Ave. NW, 202-827-1600, thewatergatehotel.com

Watergate Complex 2600 Virginia Ave. NW, watergateeast.com/watergateMall.html

route summary

1. Start at the Thompson Boat Center, 2900 Virginia Avenue NW.
2. While facing the Potomac River, turn right to head upriver along the waterfront trail. Always keep the river on the left.
3. When the waterfront trail dead-ends, follow it as it turns right, away from the river.
4. Continue north across Water Street NW and follow 34th Street NW up the hill.
5. Cross the C&O Canal and turn left into Francis Scott Key Park at the Francis Scott Key Bridge.
6. Walk left through the park and turn left to cross the bridge.
7. After crossing Key Bridge, turn left to descend to the Mount Vernon Trail.
8. Turn left to cross the footbridge to Theodore Roosevelt Island.
9. After reversing direction on the bridge, turn left to continue downriver on the trail.
10. Walk underneath the Arlington Memorial Bridge. After roughly a third of a mile, turn right to follow a paved connector trail that cloverleafs to the right up onto the bridge.
11. At the end of the bridge, turn left and cautiously cross the road to reach the sidewalk that curves left and becomes the Rock Creek Parkway waterfront trail. (If traffic prohibits a safe crossing, turn right at the end of the bridge to cloverleaf back under the bridge.)
12. Turn left for the Watergate Steps.
13. Continue on the waterfront trail.
14. Turn right to cross Rock Creek and Potomac Parkway NW to the Kennedy Center.
15. After exiting, turn left to follow New Hampshire Avenue NW to Virginia Avenue NW.
16. Turn left onto Virginia Avenue NW.
17. Cross Rock Creek and Potomac Parkway NW at the traffic light, which leads to the start.

CONNECTING THE WALKS

For Walks 6 and 7 (Georgetown), walk east on M Street NW from Key Bridge. Walk 20 (Columbia Island) also traverses the Arlington Memorial Bridge.

Georgetown edges the Potomac River.

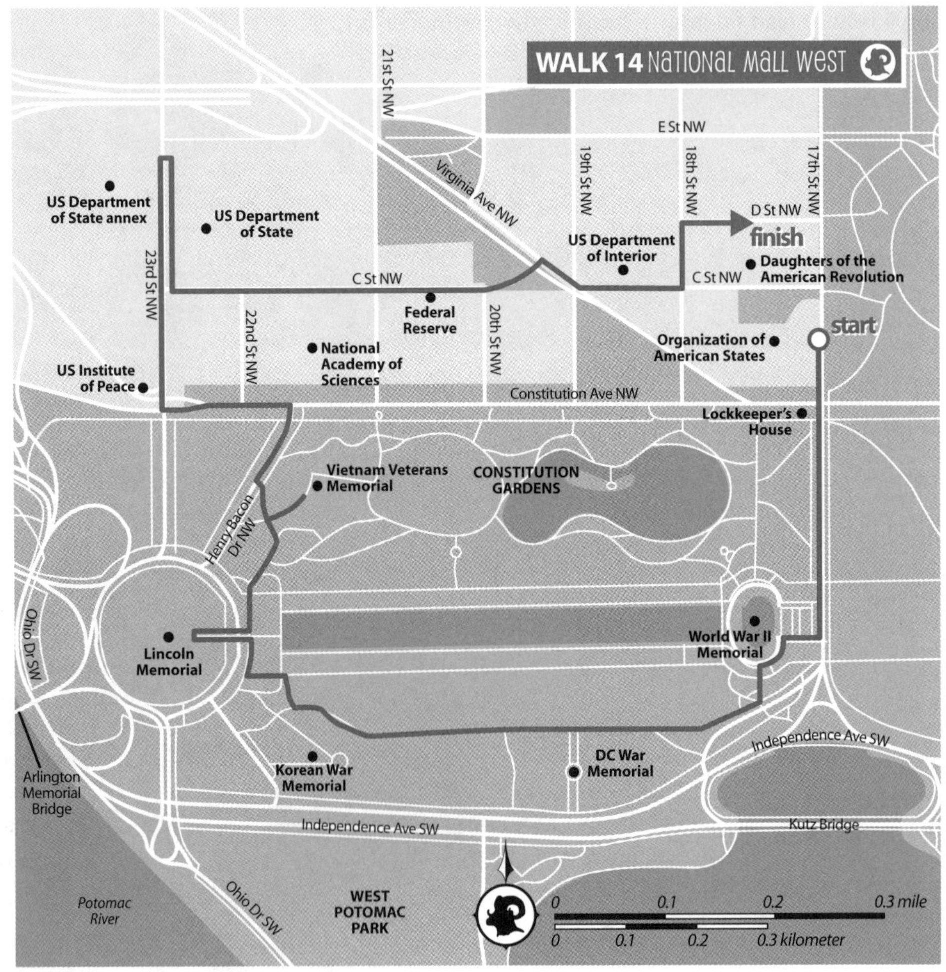
WALK 14 National Mall West
21st St NW
E St NW
19th St NW
18th St NW
17th St NW
Virginia Ave NW
D St NW
finish
US Department of State annex
US Department of State
US Department of Interior
Daughters of the American Revolution
23rd St NW
C St NW
C St NW
Federal Reserve
22nd St NW
20th St NW
National Academy of Sciences
Organization of American States
start
US Institute of Peace
Constitution Ave NW
Lockkeeper's House
Vietnam Veterans Memorial
CONSTITUTION GARDENS
Henry Bacon Dr NW
Ohio Dr SW
Lincoln Memorial
World War II Memorial
Independence Ave SW
Arlington Memorial Bridge
Korean War Memorial
DC War Memorial
Independence Ave SW
Kutz Bridge
Potomac River
Ohio Dr SW
WEST POTOMAC PARK
0 0.1 0.2 0.3 mile
0 0.1 0.2 0.3 kilometer

14 National Mall West: War and Peace

BOUNDARIES: **D Street NW, 17th Street NW, Independence Avenue SW, and 23rd Street NW**
DISTANCE: **About 2.5 miles**
DIFFICULTY: **Moderate; one hill**
PARKING: **Limited metered street parking; free three-hour parking from 6 a.m. to 1 a.m. on Ohio Drive SW by the Potomac River southeast of the Lincoln Memorial. Metro is highly recommended.**
PUBLIC TRANSIT: **Smithsonian, Foggy Bottom, Farragut West, and Federal Triangle Metro stations are within walking distance of the Mall and are served by multiple bus routes, including the $1 DC Circulator bus's National Mall route.**

War or peace? This loop delivers both—and it tosses in the CIA's original home and some impressive headquarters. The Federal Reserve, the Department of the Interior, and other federal agencies live near the Mall's famous war and peace icons. President Lincoln's Parthenon-like memorial rules the National Mall. A massive marble Lincoln sits atop a throne at the head of the Mall in tribute to our hero who won the Civil War and ended slavery. Along each side of the Mall are moving memorials to the men and women who fought other conflicts to keep America and its allies free. This trek also features our Revolutionary War roots: the White House–esque headquarters of the Daughters of the American Revolution. Peace resides at the Organization of American States' compound and at the Congressionally chartered U.S. Institute of Peace.

- **Start at the majestic Main Building of the Organization of American States at 17th Street NW and Constitution Avenue NW. Tropical trees reach for the ceiling of OAS's sunny atrium. The ornate first and second floors surrounding the courtyard are open for a quick peek. But even more accessible to the public is the OAS's free Art Museum of the Americas next door, with nearly 2,000 paintings, photos, and sculptures. It also hosts community programs and kids workshops, including one where little tykes learn to make piñatas.**

- **Continue south on 17th Street NW to the Lockkeeper's House at the corner of Constitution Gardens. The rustic-stone house is expected to open to the public in 2016 to tell the stories of the canal that once ran along the National Mall. A huge hunk of** the land was tidal mud flats of the Potomac River before the US Army Corps of Engineers filled it in.

- Continue on 17th Street NW to the World War II Memorial on the right. Dedicated in 2004, this oval memorial with a reflecting pool honors World War II's 16 million service men and women.

- Follow the path alongside the Lincoln Reflecting Pool to the DC War Memorial on the left. It's dedicated to the 26,000 D.C. residents who served in World War I. The marble structure was originally designed as a bandstand for the United States Marine Band, the NPS says.

- Continue on the path to the Korean War Veterans Memorial on the left to see 7-foot-tall soldiers in helmets and ponchos trudging through a field of cropped evergreen bushes that mimic Korea's tough terrain. Dedicated in 1995, the memorial honors the nearly 6 million soldiers who served from 1950 to 1953.

- Continue on the path to the Lincoln Memorial, the rock star of the Mall. This is where Martin Luther King delivered his famous "I Have a Dream" speech during the 1963 March on Washington. Protesters have staged countless rallies there ever since. A 19-foot-high marble statue of a seated President Lincoln is the centerpiece of the memorial. Patterned after the Greek Parthenon, the memorial is surrounded by 36 Doric columns. The north and south chambers feature inscriptions from Lincoln's second inaugural and Gettysburg addresses. The marble, limestone, and granite memorial opened in 1922. Most visitors stand at the front of the memorial to relish the postcard-perfect view of the Mall. Walk around back for a less-crowded riverfront vista.

- Continue northeast on the path to the iconic Vietnam Veterans Memorial (1982) and the lesser-known Vietnam Women's Memorial (1993). This famous polished black granite wall is inscribed with more than 58,000 names of soldiers who died. Nearby, the women's memorial features three bronze statues of nurses, one comforting a dying soldier. In 2016, construction of a long-awaited Vietnam Veterans visitor center is expected to begin nearby. This largely underground "Education Center at The Wall" will showcase photos and stories about the fallen soldiers and exhibit some of the 400,000-plus remembrances left at The Wall.

- Follow the path and turn right onto Henry Bacon Drive NW toward Constitution Avenue NW. Turn left at Constitution Avenue NW and right on 23rd Street NW for the United States Institute of Peace on the left. Its curvaceous glass canopy and modern design pop alongside its conservatively crafted neighbors. This federally funded think tank was created in 2011 by renowned architect Moshe Safdie of Habitat '67 fame. Although no tours are offered, visitors can scope out the building's glass-sided bridges and massive glass atriums when they attend public events.

- Continue north on 23rd Street NW to the fenced-in U.S. State Department annex on the left. Off-limits to the public with no signs proclaiming its storied history, Navy Hill (one of its many names) is worth more than a gander. That's where Mars's moons were discovered, and it was our nation's first modern-day spy agency headquarters. In 1844, the original U.S. Naval Observatory opened there. President Lincoln sometimes dropped by during the Civil War, according to his Lincoln Cottage papers. In 1877, Navy astronomer Asaph Hall used what was then the world's largest telescope to discover Mars's two moons. During World War II, the CIA's predecessor, the Office of Strategic Services (OSS), moved in. OSS director William J. "Wild Bill" Donovan sat at his desk in the southwest corner of the East Building (originally called the Administration Building) overlooking the river, according to records from the CIA and the OSS Society. His paneled first-floor office in this formal limestone building became part of the CIA headquarters when the OSS was dissolved after the war. Legendary chef Julia Williams Child was on his staff, handling communications with the Far East. In the Central Building, OSS's Research and Development Branch created James Bond–like devices, such as edible explosives. The East Building was

The National Mall from atop the Washington Monument

the birthplace of the CIA's U-2 spy plane (Project Aquatone). When the CIA headquarters moved to McLean, Virginia, in 1961—some offices remained there—it dragged its bright blue CIA sign with it for the agency's private museum. Fast-forward to 2012. After 70 years sharing the hill, the U.S. Navy Bureau of Medicine and Surgery vacated the compound as part of the Base Realignment and Closure Act. General Services Administration documents say the 12-acre campus is being developed into the "Potomac Hill Diplomatic Center" with 440,000 square feet of offices.

- Cross 23rd Street NW and head back south to the U.S. State Department on the left. When the agency began in 1789, then Secretary of State Thomas Jefferson oversaw two diplomatic posts in London and Paris. The State Department's lofty mission is to "shape and sustain a peaceful, prosperous, just, and democratic world and foster conditions for stability and progress for the benefit of the American people and people everywhere." And where better to do it than in the splashy Diplomatic Reception Rooms behind the agency's yawn-inducing gray exterior? These are "among the most beautiful rooms in the world," State brags on its website. That's where officials sign treaties, negotiate, host ceremonies, wine and dine visitors, and conduct other affairs. Visitors can register for free tours to sample a handful of the 42 lavish rooms and glimpse a sliver of the furniture and art collection valued in excess of $100 million. The treasures include a serpentine chest of drawers, rococo-style chandeliers, and one of the largest and most elaborate sets of American Chippendale-style chairs.

- Turn left on C Street NW for the National Academy of Sciences and its Einstein Memorial on the right. Truly a temple of science, this may be the coolest small building in Washington that most people have never seen. And this private nonprofit society of scholars actually welcomes the public with art exhibits, concerts, lectures, and impromptu visits. The ornate dome in its Great Hall represents Byzantine architectural influences and displays a dizzying array of geometric patterns and symbols of science and mythology. Outside the building is the academy's popular four-ton, bronze statue of Einstein. Tourists and locals love hopping onto the scientist's lap to take a selfie.

- Continue on C Street NW to the two main buildings of the Federal Reserve, which face each other on opposite sides of the street. The Fed is the central bank of the United States. This formidable institution oversees much of the nation's monetary policy. Only groups of 10 or more can arrange to tour the Marriner S. Eccles building to view some of its 1,000-plus donated works of art.

- **Continue on C Street NW. Turn right on Virginia Avenue NW and cross it to continue onto C Street NW to the U.S. Department of Interior. The austere-looking building is welcoming as far as federal offices go. Tourists can visit its Indian Craft Shop to buy artwork made by more than 45 American Indian tribes and stop by its basement cafeteria and gift shop to buy golf balls with the Interior's bison logo, a bison-shaped squeeze ball (for relieving stress), and other tchotchkes. The agency also runs a small museum and conducts tours of its famous murals, including some by nature photographer Ansel Adams.**

- **Continue on C Street NW, turning left on 18th Street NW and right onto D Street NW for the headquarters of the Daughters of the American Revolution. Founded in 1890, DAR is a 175,000-member nonprofit that promotes patriotism. DAR says it's open to all women who "can prove lineal descent from a patriot of the American Revolution." It now accepts DNA evidence. The DAR offers free tours of period-decorated rooms; a museum with quilts, ceramics, and Paul Revere silver spoons; a gift shop; and a genealogical library. Every president since Calvin Coolidge has attended events at its Constitution Hall concert arena. Performers and lecturers have ranged from Bob Dylan and Big Bird to the Moscow Ballet and anthropologist Jane Goodall. Its grand columned building has starred in TV shows and movies. Part of Angelina Jolie's 2010 spy thriller *Salt* was filmed there. The national historic landmark also stood in as the White House in an episode of the Emmy-winning *West Wing* TV show. The country's first female White House press secretary, Dee Dee Myers of the Clinton administration, was an original consultant for the show.**

Points of Interest

Organization of American States 17th Street NW and Constitution Avenue NW, 202-370-5000, museum.oas.org

Lockkeeper's House at Constitution Gardens 17th Street NW and Constitution Avenue NW, 202-426-6841, nps.gov/nr/travel/wash/dc34.htm

World War II Memorial 17th Street SW between Constitution Avenue NW and Independence Avenue SW, 202-426-6841, wwiimemorial.com

DC War Memorial North side of Independence Avenue SW between the World II Memorial and the Lincoln Memorial, 202-426-6841, nps.gov/nama/planyourvisit/dc-war-memorial.htm

Korean War Veterans Memorial North side of Independence Avenue SW between the DC War Memorial and the Lincoln Memorial, 202-426-6841, nps.gov/kowa

Lincoln Memorial and reflecting pool 23rd Street NW between Constitution Avenue NW and Independence Avenue SW, 202-426-6841, nps.gov/linc

Vietnam Veterans Memorial and Vietnam Women's Memorial 22nd Street NW and Constitution Avenue NW, 202-426-6841, nps.gov/vive/index.htm

United States Institute of Peace 2301 Constitution Ave. NW, 202-457-1700, usip.org

Annex of U.S. Department of State 23rd and D Streets NW, 202-647-4000, state.gov

U.S. Department of State 2201 C St. NW, 202-647-4000, state.gov

National Academy of Sciences and Einstein Memorial 2101 Constitution Ave. NW, 202-334-2000, nasonline.org

Federal Reserve 20th Street NW and Constitution Avenue NW, 202-452-3324, federalreserve.gov

U.S. Department of Interior 1849 C St. NW, 202-208-3100, doi.gov

National Society of the Daughters of the American Revolution 1776 D St. NW, 202-628-1776, dar.org

route summary

1. **Start at the Organization of American States at 17th Street NW and Constitution Avenue NW.**
2. **Walk south on 17th Street NW.**
3. **Turn right into the World War II Memorial.**
4. **Stay to the south of the memorial and turn left to follow the paved footpath.**
5. **Turn left into the DC War Memorial.**
6. **Return to the trail and turn left.**
7. **Turn left into the Korean War Veterans Memorial.**
8. **Follow the path to the right toward the Lincoln Memorial and on to the Vietnam Veterans Memorial.**
9. **Turn right on Henry Bacon Drive NW toward Constitution Avenue NW.**
10. **Turn left at Constitution Avenue NW.**
11. **Turn right on 23rd Street NW and reverse direction.**

12. **Walk south on 23rd Street NW.**
13. **Turn left on C Street NW.**
14. **Turn right on Virginia Avenue NW.**
15. **Turn left on C Street NW.**
16. **Turn left on 18th Street NW.**
17. **Turn right on D Street NW.**

Connecting the Walks

For Walk 22 (National Mall East), walk east toward the Washington Monument from the World War II Memorial. For Walk 15 (White House), walk north on 17th Street NW. For Walk 19 (Tidal Basin Cherries), walk south on 17th Street NW. For Walks 13 and 20 (Potomac River and Columbia Island), start at the Memorial Bridge south of the Lincoln Memorial.

Visitors adore the Lincoln Memorial.

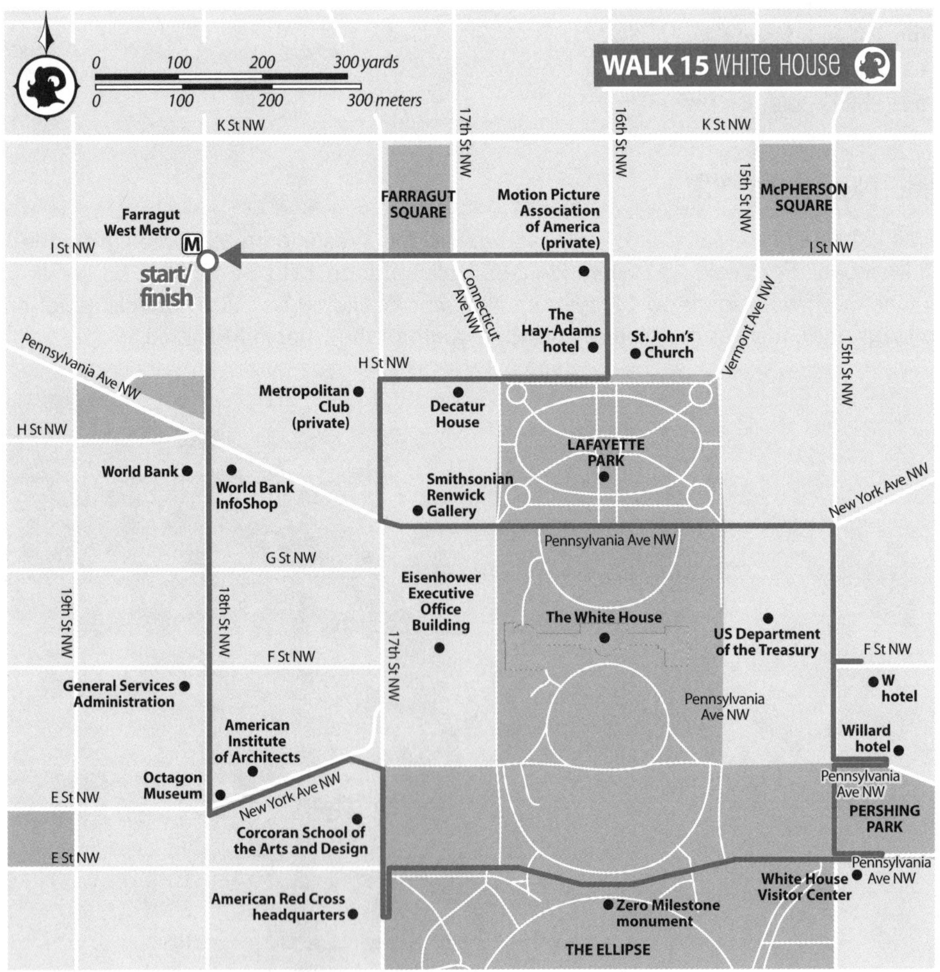
WALK 15 WHITE HOUSE
0
100
200
300 yards
0
100
200
300 meters
K St NW
K St NW
17th St NW
16th St NW
15th St NW
FARRAGUT SQUARE
Motion Picture Association of America (private)
McPHERSON SQUARE
Farragut West Metro
M
I St NW
I St NW
start/ finish
Connecticut Ave NW
The Hay-Adams hotel
St. John's Church
Vermont Ave NW
15th St NW
Pennsylvania Ave NW
H St NW
Metropolitan Club (private)
Decatur House
H St NW
LAFAYETTE PARK
World Bank
World Bank InfoShop
Smithsonian Renwick Gallery
New York Ave NW
Pennsylvania Ave NW
G St NW
Eisenhower Executive Office Building
19th St NW
18th St NW
The White House
US Department of the Treasury
F St NW
F St NW
17th St NW
W hotel
General Services Administration
Pennsylvania Ave NW
American Institute of Architects
Willard hotel
Octagon Museum
E St NW
New York Ave NW
Pennsylvania Ave NW
PERSHING PARK
Corcoran School of the Arts and Design
E St NW
Pennsylvania Ave NW
White House Visitor Center
American Red Cross headquarters
Zero Milestone monument
THE ELLIPSE

15 WHITE HOUSE: POWERFUL, PLUSH, AND ARTSY NEIGHBORS

BOUNDARIES: I Street NW, just east of 15th Street NW, E Street NW, and 18th Street NW
DISTANCE: Nearly 3 miles
DIFFICULTY: Easy
PARKING: Limited metered street parking; parking garages in office buildings; Metro recommended
PUBLIC TRANSIT: Farragut West Metro

Is this White House walk at the center of the universe? No. But it might feel that way because some of the power players here control a huge chunk of the world's future, from pollution and poverty to freedom and art. The president, of course, occupies the epicenter as arguably the single-most powerful person on the planet. But this jaunt isn't just about power. It's also a fun foray through D.C.'s storied past and its boom-time present. Visitors will find great restaurants, great architecture, great vistas, and great deals. Since this loops around a mixed business and tourist area, some shops, cafés, and museums operate only on weekdays during business hours.

- **Start this power walk at the Farragut Metro Station along a streetscape of largely humdrum, medium-rise office buildings, which house law firms, lobbyists, and some of the world's most powerful people and institutions.**

- **Walk south on 18th Street NW to the World Bank's global headquarters on the right at H Street NW. This financial institution, which aids developing countries—no tours here—hopes to end "extreme poverty" in the world by 2030.**

- **Across the street is InfoShop, the bank's gem of a public bookstore. It sells World Bank publications that make economists and policy wonks drool, along with heaps of other books, including super deals on publishers' overstocks. Another big draw: no D.C. sales tax–which may soon rise from 5.75% to 6%. *Washington City Paper* named this otherwise little-known shop the "Best Downtown Book Store" in 2014.**

- **Continue on 18th Street NW to F Street NW. On the right is the General Services Administration headquarters (and beyond that, the George Washington University** campus). This somber, gray building, which fills an entire city block, doesn't welcome tourists, but it does touch the lives of most Americans. As the federal government's chief buyer, it handles real estate, architecture, autos, and much more.

- Turn left on New York Avenue NW for the American Institute of Architects on the left. The 1801 Federal-style Octagon House served as the temporary White House for President James Madison when the British burned down the White House and the Capitol in the War of 1812. The Treaty of Ghent, which ended the war, was signed there in a fashionably round (rounded-off octagonal) room. Next door, the AIA runs a gift shop at its modern headquarters, which sells architectural books and designer-inspired curios. The AIA's D.C. chapter hosts an Architecture Week each spring.

- After exiting the AIA, continue northeast on New York Avenue NW and turn right on 17th Street NW for the magnificent French Beaux Arts building of the George Washington University's Corcoran School of the Arts and Design. In 2014, GW took over the building—formerly the Corcoran Gallery of Art—and the National Gallery of Art acquired most of its American and European art collections. NGA and GW will still stage exhibitions here in the future. The museum's trademark twin bronze lions flanking the entrance will remain. They came from Pony Express founder Bill Holliday.

- Continue south on 17th Street NW to the American Red Cross headquarters, with its monumental white columns. This "marble palace" features massive Tiffany windows in its ornate Board of Governors Hall. Some of the art and artifacts on display include founder Clara Barton's sewing kit and a Red Cross quilt signed by Microsoft founder Bill Gates, astronaut Neil Armstrong, and other notables. Just outside, the citrusy scent of cream-colored magnolia flowers reminds visitors that they're in a sultry Southern city.

- After exiting, reverse direction to return north on 17th Street NW. Turn right on E Street NW to reach the edge of the South Lawn of the White House. The thigh-high Zero Milestone monument lies just outside the fence on the Ellipse. It was conceived of in 1919 as the starting point to measure the distances of all the country's roads. It was also the departure point for the Army's first cross-country convoy to the west coast. The Federal Highway Administration says, though it "never became the American equivalent of Rome's Golden Milestone," it still "marks the place where 'a new era' " of transportation began.

- Continue on E Street NW as it crosses 15th Street NW to become Pennsylvania Avenue NW. On the right is the White House Visitor Center, which opened in 1995.
- After the visitor center, reverse direction on Pennsylvania Avenue NW. Turn right on 15th Street NW and then turn right again to reach the north side of Pennsylvania Avenue. On the left is the Willard Hotel. The lavish hotel, capped with its trademark curved mansard roof and round windows, is where Rev. Martin Luther King finished his "I Have a Dream" speech. Also popular with presidents, it sports a high tea, a harpist, and opulent restaurants and bars, with seasonal sidewalk dining. Mark Twain, Charles Dickens, and other legends overnighted in the 335-room hotel.
- After the Willard, reverse direction on Pennsylvania Avenue NW; turn right on 15th Street NW; and then turn right on F Street NW for the W hotel on the right. In 2008, this trendy chain rehabbed the historic Hotel Washington. Its incomparable outdoor rooftop bar overlooking the White House draws all types, from politicos to rock stars. Elvis Presley even stayed there in 1970 when he decided to drop in on President Nixon.
- After the W hotel, reverse direction on F Street NW; turn right on 15th Street NW, and turn left on Pennsylvania Avenue NW for the stately U.S. Department of the Treasury. Public tours guide visitors by the 1864 cast-iron "burglar-proof vault" in the Treasurer's office; the conference room where G7 leaders meet and mingle; a triple-skylighted oval room freshly gilded from a 2004 restoration; and its marble-clad, palazzo-inspired cash room. Tour-goers learn that in 1862, Treasury hired the first female federal government worker in the country's history.

Ceremonial cannon by the White House

- Continue west on Pennsylvania Avenue NW to the White House on the left and Lafayette Park on the right.

- The White House may be an ordinary building, but it's nearly mythological as an icon of freedom. This "People's House," with its white-columned porticos, draws tourists and protesters from all over the globe. It's the president's office and home, and it's the oldest public building in Washington. Construction commenced in 1793, but not too long after its completion, British soldiers burned it in 1814, leaving only sandstone walls and interior brickwork, the National Park Service says. Reconstruction was finished in 1817, and renovations continued off and on for years. The flamboyant, four-story Eisenhower Executive Office Building next door serves as White House staff offices.

- Across Pennsylvania Avenue is Lafayette Park, a 7-acre garden oasis and a respected haven for peaceful protestors. It has also been a slave market, a graveyard, a zoo, an orchard, a racetrack, and a fashionable residential district, says its caretaker, the National Park Service. It's worth a visit just to enjoy the sculpture, canons, views of the White House, and 19th-century row houses along the west side, which function as offices for the White House Historical Association and government agencies. Blair House, at the southwest corner, is the president's 14-room guesthouse. Britain's Queen Elizabeth, South Africa's President Nelson Mandela, and other heads of state have slumbered there. Underneath Lafayette Park lies a little-known geological fault. The 24-foot vertical displacement extends under Pennsylvania Avenue near the East Wing of the White House, according to U.S. Geological Survey data from 1976. The last earthquake along this District of Columbia Fault Zone, which continues north toward the National Zoo, was roughly 100,000 years ago, said D. C. Prowell and R. A. Christopher in 2010.

- Continue on Pennsylvania Avenue NW to 17th Street NW. The newly renovated Renwick Gallery of the Smithsonian American Art Museum, on the right, specializes in contemporary craft and decorative arts. James Renwick Jr., who designed the Smithsonian's "Castle" and New York City's St. Patrick's Cathedral, created this French Second Empire–style museum. The country's first purpose-built art museum, it was modeled after the Louvre's Tuileries addition in Paris. Its exterior was completed in 1861.

- Turn right on 17th Street NW. On the left at H Street NW is the private Metropolitan Club, which was founded in 1863.

Bagging a White House Tour

If you want to visit the White House, plan far in advance, but don't be disappointed if you can't get in. In the "good old days"—before 9/11—almost anyone willing to stand in line could visit their taxpayer-funded White House. Nowadays, unless you're chummy with the first family, famous like Beyoncé, part of a school or work tour group, a big contributor, or politically connected, you have to rely on a lottery. The first step is to request a tour through your member of Congress. Tours can be requested from three weeks to six months in advance. January and February appear to be the easiest times to get in. But even if you can't go eyeball to eyeball with President Lincoln's portrait in the State Dining Room, you can drop by the White House Visitor Center, which was renovated in 2014. Visitors can finally photograph their once-in-a-lifetime tours. The White House ended its more than 40-year-old photography ban in 2015 and now allows small cameras and cell phone photos.

- Turn right on H Street NW to Decatur House on the right. Designed by the father of American architect Benjamin Henry Latrobe in 1818, it's one of D.C.'s oldest surviving homes, according to its owner, the National Trust for Historic Preservation. It now hosts the National Center for White House History and a gift shop run by the White House Historical Association. The nonprofit sells its trademark White House Christmas ornaments, a French silk scarf inspired by the Blue Room, and other unique keepsakes.

- Turn left on 16th Street NW for The Hay-Adams hotel on the left and St. John's Church on the right.

  Few can afford one of The Hay-Adams hotel rooms overlooking the White House, but most visitors can at least sip a gin and tonic at its historic bar and restaurant or listen to the likes of Toni Morrison at its annual author lecture. Renowned guests at this tony yet tasteful getaway have included Amelia Earhart and Sinclair Lewis.

  St. John's Church, a yellow and white Episcopal church designed by Latrobe, reserves pew number 54 for presidents. The National Park Service says, "Every president since James Madison has worshiped here on some occasion."

- **Continue on 16th Street NW. Turn left on I Street NW for the headquarters and political arm of the Motion Picture Association of America. This private trade association, whose members include Walt Disney Studios Motion Pictures, hosts invitation-only events at its theater. The MPAA created the rating system for America's movies.**

- **Continue on I Street NW to the Metro on the right at 18th Street NW.**

POINTS OF INTEREST

Farragut West Metro 900 18th St. NW, 202-637-7000, wmata.com/rail/station_detail.cfm?station_id=38

The World Bank 1818 H St. NW, 202-473-1000, worldbank.org

World Bank InfoShop 701 18th St. NW, 202-458-4500, worldbank.org/infoshop

General Services Administration 1800 F St. NW, gsa.gov

American Institute of Architects and the Octagon 1735 New York Ave. NW, 800-AIA-3837, aia.org

Corcoran School of the Arts and Design 500 17th St. NW, 202-639-1700, corcoran.org

American Red Cross headquarters 430 17th St. NW, tours@redcross.org, redcross.org/about-us/history/explore-our-history

Zero Milestone On the Ellipse by the South Lawn of the White House, www.fhwa.dot.gov/infrastructure/zero.cfm

White House Visitor Center 1450 Pennsylvania Ave. NW, 202-208-1631, nps.gov/whho/planyourvisit/white-house-tours.htm

The Willard Washington D.C. 1401 Pennsylvania Ave. NW, 202-628-9100, washington.intercontinental.com

W Washington D.C. 515 15th St. NW, 202-661-2400, wwashingtondc.com

U.S. Department of the Treasury 15th Street NW and Hamilton Place NW, treasury.gov/about/education/Pages/tours.aspx

The White House 1600 Pennsylvania Ave. NW; 202-456-1111 (public comment line), 202-456-1414 (switchboard); whitehouse.gov

Lafayette Park and President's Park H Street NW to Pennsylvania Avenue NW and Madison Place NW to Jackson Place NW, 202-208-1631, nps.gov/whho/index.htm

Renwick Gallery of the Smithsonian American Art Museum 1661 Pennsylvania Ave. NW, 202-633-7970, americanart.si.edu/renwick

The Metropolitan Club 1700 H St. NW, 202-835-2500, metroclub.com

Decatur House 1610 H St. NW, 202-842-0917, whitehousehistory.org/decatur-house

The Hay-Adams 800 16th St. NW, 202-638-6600, hayadams.com

St. John's Church 1525 H St. NW, 202-347-8766, stjohns-dc.org

Motion Picture Association of America 1600 I St. NW, 202-293-1966, mpaa.org

route summary

1. **Start at the Farragut West Metro, 900 18th Street NW.**
2. **Walk south on 18th Street NW.**
3. **Turn left on New York Avenue NW.**
4. **Turn right on 17th Street NW and then reverse direction.**
5. **Turn right on E Street NW.**
6. **Continue on E Street NW, and follow it past the White House until it becomes Pennsylvania Avenue NW, and then reverse direction.**
7. **Turn right on 15th Street NW.**
8. **Turn right on Pennsylvania Avenue NW and then reverse direction.**
9. **Turn right on 15th Street NW.**
10. **Turn right on F Street NW and reverse direction.**
11. **Turn right on 15th Street NW.**
12. **Turn left on Pennsylvania Avenue NW.**
13. **Turn right on 17th Street NW.**
14. **Turn right on H Street NW.**
15. **Turn left on 16th Street NW.**
16. **Turn left on I Street NW toward the Metro on the right.**

connecting the walks

For Walks 14 and 22 on the National Mall, continue south on 17th Street NW to Constitution Avenue NW. For Walk 16 (Downtown: News Junkies West), continue north on 17th Street NW to I Street NW.

WALK 16 DOWNTOWN: News Junkies West
O St NW
17th St NW
16th St NW
Massachusetts Ave NW
Rhode Island Ave NW
14th St NW
Vermont Ave NW
N St NW
13th St NW
12th St NW
Connecticut Ave NW
15th St NW
The Jefferson hotel
M St NW
Westin hotel
ABC News
National Geographic
Russian Federation/ ambassador's residence (private)
Boston Globe
Desales St NW
Mayflower hotel
Washington Post (old)
L St NW
Wall Street Journal
18th St NW
Farragut North Metro
Washington Post (new)
K St NW
FARRAGUT SQUARE
McPHERSON SQUARE
FRANKLIN SQUARE
Farragut West Metro
New York Times
I St NW
start
Reuters
11th St NW
H St NW
Bloomberg News
National Museum of Women in the Arts
LAFAYETTE PARK
Jackson Pl NW
Madison Pl NW
Pennsylvania Ave NW
New York Ave NW
Hearst News/ McClatchy Company
Metro Center Metro
G St NW
finish
0 0.05 0.1 0.15 mile
0 0.05 0.1 0.15 kilometer
The White House

16 DOWNTOWN: NEWS JUNKIES WEST: SCANDALS AND SCRIBES

BOUNDARIES: **M Street NW, 12th Street NW, G Street NW, and Connecticut Avenue NW**
DISTANCE: **2.3 miles**
DIFFICULTY: **Easy**
PARKING: **Rare 2-hour metered street parking; parking garages in some office buildings; Metro recommended**
PUBLIC TRANSIT: **Farragut West, Farragut North, and Metro Center Metro stations, served by multiple buses**

"Dateline: Washington." That's splattered across newspapers from Portland, Oregon, to Portland, Maine. D.C. makes news. D.C. covers news. Even in this digital news age, with many newspapers folding, the capital is still arguably the biggest newshounds' town. TV, print, radio, and online news bureaus are scattered across the city, sometimes right next door to the people and institutions they report on. Typically, the stories they report are serious or sad, but some are quirky or scandalous. Here's a short loop past some spots where newsmakers and news-breakers work and play.

- **Start at the Farragut West Metro station at 18th and I Streets NW. Turn right to walk east on I Street NW past Farragut Square park to 17th Street NW for the *New York Times'* Washington Bureau on the left, in the buff-colored brick building topped with a modern tower. Although this and *all the news bureaus are private,* it's neat to know where they are when you're reading their Washington news stories.**

- **Turn left to walk north on 17th Street NW. Turn left on K Street NW and right on Connecticut Avenue NW for the *Wall Street Journal's* brown steel and glass office building on the right.**

- **Continue north on Connecticut Avenue NW for *The Boston Globe* on the left in an office building with curved glass in the middle. On the right is the elegant Mayflower Renaissance Hotel, a social landmark since 1925. FBI Director J. Edgar Hoover lunched there daily for two decades; President Harry Truman lived there briefly; and**

Franklin Roosevelt lived in suite 776 when he wrote his famous "We have nothing to fear but fear itself" speech, the National Park Service says. In 1999, Monica Lewinsky was grilled by prosecutors in the presidential suite "when she testified about her tryst" with President Clinton, according to news accounts. Scandal struck again in 2008 when married New York Gov. Eliot Spitzer stayed in room 871 with a pricey, 105-pound prostitute, the *New York Times* said.

- Turn right on Desales Street NW for ABC News on the left in a building with glass blocks.

- Turn left on 17th Street NW for the *National Geographic* headquarters on the right. Founded in 1888, "Nat Geo," as it's known to its newest generation of readers and TV viewers, welcomes visitors to its public exhibits, films, café, and gift shop.

- Turn right on M Street NW for The Jefferson hotel on the left at 16th Street NW. Most folks head to this 1923 landmark for its sumptuous setting and romantic restaurant. Bill Clinton's longtime political strategist, Dick Morris, came for a call girl in suite 205. The news broke right before Clinton accepted the presidential nomination at the 1996 Democratic convention. A photo of the married Morris "being amorous on the balcony of his hotel suite clinched the story," *The Washington Post* wrote.

- Turn right on 16th Street NW and walk past the redbrick University Club of Washington DC to the private residence of the ambassador of the Russian Federation on the left. Built in 1910 by railroad-car magnate George Pullman's wife, this limestone, French Baroque–style mansion has also served as the embassy for the Soviet Union and Russia.

- Turn left on L Street NW for the *Washington Post* on the left at 15th Street NW—at least until around 2016. Its vintage headquarters is destined for the wrecking ball after the paper moves, the developer says. That probably wouldn't bother former publisher Katharine Graham too much. In her memoir, she called the building plain and dowdy. Graham hired architect I. M. Pei to design a more striking structure, but the plans fell through. The *Post* itself became legendary when it won a Pulitzer Prize for its Watergate reporting. Robert Redford, Dustin Hoffman, and others hung out in the fifth-floor newsroom to study the paper while producing the 1976 classic flick about Watergate, *All the President's Men.* Graham vehemently nixed filming in the newsroom, so the movie company built an "exact duplicate" in Hollywood, complete with reporters' trash as props.

- Turn left on 15th Street NW and right on M Street NW for The Westin Washington, D.C. City Center hotel on the right. In 1990, when it was the Vista International Hotel, D.C.'s Mayor Marion Barry was videotaped and arrested in Room 727 for smoking crack. He served six months in prison. Later Barry was reelected mayor and then city councilman. Barry returned to the hotel for dinner in 2014, the year he died, the hotel said.

- Continue east on M Street NW; turn right on Thomas Circle NW; and turn right on Vermont Avenue NW for McPherson Square, across K Street NW. Named for Civil War General James B. McPherson, the park offers a respite for cooped-up office workers at lunch. In January 2014, it was a nighttime hangout for the "DC Snowy Owl" and some fans.

- Standing on K Street NW, with the park to the rear, turn right to continue east on K Street. Cross 14th Street for *The Washington Post*'s new headquarters on the left. One Franklin Square, a 1.1-million-square-foot, rose-tinged granite building with twin spires was designed by D.C.-based Hartman-Cox architects in 1990. It's slated to become the *Post*'s new home in 2016. Amazon founder Jeffrey P. Bezos bought the paper in 2013.

- Turn right on 13th Street NW for Franklin Square park, a hot spot for D.C.'s food trucks. Turn right on Eye Street NW and left on 14th Street NW for Reuters news agency's modern gray office building one door down on the left at H Street NW.

Washington Post's soon-to-be former home

Hedwig Came Calling

Once upon a time, a snowy owl like Harry Potter's pet, Hedwig, came to Washington. This Arctic owl was one of the rarest creatures ever spotted in the city, said D.C. government biologist Daniel Rauch. Maybe the snow-white bird had heard how I helped make another flyer famous. The previous winter, I successfully persuaded *The Washington Post* to assign a story about a somewhat rare rufous hummingbird overwintering near D.C. But this time the editors where I used to work wouldn't bite. I pleaded: This is like a polar bear coming to visit. We were seeing more snowy owls than we'd seen in decades, said Project SNOWstorm's Scott Weidensaul, an expert studying these rodent-guzzling raptors, which seldom migrate this far south from their desolate tundra homes. But no one would listen. No one would write. Until one brave snowy owl flew straight to the *Post* and camped out for days on its second-story window ledge to tell the story himself. The editors and reporters were stunned. Crowds began huddling inside and outside the newspaper to ogle the roughly 2-foot-tall bird with big yellow eyes and feathery feet. They watched him at night as he lurked on a CVS drugstore awning in nearby McPherson Square. After the *Post* and others wrote about him, he became a celebrity with his own Twitter account: @DCSnowyOwl. Then in the wee hours of January, 30, 2014, a bus and an SUV struck the penguin-like owl on 14th Street at K Street, the *Post* reported. The bloody bird flew near the White House, where three D.C. cops rescued him. After local rehab, he wound up at the University of Minnesota's Raptor Center, where he had temporary feather "prosthetics" installed and his fame spread even farther. In April, the center released the banded bird along the Minnesota-Wisconsin border. Unfortunately, just like Hedwig, he never made it home. He was spotted four weeks later along a nearby highway, smashed by yet another motor vehicle, the center said. If only the newspaper had written about him at first, the poor critter wouldn't have needed to swoop through the dangerous downtown streets to visit the *Post* in person. But then we all would have missed meeting our beloved DC Snowy Owl. Maybe one day we'll be lucky enough to meet his brother or sister. One banded snowy owl lived to be about 17 years old.

- Continue south on 14th Street NW for Bloomberg News's curvy glass and concrete building on the left at New York Avenue NW. This financial news and information company was founded by former New York Mayor Michael Bloomberg in 1982.

- Turn left on New York Avenue NW for the National Museum of Women in the Arts on the right. The nonprofit museum refurbished this wedge-shaped Masonic temple in 1987 to showcase more than 4,500 works of art by more than 1,000 female artists.

- Turn right on 12th Street NW for the Metro Center Metro station on the left and the Hearst and McClatchy news bureaus on the right, in a building with three angled glass awnings.

  The holdings of New York City–based Hearst Corporation include TV, radio, magazines, and newspapers (15 dailies and 34 weeklies). Back in 1945, President John F. Kennedy worked as a reporter—a "special correspondent"—for Hearst Newspapers, according to his records at the JFK Presidential Library and Museum.

  The D.C. bureau of California-based McClatchy Company employs 40 journalists, the company says on its website. It owns 29 daily newspapers, including the *Miami Herald,* which broke the story about married presidential candidate Gary Hart "dating" a young model in 1987. That "began a new era of political journalism in which politicians' private lives, which had been mostly exempt from media scrutiny, were now considered measurements of 'character' and thus fair game for reporters," the *Herald* wrote in 2014—after *The New York Times* reportedly "outted" the story's anonymous source.

Beloved DC Snowy Owl; photo by Daniel Rauch

POINTS OF INTEREST

Farragut West Metro station 18th and Eye Streets NW, 202-637-7000, mata.com/rail/station_detail.cfm?station_id=38

The New York Times 1627 Eye St. NW, 888-698-6397, nytimes.com

The Wall Street Journal 1025 Connecticut Ave. NW, 800-568-7625, wsj.com

The Mayflower Renaissance Hotel 1127 Connecticut Ave. NW, 202-347-3000, marriott.com

The Boston Globe 1130 Connecticut Ave. NW, 888-694-5623, bostonglobe.com

ABC News 1717 DeSales St. NW, 212-456-7777, abcnews.go.com

National Geographic 1145 17th St. NW, 202-857-7588, nationalgeographic.com

The Jefferson 1200 16th St. NW, 202-448-2300, jeffersondc.com

(Private) residence of the Ambassador of the Russian Federation 1125 16th St. NW, 202-298-5700, ussianembassy.org

***The Washington Post* (until 2016)** 1150 15th St. NW, 202-334-6000, washingtonpost.com

The Westin Washington, D.C. City Center 1400 M St. NW, 202-429-1700, westinwashingtondccitycenter.com

McPherson Square 13th to 14th Streets NW between I and K Streets NW

***The Washington Post* (future)** 1301 K St. NW, 202-334-6000, washingtonpost.com

Reuters News Agency 1333 H St. NW, 646-223-4000, reuters.com

Bloomberg News 1399 New York Ave. NW, 212-318-2000, bloomberg.com

National Museum of Women in the Arts 1250 New York Ave. NW, 202-783-5000, nmwa.org

Hearst News Service 700 12th St. NW, 212-649-2000, hearst.com

The McClatchy Company 700 12th St. NW, 916-321-1855, mcclatchydc.com

Metro Center Metro station 12th and G Streets NW, 202-637-7000, wmata.com/rail/station_detail.cfm?station_id=1

route summary

1. Start at the Farragut West Metro station at 18th and I Streets NW.
2. Walk east on I Street NW.
3. Turn left on 17th Street NW.
4. Turn left on K Street NW.
5. Turn right on Connecticut Avenue NW.
6. Turn right on Desales Street NW.
7. Turn left on 17th Street NW.
8. Turn right on M Street NW.
9. Turn right on 16th Street NW.
10. Turn left on L Street NW.
11. Turn left on 15th Street NW.
12. Turn right on M Street NW.
13. Turn right at Thomas Circle NW.
14. Turn right on Vermont Avenue NW.
15. Cross K Street for McPherson Square on the right.
16. Standing on K Street NW, with the park to the rear, turn right to continue east on K Street NW.
17. Turn right on 13th Street NW.
18. Turn right on I Street NW.
19. Turn left on 14th Street NW.
20. Turn left on New York Avenue NW.
21. Turn right on 12th Street NW.

connecting the walks

For companion Walk 18 (Downtown: News Junkies East), at Metro Center station, continue south on 12th Street NW. For Walk 12 (Dupont Circle), continue north on Connecticut Avenue NW. For Walk 15 (White House), walk south on Connecticut Avenue NW from Farragut Square.

Dinosaurs rule at National Geographic.

WALK 17 PENN QUARTER–CHINATOWN
L St NW
Massachusetts Ave NW
K St NW
Historical Society of Washington, D.C.
7th St NW
5th St NW
4th St NW
3rd St NW
I St NW
New York Ave NW
Destination DC
Goethe-Institut
9th St NW
U.S. Mint
8th St NW
10th St NW
Friendship Arch
H St NW
Smithsonian National Portrait Gallery
finish
Gallery Place–Chinatown Metro
Martin Luther King, Jr. Memorial Library
13th St NW
12th St NW
11th St NW
G St NW
National Building Museum
Gallup headquarters
Verizon Center
F St NW
National Law Enforcement Officers Memorial
Shakespeare Theatre Company's Harman Center for the Arts
International Spy Museum
E St NW
National Academy of Sciences
District Architecture Center
Shakespeare Theatre Company's Lansburgh Theatre
Woolly Mammoth Theatre Company
D St NW
Pennsylvania Ave NW
Indiana Ave NW
start
Archives–Navy Memorial–Penn Quarter Metro
C St NW
6th St NW
0 0.1 0.2 0.3 mile
0 0.1 0.2 0.3 kilometer

17 Penn Quarter–Chinatown: A Cultural Buffet

BOUNDARIES: Ninth Street NW, K Street NW, Fourth Street NW, and Pennsylvania Avenue NW
DISTANCE: 1.8 miles
DIFFICULTY: Easy
PARKING: Extremely limited 2-hour metered street parking; Metro recommended; public parking garages in several office buildings
PUBLIC TRANSIT: Archives, Gallery Place, and Judiciary Square Metro stations, which are served by multiple buses

There's no room for "dull" here. Even if you closed your eyes and headed into a random building in Penn Quarter or Chinatown, you'd likely find food, fun, or something fantastic—and maybe all three. Not that it's all play. This is still a downtown office hub near the Capitol—with the headquarters of the U.S. Mint, the U.S. Secret Service, and the Gallup Poll, among others. But alongside their offices are brand-new buildings, "façade-omies" (new structures wrapped in the preserved façades of vintage buildings), and rehabbed buildings that are overflowing with restaurants, bars, unusual museums, theaters, shops, and hotels. The 20,000-seat Verizon Center, with its ice-skating princes and princesses, basketball giants, and rock stars, is the biggest nighttime draw. When it opened as the MCI Center in 1997, some streets were still seedy. Now the neighborhood's rebuilding is nearly complete, with an eye-pleasing mix of buildings in a smorgasbord of materials, sizes, shapes, colors, and architectural details. Although there is still some yummy Chinese food here, only a handful of the old-school restaurants are left on H Street NW. Some locals refer to Chinatown as Chinablock. These days, Spanish tapas, Mediterranean mezze, and happy-hour appetizers are more common than dim sum. The entire neighborhood is like a small-plates tasting menu of D.C.'s primo urban adventures.

- **Start at the Archives–Navy Memorial–Penn Quarter Metro station, 701 Pennsylvania Avenue NW. At the top of the Metro escalator, make a U-turn to reach Seventh Street NW. Turn left on Seventh Street NW and then turn right on D Street NW for the 265-seat Woolly Mammoth Theatre Company on the left. This nonprofit, which began in 1980 and moved here in 2005, bills itself as "Washington's most daring theatre company."**

- **Reverse direction on D Street NW and turn right to follow the brick sidewalks on Seventh Street NW. On the right is the District Architecture Center. This storefront** headquarters of the Washington chapter of the American Institute of Architects has run exhibits, films, workshops, and other public events since it moved here in 2011. In 1998, the group began hosting an Architecture Week each spring with lectures and tours.

- Across the street is another award-winning theater. The Shakespeare Theatre Company produces classic plays at this location; the 451-seat Lansburgh Theatre, which opened in 1992; and nearby in the 774-seat Sidney Harman Hall, which opened in 2007. The company also offers acting classes. The Lansburgh apartment building next door is where the first female attorney general (Janet Reno) lived during the Clinton administration.

- Turn right on E Street NW and walk past AARP's headquarters for the National Academy of Sciences on the left at Sixth Street. On the southeast corner is NAS's Marian Koshland Science Museum, which opened in 2004 to help "people use science to solve problems in their communities." Around the corner at 500 Fifth Street NW is NAS's bookstore. It mainly sells tomes on grave subjects, such as nuclear power safety, which are published by this private, nonprofit research organization chartered by Congress in 1863. But it also sells T-shirts emblazoned with the popular Einstein statue at its headquarters, along with Infectious Awareables' cuddly Giant Microbe stuffed toys (herpes resembles a floppy yellow flower with eyes).

- After NAS, walk north on Fifth Street NW and turn right on F Street NW for the National Building Museum on the left. Designed as the Pension Building in 1887 by Montgomery C. Meigs to serve Civil War veterans, it now exhibits architecture, engineering, and design. The museum's cavernous, Roman palace–inspired atrium with colossal gold columns has hosted 17 presidential inaugural balls.

- Across F Street NW is the National Law Enforcement Officers Memorial, which opened in 1991. The names of more than 20,000 law enforcement officers are carved on two short, curved marble walls flanked by allées of fragrant linden trees on opposite sides of the oval memorial. A museum is in the works.

- Reverse direction on F Street NW for the Shakespeare Theatre Company's modern, glass-clad home at Sidney Harman Hall just past Sixth Street NW.

- Across F Street NW is the Verizon Center. When it's not hosting the Washington Wizards, the Washington Mystics, the Washington Capitals, or the Georgetown Hoyas, the arena is a stage for Rolling Stones concerts, Disney on Ice, the Washington International Horse Show, and other class acts.

- Continue on F Street NW for the mammoth Greek Revival building on the right that houses the Donald W. Reynolds Center for American Art and Portraiture, otherwise known as the Smithsonian American Art Museum and the National Portrait Gallery. Inside this somber gray stone shell, it's bursting with color, creativity, texture, and history. The 1785 oil painting of Benjamin Franklin that's featured on the $100 bill and the Constitution's preamble spelled out in license plates are among its approximately 66,000 works of art. Three of the biggest stars are the upper floors of the south and west wings, the Luce Foundation Center for American Art and the Lunder Conservation Center. At the Luce, visitors go eye-to-eye with more than 3,300 paintings, sculptures, jewelry, and other art displayed in rows of glass cases on three luscious floors. That's how thousands of patent models were displayed, including the first telephone, when it was the old Patent Office. It feels like a Victorian dollhouse, with a black-and-white marble floor in a three-story-high atrium under a nearly block-long pitched skylight. On the lower mezzanine, 10 curvaceous balconies cantilever into the space with filigreed bronze and glass railings. Just steps away at the Lunder, master conservators preserve and repair artwork in floor-to-ceiling glass studios right in front of visitors. It's the first of its kind, the museum says. The museum was renovated in 2006, including the Victorian-style Great Hall on the south wing's third floor. Its popular courtyard was capped with a curving glass roof in 2007.

Chinatown's dazzling arch

- Across F Street NW is the privately owned International Spy Museum. The 64,000-square-foot museum, with stealthy gadgets like a lipstick pistol, and its spy school and other interactive exhibits, opened in 2002. Don't tell anyone, but as of 2015, the spies were reconnoitering for a new, larger home in D.C.

- Continue on F Street and turn right on Ninth Street NW for the world headquarters of the private Gallup company on the left. It's known for its Gallup Poll, which began in 1935. Gallup moved here from Princeton, New Jersey, in 1999.

- Continue north on Ninth Street NW for the Martin Luther King Jr. Memorial Library on the left. D.C.'s only building designed by legendary German architect Ludwig Mies van der Rohe, this black steel and smoky-glass landmark from 1972 is about to be renovated.

- After the library and just past H Street NW is the U.S. Mint headquarters on the right. It's not Fort Knox (which safeguards 147.3 million ounces of gold), but it is one of the federal agency's six main facilities. A mini-store in the lobby sells 1-ounce, 24-karat-gold American Buffalo coins; America the Beautiful quarter sets; and other products that it makes outside of D.C.

- Continue on Ninth Street NW and turn right on K Street NW for the Historical Society of Washington, D.C., on the left in a monumental Vermont marble landmark. Founded in 1894 as the Columbia Historical Society, the nonprofit moved into the Carnegie Library at Mount Vernon Square in 1999. It stages exhibits and lectures and welcomes researchers. The Beaux Arts building with a façade of 11 huge Roman arches was dedicated in 1903. D.C.'s central public library operated here for about 70 years until it built the MLK library.

- Turn right on Seventh Street NW for the Goethe-Institut on the right at I Street NW. This German-supported cultural and educational organization has hosted films, exhibits, language classes, and other events to teach Americans about Germany since 1996.

- Facing the institute, turn left on I Street NW for Destination DC's headquarters in a vintage office building on the left. It's Washington's official tourism agency.

- Reverse direction on I Street NW and turn left on Seventh Street NW. The Friendship Arch on the left at H Street NW was built in 1986 in collaboration with Beijing two years after it became one of D.C.'s sister cities. The roughly 47-foot-high and 75-foot-wide archway with seven pagodalike roofs was designed in the style of China's Qing Dynasty, says *The Washington Post.* The red, aqua, green, and blue arch "features 272 decorative dragons, 35,000 gold leaf adornments and 7,000 roof tiles." Several Chinese restaurants and a knickknack store still operate on that block, but they now share the street with four chain stores. In 2007, Chinatown began its annual Chinese New Year festival and parade.

- Continue south on Seventh Street NW for the Gallery Place–Chinatown Metro on the left.

POINTS OF INTEREST

Archives–Navy Memorial–Penn Quarter Metro Station 701 Pennsylvania Ave. NW, 202-637-7000, wmata.com/rail/station_detail.cfm?station_id=81

Woolly Mammoth Theatre Company 641 D St. NW, 202-393-3939, woollymammoth.net

District Architecture Center 421 Seventh St. NW, 202-347-9403, aiadac.com

Shakespeare Theatre Company 450 Seventh St. NW, 202-547-1122, shakespearetheatre.org

National Academy of Sciences 525 E St. NW, 202-334-1201, koshland-science-museum.org

National Building Museum 401 F St. NW, 202-272-2448, nbm.org

National Law Enforcement Officers Memorial E Street between Fourth and Fifth Streets NW, 202-737-3400, nleomf.org/memorial

Shakespeare Theatre Company 610 F St. NW, 202-547-1122, shakespearetheatre.org

Verizon Center 601 F St. NW, 202-628-3200, verizoncenter.monumentalnetwork.com

Donald W. Reynolds Center for American Art and Portraiture Eight and F Streets NW, 202-633-7970, americanart.si.edu

International Spy Museum 800 F St. NW, 202-393-7798, spymuseum.org

Gallup 901 F St. NW, 202-715-3030, gallup.com

Martin Luther King Jr. Memorial Library 901 G St. NW, 202-727-0321, dclibrary.org/mlk

U.S. Mint 801 Ninth St. NW, 800-USA-MINT, usmint.gov

Historical Society of Washington, D.C. 801 K St. NW, 202-249-3955, dchistory.org

Goethe-Institut 812 Seventh St. NW, 202-289-1200, goethe.de/ins/us/was/uun/enindex.htm

Destination DC 901 Seventh St. NW, 202-789-7000, washington.org

Friendship Arch H and Seventh Streets NW

Gallery Place–Chinatown Metro Seventh and G Streets NW, 202-637-7000, wmata.com/rail/station_detail.cfm?station_id=21

route summary

1. Start at the Archives–Navy Memorial–Penn Quarter Metro station, 701 Pennsylvania Avenue NW. After exiting the Metro escalator, make a U-turn to reach Seventh Street NW.
2. Turn left on Seventh Street NW.
3. Turn right on D Street NW and then reverse direction.
4. Turn right on Seventh Street NW.
5. Turn right on E Street NW.
6. Turn left on Fifth Street NW.
7. Turn right on F Street NW and then reverse direction.
8. Turn right on Ninth Street NW.
9. Turn right on K Street NW.
10. Turn right on Seventh Street NW.
11. Turn left on I Street NW and then reverse direction.
12. Turn left on Seventh Street NW for the Metro just past G Street NW on the left.

CONNECTING THE WALKS

Walk 16 (Downtown: News Junkies West) runs past the Archives–Navy Memorial–Penn Quarter Metro station. For Walk 22 (National Mall East), walk south on Seventh Street NW for two blocks to the Mall.

The National Building Museum's monumental atrium has hosted presidential inaugural balls since 1885.

WALK 18 DOWNTOWN: News Junkies east
G St NW
F St NW
E St NW
D St NW
C St NW
14th St NW
13th St NW
12th St NW
11th St NW
10th St NW
9th St NW
8th St NW
7th St NW
5th St NW
4th St NW
3rd St NW
Madame Tussauds
National Press Club
National Theatre
Warner Theatre
Ford's Theatre
Pennsylvania Ave NW
former Evening Star building (private)
FBI
Corporation for Public Broadcasting
Old Post Office Pavilion/Trump Int'l Hotel
start
M
Federal Triangle Metro/ Environmental Protection Agency
US Department of Justice
US Navy Memorial
Indiana Ave NW
National Archives and Records Administration
Federal Trade Commission
Newseum
Embassy of Canada
Constitution Ave NW
Madison Dr NW
Jefferson Dr SW
Independence Ave SW
Maryland Ave SW
C St SW
finish
Voice of America
To Federal Center SW Metro
0 0.1 0.2 0.3 mile
0 0.1 0.2 0.3 kilometer

18 DOWNTOWN: NEWS JUNKIES EAST: FEDS, FREEDOM, AND THE PRESS

BOUNDARIES: F Street NW, Fourth Street SW, Independence Avenue SW, and 14th Street NW
DISTANCE: 2 miles
DIFFICULTY: Easy
PARKING: Limited 2-hour metered parking; parking garages in some office buildings; Metro recommended
PUBLIC TRANSIT: Federal Triangle Metro station at the start. Federal Center SW Metro station one block south of the finish at 401 Third Street SW. Both are served by multiple buses.

What happens in Vegas might stay in Vegas, but what happens in D.C. might spread around the globe at the speed of sound. Savvy locals have learned not to blab newsy tidbits in public where journalists and others can overhear. Of course, no one would utter a word without the First Amendment's protections, which include freedom of speech and freedom of the press. Here's a little trek to some of the institutions that help protect those rights, some news outlets, and some spots that are just plain fun. After all, "pursuit of happiness" is one of our coolest constitutional guarantees.

- **Start at the Federal Triangle Metro station's exit on the west side of 12th Street NW. Step off the escalator and turn left to walk through the barrel-vaulted breezeway of the Environmental Protection Agency's headquarters. This curvaceous masterpiece opened in 1934 to house the headquarters of the United States Post Office Department. It's one of several federal buildings that form the Federal Triangle. As part of a massive building program authorized by Congress in 1926, based on the McMillan Plan (See Walk 26, Eastern Market to Barracks Row), most of these structures feature limestone façades, red-tiled roofs, classical colonnades, and courtyards, says the Federal Triangle Heritage Trail booklet.**

- **Turn left to walk north on 12th Street NW. Across 12th Street is the Old Post Office Pavilion, which is slated to be reborn in 2016 as a luxe Trump International Hotel. This Romanesque Revival landmark was built in 1899 as an earlier headquarters for the U.S.**

Post Office Department. Its 315-foot-high clock tower will remain open to the public for its panoramic view of Pennsylvania Avenue NW from the White House to the Capitol.

- Cross Pennsylvania Avenue NW for the 10-story marble and limestone Beaux Arts *Evening Star* building one door down on the right. The paper was also called the *Washington Star,* among other names, during its 129 years. Some of its own stars, like Mary McGrory, migrated to *The Washington Post* when the *Post* bought its assets in 1981.

- Turn left on E Street NW, which becomes Pennsylvania Avenue NW. The Warner Theatre is on the right at 13th Street NW. It's hard to imagine that this lavish, gilded theater from 1924 showed porn flicks during the neighborhood's dark days in the early 1970s.

- Continue west on Pennsylvania Avenue past 1335 E Street NW, where Eugene Meyer stood on the steps of *The Washington Post*'s 1893 headquarters in 1933 to buy the bankrupt paper. The *Post* building is gone, but its next-door neighbor, the National Theatre, is still there, wowing audiences since 1835.

- Continue on Pennsylvania Avenue NW to 14th Street NW and turn right for the National Press Club on the right. This private club for journalists and communications professionals got its start in 1908. In 1971, it began accepting women. Many national and international media outlets have news bureaus in the building. Originally some ran their own offices along Pennsylvania Avenue and 14th Street, which was once dubbed Newspaper Row. The public can visit the club's 13th-floor penthouse to chow down in the Fourth Estate restaurant. It earned its name because the media is sometimes called the fourth branch—or estate—of government for its important role in providing checks and balances on those wielding power in the executive, judiciary, and legislative branches.

- Continue north on 14th Street NW and turn right on F Street NW for Madame Tussauds museum on the left at 10th Street NW. D.C.-born Stephen Colbert's wax lookalike hobnobs with those of 44 presidents, celebrities such as George Clooney (whose dad, Nicholas, teaches journalism at D.C.'s American University), and news icons such as Katie Couric and Dan Rather.

- Turn right on 10th Street NW for Ford's Theatre on the left. Stop by for a play or a tour to see where John Wilkes Booth shot President Lincoln in 1865. It took 12 days for

Reuters's report of his assassination to cruise across the Atlantic Ocean to Britain, the news wire says.

- Continue south on 10th Street and turn left on E Street NW for the Federal Bureau of Investigation's concrete behemoth on the right. When FBI Director James Comey was a kid, he attended the agency's übercool public tour. Comey restarted the tours in 2014 for the first time since they were halted following the September 11, 2001, terrorist attacks. The chilling pink "martyr letter" that hijacker Mohamed Atta wrote to instruct his fellow 9/11 terrorists is one of the many moving educational displays. Visitors also see John Dillinger's death mask, John Hinckley's gun, and other exhibits that show how the FBI's varied departments fight terrorism, cybercrime, and other menaces. While the tours aren't quite like the old days—and they have to be arranged through one's member of Congress—one thing remains the same: visitors can watch agents firing their Glocks and other firearms with the same pinpoint precision they use to nail the bad guys.

- Turn right on Ninth Street NW for the private Corporation for Public Broadcasting on the left in a pink granite-faced office building. Congress created this federally funded, nonprofit corporation in 1967 to promote the growth and development of public TV and radio broadcasting and telecommunications.

- Continue south on Ninth Street NW to Pennsylvania Avenue NW. On the right, near the corner of the FBI building, is where *The Washington Post* built its first headquarters in 1877. On the left is the United States Navy Memorial. A lone sailor guards its 100-foot-diameter plaza atop a small museum.

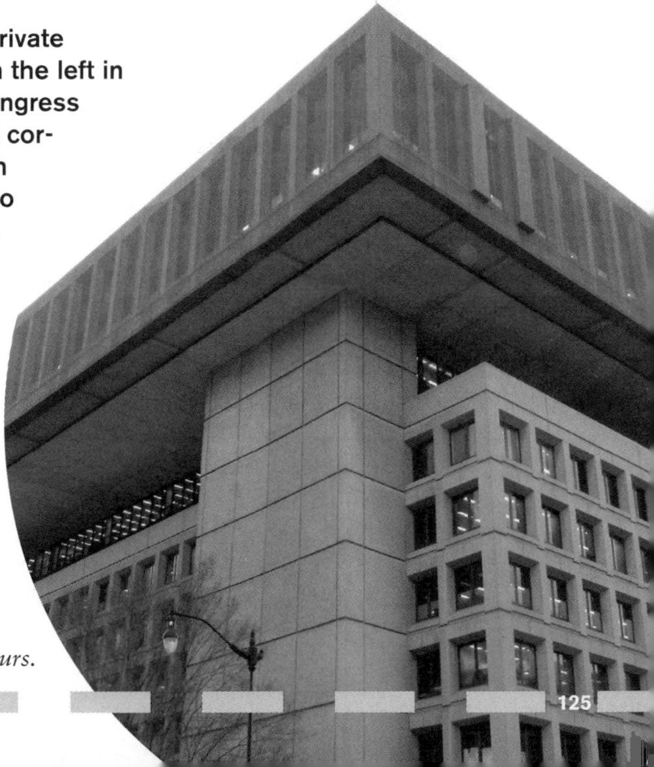

The FBI recently restarted its acclaimed tours.

- Across Pennsylvania Avenue NW on the right is the United States Department of Justice's classic 1935 limestone-clad home with touches of Art Deco. Created in 1789, this cabinet-level department, whose small to massive agencies include the Civil Rights division, the Office of Privacy and Civil Liberties, the U.S. Marshals Service, and the FBI, calls itself "the world's largest law office and the central agency for enforcement of federal laws."

- Across Pennsylvania Avenue NW on the left is the headquarters of the National Archives and Records Administration. Visitors queue up at the Constitution Avenue entrance to view America's most valuable documents—the Constitution, the Bill of Rights, and the Declaration of Independence—in this federal agency's grand rotunda. They also can visit the National Archives Museum, gift shop, and café. Members of the Foundation for the National Archives get store discounts. In 2014, that independent nonprofit began hosting sleepovers for kids in the Rotunda. On the Pennsylvania Avenue side of the stately structure with 72 giant Corinthian columns, researchers tap NARA's genealogy and other largely pre–World War I records. The Nixon tapes, the bullet-pocked windshield from President Kennedy's limousine, and other artifacts and records reside at NARA's larger College Park, Maryland, campus.

- Walk one block east on Pennsylvania Avenue NW past the site of a former slave market, at Seventh Street NW, and see the current home of the National Council for Negro Women, in the twin-turreted building on the left. Across the street on the right is the Federal Trade Commission's triangular-shaped building, the last piece in the Federal Triangle. Established in 1914, the FTC protects consumers and promotes competition.

- Catty-corner on the left is the Freedom Forum foundation's Newseum, a dazzling glass treasure box built in 2008 to champion "the First Amendment as a cornerstone of democracy." If the Newseum were in founder Al Neuharth's frigid home state of South Dakota, it would still be worth venturing there. But since it's in D.C., with a sixth-floor outdoor balcony overlooking the Capitol dome and filled with fun and factoids, it's a must-see. Everyone seems to enjoy playing TV reporter at its interactive news center and its other hands-on exhibits. The Newseum also showcases part of the 12-foot-tall Berlin wall, the dingy door to the Watergate building, Unabomber Ted Kaczynski's hermit cabin, and Pulitzer Prize–winning photos. Celeb chef Wolfgang

Puck serves his goodies in the museum's café and in The Source, his fine-dining restaurant next door on Sixth Street.

- Next door on Pennsylvania Avenue is the Embassy of Canada, America's largest trading partner. Native son Arthur Erickson designed this marble landmark with a grand plaza and monumental columns in 1989. Visitors can pop into its outdoor rotunda—it's an echo chamber—or visit the embassy's first-floor art gallery.

- With the embassy to the left, turn right on Fourth Street NW and then turn left on Independence Avenue SW for the Voice of America on the right. Visitors can watch live TV and radio broadcasts at this federally funded agency, which calls itself "the largest U.S. international broadcaster." VOA began after World War II to provide reliable news to "closed and war-torn societies" in Europe. Now it broadcasts news, music, and other programs in 45 languages.

Points of Interest

Federal Triangle Metro 302 12th St. NW, 202-637-7000, wmata.com/rail/station_detail.cfm?station_id=53

Trump International Hotel (Old Post Office Pavilion) 1100 Pennsylvania Ave. NW, 855-878-6700, trumphotelcollection.com/washington-dc

(Private) former *Evening Star* newspaper building 1101 Pennsylvania Ave. NW

Warner Theatre 513 13th St. NW, 202-783-4000, warnertheatredc.com

National Theatre 1321 Pennsylvania Ave. NW, 202-628-6161, nationaltheatre.org

National Press Club 529 14th St. NW, 202-662-7500, press.org

Madame Tussauds 1001 F St. NW, 866-823-9565, madametussauds.com/washington

Ford's Theatre 511 10th St. NW, 202-347-4833, fordstheatre.org

Federal Bureau of Investigation 935 Pennsylvania Ave. NW, 202-324-3000, fbi.gov

Corporation for Public Broadcasting 401 Ninth St. NW, 202-879-9600, cpb.org

The United States Navy Memorial 701 Pennsylvania Ave. NW, 202-737-2300, navymemorial.org

The United States Department of Justice 950 Pennsylvania Ave. NW, 202-514-2000, justice.gov

National Archives and Records Administration 700 Pennsylvania Ave. NW, 202-357-5000, archives.gov

Federal Trade Commission 600 Pennsylvania Ave. NW, 202-326-2222, ftc.gov

Newseum 500 Pennsylvania Ave. NW, 202-292-6100, newseum.org

Embassy of Canada 501 Pennsylvania Ave. NW, 202-682-1740, can-am.gc.ca/washington

Voice of America 330 Independence Ave. SW, 202-203-4990, voanews.com

route summary

1. Start at the Federal Triangle Metro station, 302 12th Street NW. (Take the west exit to the Environmental Protection Agency.)
2. At the top of the escalator, turn left to reach 12th Street NW.
3. Turn left on 12th Street NW to walk north.
4. Turn left on E Street NW, which becomes Pennsylvania Avenue NW.
5. Turn right on 14th Street NW.
6. Turn right on F Street NW.
7. Turn right on 10th Street NW.
8. Turn left on E Street NW.
9. Turn right on Ninth Street NW.
10. Turn left on Pennsylvania Avenue NW.
11. Turn right on Fourth Street NW.
12. Turn left on Independence Avenue SW.

CONNECTING THE WALKS

For companion Walk 16 (Downtown: News Junkies West), at F Street, continue north on 12th Street NW. For Walk 23 (Capitol Hill), continue east on Pennsylvania Avenue NW. This walk passes the National Mall (Walks 14 and 22) and the Archives Metro station, where Walk 17 (Penn Quarter–Chinatown) begins.

Luxe Warner Theatre debuted in 1924.

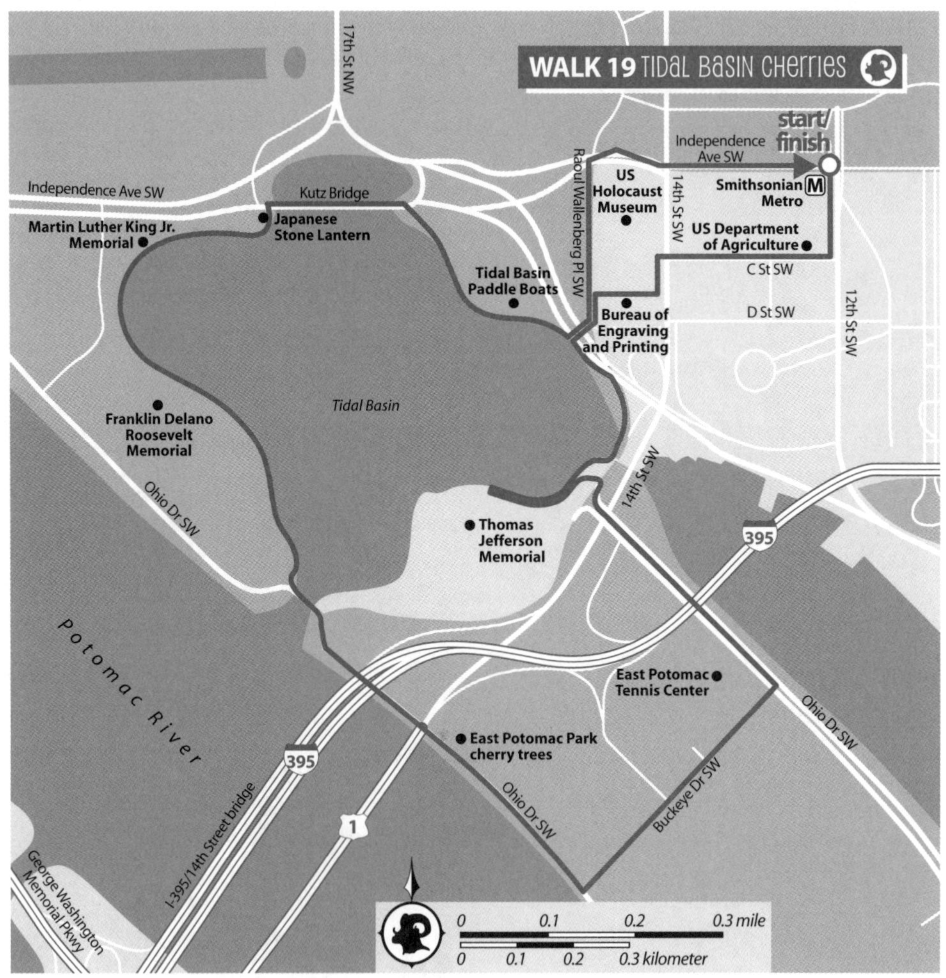
WALK 19 Tidal Basin Cherries
start/finish
Independence Ave SW
Smithsonian Metro
US Holocaust Museum
US Department of Agriculture
14th St SW
C St SW
D St SW
12th St SW
Raoul Wallenberg Pl SW
17th St NW
Independence Ave SW
Kutz Bridge
Japanese Stone Lantern
Martin Luther King Jr. Memorial
Tidal Basin Paddle Boats
Bureau of Engraving and Printing
Tidal Basin
Franklin Delano Roosevelt Memorial
Ohio Dr SW
14th St SW
Thomas Jefferson Memorial
395
Potomac River
East Potomac Tennis Center
East Potomac Park cherry trees
Ohio Dr SW
Buckeye Dr SW
395
1
I-395/14th Street bridge
George Washington Memorial Pkwy
0 0.1 0.2 0.3 mile
0 0.1 0.2 0.3 kilometer

19 Tidal Basin Cherries: Spectacular Flower Power

BOUNDARIES: **Buckeye Drive SW, Ohio Drive SW, Independence Avenue SW, and 12th Street SW**
DISTANCE: **Just over 4 miles**
DIFFICULTY: **Easy**
PARKING: **Extremely limited street parking; Metro recommended**
PUBLIC TRANSIT: **Smithsonian Metro station, 1200 Independence Avenue SW, and the $1 DC Circulator bus's National Mall route**

Come for the cherries. About 1.5 million "blossom gawkers" trek to the Tidal Basin every year. But stick around afterward for its notable neighbors too—like the Bureau of Engraving and Printing. Visitors can buy sheets of uncut $1 or $100 paper bills following a free tour. Next door is a somber memorial to the 6 million victims killed during the Holocaust. While the United States Holocaust Memorial Museum commemorates one of the biggest abominations in world history, it also offers hope: One of its missions is to inspire citizens "to confront hatred, prevent genocide, and promote human dignity." All the memorials surrounding the Tidal Basin offer similar inspiration. All that inspiration—and all that walking—works up an appetite. So before hopping back on the subway, grab a homegrown tomato or a hot meal from the good old United States Department of Agriculture.

- **Start at the Smithsonian Metro Station, 1200 Independence Avenue SW. This station opened on July 1, 1977. The first leg of the Washington Metropolitan Area Transit Authority's Metro debuted in 1976. The USDA runs a farmers' market on the corner from June to November.**

- **Head south on 12th Street SW. Turn right on C Street SW and turn right into Wing 2 of the USDA's South Building. Drop by for some bacon and eggs in the South Café or to buy a turkey "stress squeeze ball" or a "USDA Organic" T-shirt from its employee gift shop. This is one of the few federal offices that still allows the public inside post-9/11.**

- **Exit the USDA and turn right onto C Street SW. Cross 14th Street SW and turn left. Turn right into the Bureau of Engraving and Printing. Who can resist a free tour to** watch millions of dollars being created? Even pop star Michael Jackson once stopped by, a tour guide said. Visitors parade along an elevated, enclosed walkway above massive machines that print and cut the newly colorful bills. Some employees even yuk it up with handheld or posted signs. "Just think how I feel," says one. "I printed my lifetime salary in a few minutes."

- Exit the museum through the west doors and turn left onto Raoul Wallenberg Place SW. Cross Maine Avenue SW; turn left onto the paved trail along the Tidal Basin and follow it to the Thomas Jefferson Memorial. Jefferson was the primary author of the Declaration of Independence, George Washington's first Secretary of State, the nation's third president, founder of the University of Virginia, fluent in six languages—and an architect. His memorial reflects the classical architecture he adored. Modeled after the Pantheon and designed by John Russell Pope, the partially open-air structure features a rotunda with an entrance portico flanked by colossal Ionic columns. The exterior is crafted from white Vermont Imperial Danby marble. Inside the center of the rotunda, a bronze statue of a regal-looking Jefferson stands 19 feet tall. Construction of the memorial began in 1939, and it was dedicated in 1943.

- With the memorial to the rear, reverse direction to backtrack along the Tidal Basin trail. When the trail forks, stay right to cross East Basin Drive SW at Ohio Drive SW. Follow Ohio Drive SW into East Potomac Park, more commonly called Hains Point. On the right is East Potomac Tennis Center, public courts where Supreme Court Chief Justice William H. Rehnquist played before his death in 2005.

- Continue on Ohio Drive SW. Instead of continuing straight to follow a 3-mile cherry blossom loop around this man-made peninsula, turn right on Buckeye Drive SW. After one long block, turn right again back onto Ohio Drive SW. About 1,700 cherry trees line the riverfront trail: 995 Yoshino cherry trees, 414 Kwanzan cherries, 60 graceful Weeping Japanese cherries, and 8 other varieties, with monikers like Afterglow. Continue on Ohio Drive SW. Cross the inlet bridge and then stay to the right to continue on the Tidal Basin trail.

- Turn left into the Franklin Delano Roosevelt Memorial, created in 1997. Unlike most of the Mall's white marble or limestone monuments, this stands out for its rose-tinged and rustic-cut Carnelian granite from South Dakota. These brawny blocks create four outdoor rooms with waterfalls and pools. They symbolize the 32nd president's strength of character facing the Great Depression and World War II. FDR's legs were paralyzed by polio at age 39, but he hid his disability in public. Now a wheelchair he designed is showcased in the gift shop.

- Exit the memorial to return to the Tidal Basin trail. Follow it along the water under a canopy of old cherry trees to the Martin Luther King Jr. Memorial on the left. The memorial debuted in 2011, 48 years after the nonviolent civil rights leader's "I Have a Dream" speech during the 1963 March on Washington. King, whose original name was Michael, was the youngest man to receive the Nobel Peace Prize. A 28-foot 6-inch statue of the pastor is carved into a mammoth boulder. A whites-only beach operated on the Tidal Basin until 1925.

- After exiting the memorial, turn left to continue on the trail. Turn left at the Japanese Stone Lantern. The 4,000-pound lantern marks the spot of the original cherry tree plantings. Japan gave the United States 3,020 trees and the nearly 400-year-old lantern in 1912 as a symbol of friendship. Park rangers lead walks there during the National Cherry Blossom Festival.

- After the lantern, follow the Tidal Basin trail as it curves right onto the Kutz Bridge. After crossing the bridge's narrow sidewalk, keep right to stay on the trail. Some of the oldest cherry trees hang low over the trail around here, their gnarled trunks like wrinkles on a wise elder's face. Turn right into Tidal Basin Paddle Boats. Even at the height of the cherry blossom crunch, paddleboaters enjoy a panoramic view of the flowers without having to squish their way through the crowds.

The Jefferson Memorial inspires.

Cherry Blossom Peak and Festival

Timing, as the adage goes, is everything. Especially when it comes to the must-see cherry blossom peak bloom at the Tidal Basin. The climax lasts a handful of days and it depends on Washington's sometimes wild and sometimes mild weather. The National Park Service says the "average peak bloom date from 1992 through 2013" was March 31. The peak is when "70 percent of the Yoshino Cherry blossoms are open." The flowers are still stunning prepeak and post-peak. But it's just not perfection to an artist's eye when even a smidgen of green peeks through the puffy pink and white cloud of blossoms. For the current bloom forecast, visit **nps.gov/cherry/cherry-blossom-bloom.htm.** To check out the National Cherry Blossom Festival's schedule, visit **nationalcherryblossomfestival.org.** Everyone seems to celebrate during the month-long festival: from restaurants' cherry-inspired menus to Japanese art exhibits to fireworks to ranger-led walks and runs at the Tidal Basin. The whole shebang got its start in 1912, when Japan donated the trees as a gesture of friendship. The festival began in 1927. Although there's no festival in autumn, the cherry trees also put on a show then. Their foliage lights up like an orange halo each October. Plus, there are no crowds.

- **With the boats to the rear, cross Maine and Independence Avenues to Raoul Wallenberg Place SW. Turn left on Raoul Wallenberg Place SW for the the United States Holocaust Memorial Museum on the right. Opened in 1993, this memorial to the 6 million Jews and other victims who were murdered between 1933 and 1945 is one of Washington's most solemn sites. After entering, each visitor takes an ID card that details how one person was persecuted by Nazi Germany. Visitors are then channeled through three floors of exhibits to learn about the Nazi Party's rise to power, the systematic mass execution of Jews in gas chambers, and the liberation of the notorious prison camps at the end of World War II.**

- **Exit the museum and turn right (north) onto Raoul Wallenberg Place SW. Turn right onto Independence Avenue SW and follow it back to the Metro.**

POINTS OF INTEREST

Smithsonian Metro Station 1200 Independence Ave. SW, 202-637-7000, wmata.com/rail/station_detail.cfm?station_id=54

U.S. Department of Agriculture, Wing 2 C Street SW west of 12th Street SW, 202-488-7279, www.dm.usda.gov/oo/cafemenu.htm

Bureau of Engraving and Printing 14th and C Streets SW, 202-874-2330, moneyfactory.gov/home.html

Thomas Jefferson Memorial East Basin Drive SW at Ohio Drive SW, 202-426-6841, nps.gov/thje/index.htm

East Potomac Tennis Center 1090 Ohio Dr. SW, 202-554-5962, eastpotomactennis.com

East Potomac Park cherry trees Ohio Drive SW, East Potomac Park; 202-426-6841; npca.org/parks/east-potomac-park.html

Franklin Delano Roosevelt Memorial 400 W. Basin Dr. SW, 202-426-6841, nps.gov/frde/index.htm

Martin Luther King Jr. Memorial 1850 W. Basin Dr. SW, 202-426-6841, nps.gov/mlkm/index.htm

Japanese stone lantern Independence Avenue SW at the Tidal Basin southwest of 17th St. SW, 202-426-6841, nps.gov/cherry/index.htm and nationalcherryblossomfestival.org

Tidal Basin Paddle Boats 1501 Maine Ave. SW, 202-479-2426, tidalbasinpaddleboats.com

United States Holocaust Memorial Museum 100 Raoul Wallenberg Place SW, 202-488-0400, ushmm.org

ROUTE SUMMARY

1. **Start at the Smithsonian Metro Station, 1200 Independence Avenue SW.**
2. **Walk south on 12th Street SW.**
3. **Turn right onto C Street SW.**
4. **Turn left onto 14th Street SW and enter the Bureau of Engraving and Printing on the right.**
5. **Exit the Bureau of Engraving and Printing onto Raoul Wallenberg Place SW.**

6. Turn left on Raoul Wallenberg Place SW.
7. Cross Maine and Independence Avenues SW.
8. Turn left onto the paved trail along the Tidal Basin.
9. Follow the trail to the Thomas Jefferson Memorial on the left.
10. Reverse direction at the Jefferson Memorial to backtrack on the Tidal Basin trail.
11. Where the trail forks, stay right onto a mini connector trail to East Basin Drive SW.
12. Cross East Basin Drive SW to reach Ohio Drive SW.
13. Continue east on Ohio Drive SW.
14. Turn right on Buckeye Drive SW.
15. Turn right onto Ohio Drive SW.
16. After crossing the Inlet Bridge, stay right to return to the Tidal Basin trail.
17. Continue on the trail and turn left to the Japanese Stone Lantern.
18. Follow the trail as it curves right onto the Kutz Bridge.
19. Stay right after crossing the bridge to continue on the Tidal Basin trail.
20. With the paddleboats to the rear, cross Maine and Independence Avenues to Raoul Wallenberg Place SW.
21. Turn left on Raoul Wallenberg Place SW.
22. Turn right into the Holocaust Museum.
23. Exit the museum and turn right (north) onto Raoul Wallenberg Place SW.
24. Turn right onto Independence Avenue SW and follow it back to the Metro.

CONNECTING THE WALKS

For Walk 20 (Columbia Island), turn right into the George Mason Memorial just before the Inlet Bridge. For Walk 14 (National Mall West), cross Independence Avenue SW by the stone lantern toward the World War II Memorial. For Walk 22 (National Mall East), take the National Mall exit at the Smithsonian Metro station.

Four-century-old Japanese stone lantern

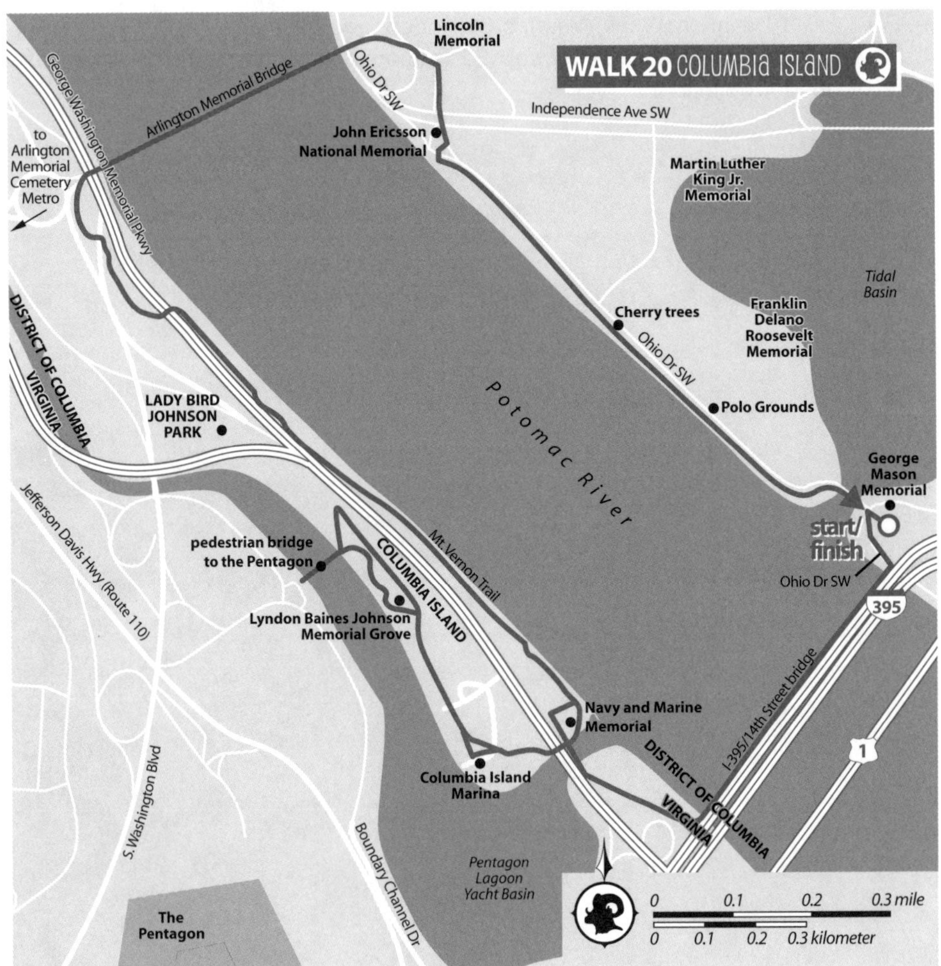

WALK 20 COLUMBIA ISLAND
Lincoln Memorial
Arlington Memorial Bridge
George Washington Memorial Pkwy
Ohio Dr SW
Independence Ave SW
John Ericsson National Memorial
to Arlington Memorial Cemetery Metro
Martin Luther King Jr. Memorial
Tidal Basin
Franklin Delano Roosevelt Memorial
Cherry trees
Polo Grounds
DISTRICT OF COLUMBIA
VIRGINIA
LADY BIRD JOHNSON PARK
Potomac River
George Mason Memorial
start/finish
pedestrian bridge to the Pentagon
COLUMBIA ISLAND
Mt. Vernon Trail
Jefferson Davis Hwy (Route 110)
Lyndon Baines Johnson Memorial Grove
395
I-395/14th Street bridge
Navy and Marine Memorial
1
Columbia Island Marina
S. Washington Blvd
Boundary Channel Dr
Pentagon Lagoon Yacht Basin
The Pentagon
0 0.1 0.2 0.3 mile
0 0.1 0.2 0.3 kilometer

20 COLUMBIA ISLAND: LBJ AND CHERRY VIEWS

BOUNDARIES: Arlington Memorial Bridge, Ohio Drive SW, I-395/14th Street bridge, and Boundary Channel
DISTANCE: About 4.5 miles
DIFFICULTY: Easy
PARKING: Limited free street parking on Ohio Drive SW; free parking on Columbia Island; Metro recommended
PUBLIC TRANSIT: Smithsonian Metro station, which is served by many bus routes, including the $1 DC Circulator bus's National Mall route

LBJ had a hideaway. When the Vietnam War and other travails of the presidency tightened their grip, he escaped to Columbia Island for its placid Potomac River views. While the man-made island is no secret today, the Lyndon Baines Johnson Memorial Grove there remains serene and perhaps even more scenic since his namesake park was created to honor him. It can be downright empty there, while on the opposite side of the parking lot, the Columbia Marina and its café are hopping in warm weather. Even more popular is the Mount Vernon Trail, which skims the edge of the island. The paved trail provides a haven for walkers, runners, and cyclists. Spring is a delicious time to visit, with sunshine-colored daffodils, red tulips, and weeping willow trees. Canada geese waddle along the riverbank like mini soldiers patrolling the idyllic turf.

- **Start at the George Mason Memorial, which is marked by an explosion of pink magnolias and yellow forsythia in the early spring. It showcases a statue of the Virginia gentleman in his buckled shoes and ruffled sleeves. Mason is often called the father of our Constitution's Bill of Rights. The memorial's historical marker says he "wrote the landmark Virginia Declaration of Rights that not only inspired the American Declaration of Independence, but also France's 1789 Declaration of the Rights of Man." With the statue to the left, walk to Ohio Drive SW and turn left. At the bottom of the I-395/14th Street bridge, turn left to climb the stairs. At the top, turn right to cross the Potomac River.**

- **At the end of the bridge, turn right to follow the pedestrian trail down to the river for the Navy and Marine Memorial on the right. This sculpture of waves and gulls is dedicated to the thousands of sailors in the United States Navy and Merchant Marine who perished at sea. It was designed by Harvey Wiley Corbett, who also designed the**

George Washington National Masonic Temple Memorial in Alexandria, Virginia, and the Criminal Courts Building in New York City.

- With the memorial to the rear, walk toward the river and turn right on the paved trail. Follow it as it curves along Boundary Channel through a tunnel to the Columbia Island Marina on the left. Columbia Island Marina's café and outdoor picnic tables offer prime viewing of the Pentagon from this 380-slip marina. Run by Guest Services for the National Park Service, it stays open year-round but only serves its home-style barbecue and other hot chow from Memorial Day to Labor Day. Kayakers and others can launch their boats at the marina. Nonboaters can chill out by gazing at mallards and other birds, including bald eagles, which sometimes lurk atop trees before swooping down to nab their sushi-like supper from the Pentagon Lagoon.

- Facing away from the marina, head north through the parking lot to the Lyndon Baines Johnson Memorial Grove. Follow the trail through the park, staying left if you want to cross the wooden pedestrian bridge over D.C.'s Boundary Channel to the Pentagon in Arlington, Virginia. Although it's in Virginia, the Pentagon's mailing address, with six zip codes, is in Washington, D.C. LBJ's legacy is forever linked to the Pentagon and the Vietnam War. But he's also remembered for something more far-reaching: he helped pass the Civil Rights Act of 1964 and the Voting Rights Act of 1965.

- In the 1960s, President Johnson began using the island paradise as a getaway to decompress from the pressures of office. Now a grove of white pine trees, a meadow, and a 19-foot-high granite megalith quarried near his Texas ranch serve as a living memorial to our 36th president. Columbia Island was renamed Lady Bird Johnson Park in 1968, NPS says in its brochure, but locals and maps usually call it Columbia Island. To reach the riverside part of her park, return to the marina and turn left onto the connector trail, which returns through the arched tunnel and merges with the Mount Vernon Trail.

- The trail runs along the river from George Washington's former home to Roosevelt Island. This leg glows with flaming orange maple trees each fall. In the early spring, huge patches of bright yellow daffodils seem Instagram-perfect against the panorama of pink and white cherry blossoms across the river. Continue northwest on the trail. Just before the Arlington Memorial Bridge, turn left onto a connector trail, which then curves right up onto the bridge.

- Cross the bridge and turn right at the end to stay on the sidewalk. Turn right onto 23rd Street SW and cross Independence Avenue SW to the John Ericsson National Memorial. Engineer, inventor, and former Swedish Army Captain John Ericsson "possessed one of the greater engineering minds that ever existed," NPS proclaims. Though his name is seldom recognized, Ericsson's iron-plated *USS Monitor* revolutionized naval warfare and helped save the Union during the Civil War. His sculpture was created by James Earle Fraser, who designed the Buffalo nickel.

- With the statue to the left and the river to the right, follow the riverfront trail along Ohio Drive SW. Double-pink Fugenzo and Akebono cherries line the trail here. Continue to the Polo Grounds on the left. Rarely the site of a polo match these days, it's most famous for blazing aeronautical history: On May 15, 1918, the "Post Office Department began the nation's first regularly scheduled airmail service" there, says the National Postal Museum. It didn't start out smoothly for these pioneer pilots. Army Lieutenant George Boyle took off in his Curtiss Jenny airplane bound for New York via Philadelphia—but he got lost and crashed in a farmer's field in nearby Waldorf, Maryland. He reportedly wasn't hurt, but his "airmail" had to be delivered by train. His colleague who flew the New York–to-Washington route a few hours later arrived safely.

- To return to the start of this walk, continue on the trail and follow it over the Ohio Drive SW inlet bridge to the George Mason Memorial.

POINTS OF INTEREST

George Mason Memorial Ohio and East Basin Drives SW, 202-426-6841, nps.gov/gemm/index.htm

Navy and Marine Memorial Mount Vernon Trail northwest of the I-395/14th Street bridge, 703-289-2500, nps.gov/gwmp/planyourvisit/brochures.htm

Columbia Island Marina George Washington Memorial Parkway, 202-347-0173, columbiaisland.com

Pedestrian bridge to the Pentagon Boundary Channel, Columbia Island

Lyndon Baines Johnson Memorial Grove Columbia Island, 202-289-2500, nps.gov/lyba/index.htm

Lady Bird Johnson Park Columbia Island, 703-289-2500, nps.gov/gwmp/planyourvisit/ladybirdjohnsonpark.htm

John Ericsson National Memorial 23rd Street and Ohio Drive SW, 202-426-6841, nps.gov/joer/index.htm

Cherry trees Ohio Drive SW, 202-426-6841, nps.gov/cherry/loader.cfm?csModule=security/getfile&PageID=223322 and nps.gov/nacc/index.htm

West Potomac Park Polo Grounds Ohio Drive SW, 202-426-6841, nps.gov/nacc/index.htm and postalmuseum.si.edu/airmail/airmail/foundation/airmail_foundation_schedule_long.html

route summary

1. **Start at the George Mason Memorial. With the statue to your left, walk to Ohio Drive SW, and turn left.**
2. **At the bottom of the I-395/14th Street bridge, turn left to climb the stairs.**
3. **At the top of the stairs, turn right to cross the Potomac River.**
4. **At the end of the bridge, turn right to follow the pedestrian trail down to the river.**
5. **Turn right for the Navy and Marine Memorial.**
6. **With the memorial to the rear, walk toward the river and turn right on the paved trail.**
7. **Follow the trail as it curves right along Boundary Channel through a tunnel to the Columbia Island Marina on the left.**
8. **With the marina to the rear, walk north through the parking lot to the Lyndon Baines Johnson Memorial Grove.**
9. **Follow the trail through the park. (Stay left for the pedestrian bridge to the Pentagon.)**
10. **Reverse direction and return to the marina.**
11. **At the marina, turn left onto the connector trail and return through the tunnel.**
12. **After the tunnel, follow the trail as it curves left and merges with the main Mount Vernon Trail.**
13. **Continue northwest on the trail.**
14. **Just before the Arlington Memorial Bridge, turn left onto a connector trail that curves right up onto the bridge.**
15. **Cross the bridge.**
16. **At the end of the bridge, turn right to stay on the sidewalk.**
17. **Turn right onto 23rd Street SW.**
18. **Cross Independence Avenue SW.**
19. **Turn left on the trail and follow it along the river.**
20. **Continue on the trail across the Ohio Drive SW inlet bridge to the George Mason Memorial.**

Connecting the Walks

For Walk 13 (Potomac River Panorama and Watergates), continue on the Mount Vernon Trail *under* the Arlington Memorial Bridge instead of veering left onto a connector trail. For Walk 14 (National Mall West), turn left instead of right at 23rd Street SW toward the Lincoln Memorial. Walk 19 (Tidal Basin Cherries) is right across the street (East Basin Drive SW) from the George Mason Memorial.

The Navy and Marine Memorial honors seafarers.

WALK 21 SOUTHWEST WATERFRONT
Jefferson Dr SW
start
Independence Ave SW
Smithsonian Metro
15th St NW
14th St NW
12th St SW
C St SW
D St SW
Mandarin Oriental hotel
US Immigration and Customs Enforcement
Federal Communications Commission
Tidal Basin
C St SW
3rd St SW
2nd St SW
6th St SW
E St SW
395
7th St SW
G St SW
395
seafood markets
E Basin Dr SW
395
Maine Ave SW
The Wharf offices
I.M. Pei–designed buildings (private)
I St SW
K St SW
Washington, DC city offices
Arena Stage
Water St
Ohio Dr SW
The Washington Channel
Buckeye Dr SW
Ohio Dr SW
Gangplank Marina
M St SW
Waterfront Metro
finish
Potomac River
Thomas Law House (private)
N St SW
4th St SW
Canal St SW
HAINS POINT (EAST POTOMAC PARK)
Titanic Memorial
P St SW
Fort Lesley J. McNair
0 0.1 0.2 0.3 mile
0 0.1 0.2 0.3 kilometer

21 SOUTHWEST WATERFRONT: PARDON THE DUST

BOUNDARIES: Independence Avenue SW, Fourth Street SW, P Street SW, and 12th Street SW
DISTANCE: 2 miles
DIFFICULTY: Easy
PARKING: Limited street parking by the National Mall; 4-hour metered parking by Water Street SW
PUBLIC TRANSIT: Smithsonian and Waterfront Metro stations

Whack. Whirrrrrr. Bam! Don't let the construction noise and mayhem distract you. There's still much to see, hear, smell, taste, and do along the Southwest Waterfront during its latest overhaul. Even before the construction adds new destinations, you'll find many existing "bests" here: one of D.C.'s best hotels, theaters, local cruise lines, vistas, and architectural designs. In 2014, the city and developers cranked into high gear on the second modern-day renaissance of this neighborhood—but this time some historic structures are sticking around. In the 1950s and 1960s, the neighborhood was virtually flattened during one of the nation's first major urban-renewal projects. During that era, high-rises and other homes were mainly built inland. Now much of the focus has switched to erecting high-rises right on the water. Call first before heading out. Southwest will continue to be a work in progress until about 2020.

- **Start at the Smithsonian Metro Station and walk south on 12th Street SW. Turn right on Maryland Avenue SW for the Mandarin Oriental hotel at the end of the cul-de-sac on the left. Insiders head to this posh hotel for its high tea, spa, and luxe rooms overlooking the Tidal Basin's cherry blossoms.**

- **Head back on Maryland Avenue to 12th Street SW. After turning right, the headquarters for the Federal Communications Commission is on the right and the U.S. Immigration and Customs Enforcement is on the left. Walk through the tunnel underneath the Southwest Freeway (I-395) with bright mosaic art adorning its walls. Exit the tunnel and turn right to cross Maine Avenue SW. Follow the scent of seawater and Old Bay Seasoning to the waterfront fish markets.**

- **Vendors have peddled blue crabs, oysters, and other seafood at outdoor fish markets on the Washington Channel for more than 100 years. Even after a condo is built on** the colorful markets' doorstep, the fish markets will stick around, along with a new market hall, says the developer, Hoffman-Madison Waterfront.

- With the markets to the rear, turn right to head southeast onto Maine Avenue SW, which parallels the channel. The well-worn waterfront is getting a $3 billion makeover to become "The Wharf," with condos, apartments, offices, hotels, shops, cafés, a marina, a cultural venue, water taxis, and public promenades, the developer says.

- A few blocks down on the left is another longtime fixture in the neighborhood, the Arena Stage at the Mead Center for American Theater. It opened there in 1961. In 2010, it got an extreme makeover by renowned Canadian designer Bing Thom Architects. Now it's a space-age looking structure with curving glass walls and a cantilevered roof, which encloses its two original landmark Fichandler and Kreeger theaters and a new theater.

- Across the street on the water is a cluster of goodies. Sneak a peek at the former presidential yacht, the *USS Sequoia,* which is moored at the Gangplank Marina. This privately owned mahogany, teak, and pine yacht can be chartered. Rates start at $10,000 for 45 minutes. Built in 1925 and owned by the federal government from 1933 to 2000, it's where Presidents Roosevelt and Eisenhower strategized with Winston Churchill during World War II, President Nixon decided to resign, and President Kennedy celebrated his 46th and final birthday, reports Gary Silversmith, who bought it. Next to the hoity-toity, 104-foot yacht is the down-home Cantina Marina bar and restaurant. Also nearby are the glass-enclosed *Odyssey* cruise ship and the more traditional-looking *Spirit of Washington.* Their dancing and dining cruises sail along the Potomac River year-round.

- Continue south on the broad riverwalk. Just before Water Street dead-ends at a circle, the Thomas Law House is on the left. First Lady Martha Washington's eldest granddaughter lived in this 1794 Federal-style house, says a historical marker there. It's now the community center for the 1966 Tiber Island Cooperative Homes development, with its four eight-story towers and 21 town houses.

- At the end of the riverwalk is the Titanic Memorial. Designed in 1933, this 13-foot-tall granite statue of a man with outstretched arms is dedicated to the men who died in the famous 1912 shipwreck. It used to be upriver, but it was moved when the Kennedy

Center was built in 1966. Now it has something the Kennedy Center could never claim: a glorious view of the cherry trees edging Hains Point across the channel.

- With the statue to the right, follow the sidewalk along the brick wall to P and Fourth Streets SW. On the right is Fort Lesley J. McNair. A military installation since L'Enfant drew the city's first map in 1791, this is where Mary Surratt and some of the other Lincoln assassination conspirators were hanged in 1865. Its 1905 Generals' Row houses and the neoclassical, domed Army War College building are visible from Hains Point. (See Walk 19, Tidal Basin Cherries.)

- Turn left onto Fourth Street SW. The intersection of Fourth and N Street SW is approximately where then-64-year-old Supreme Court Justice David H. Souter was mugged while jogging in 2004. He lived near there before he retired and returned to his rural New Hampshire home in 2009. The southwest neighborhood was also home to Thurgood Marshall, the grandson of a slave who became the first African American on the Supreme Court.

- Continue on Fourth Street SW across M Street SW. The Waterfront Metro station, which opened in 1991, is on the right. North of the station on both sides of Fourth Street SW are two D.C. government office buildings. Flanking them at Third and M Streets SW and Sixth and M Streets SW are four private apartment and condo towers designed by I. M. Pei in the early 1960s. When Pei's glass-clad Town Center East was granted historic status in 2013, D.C.'s Historic Preservation Review Board said, "It embodies the distinguishing characteristics of the rationalist school of the International Style and is a high-quality example of the architectural use of reinforced-concrete designed by an acknowledged master."

Points of Interest

Smithsonian Metro 1200 Independence Ave. SW, 202-637-7000, wmata.com/rail/station_detail.cfm?station_id=54

Mandarin Oriental 1330 Maryland Ave. SW, 202-554-8588, mandarinoriental.com

Federal Communications Commission 445 12th St. SW, 888-225-5322, fcc.gov

U.S. Immigration and Customs Enforcement 500 12th St. SW, ice.gov

Seafood markets 1100 Maine Ave. SW

The Wharf 690 Water St. SW, info@swdcwaterfront.com, swdcwaterfront.com/index.htm

Arena Stage at the Mead Center for American Theater 1101 Sixth St. SW, 202-554-9066, arenastage.org

Gangplank Marina 600 Water St. SW, 202-554-5000, gangplank.com

USS Sequoia Presidential Yacht 202-337-7300, sequoiayacht.com

Cantina Marina 202-554-8396, cantinamarina.com

Odyssey cruises 866-306-2469, odysseycruises.com/washington-dc

Spirit of Washington cruises 866-404-8439, spiritcruises.com/washington-dc

Thomas Law House (Tiber Island Cooperative Homes) Sixth and N Streets SW, 202-554-4844, tiberisland.com

Titanic Memorial On the Washington Channel at P Street SW

Fort Lesley J. McNair P Street SW and Third Avenue SW, www.jbmhh.army.mil/web/jbmhh/AboutJBMHH/FortMcNairHistory.html

Washington, D.C., city offices 1100 and 1101 Fourth St. SW, dc.gov

I. M. Pei–designed buildings M and Sixth Streets SW and M and Third Streets SW

Waterfront Metro station 399 M St. SW, 637-7000, wmata.com/rail/station_detail.cfm?station_id=83

route summary

1. Start at the Smithsonian Metro station, 1200 Independence Avenue SW.
2. Head south on 12th Street SW.
3. Turn right on Maryland Avenue SW and then reverse direction.
4. Turn right on 12th Street SW.
5. Exit the freeway tunnel and turn right to cross Maine Avenue SW to the waterfront fish market.
6. With the seafood markets to the rear, turn right to head southeast onto Maine Avenue SW.
7. With the Arena Stage on the left, turn right to reach Water Street SW.
8. Turn left onto Water Street SW.
9. At the end of Water Street SW, continue on the sidewalk along the river.

10. When the sidewalk dead-ends, follow it to the left past the wall surrounding Fort Lesley J. McNair.
11. Turn left on Fourth Street NW.
12. Cross M Street SW for the Waterfront Metro Station, D.C. government offices, and Pei-designed buildings.

CONNECTING THE WALKS

Walk 19 (Tidal Basin Cherries) and Walk 22 (National Mall East) also begin at the Smithsonian Metro station. To reach Walk 27 (Navy Yard), take the Waterfront Metro one stop to the Navy Yard Metro.

Seafood markets hawk yummy blue crabs.

WALK 22 National Mall East
F St NW
E St NW
D St NW
C St NW
15th St NW
14th St NW
13th St NW
12th St NW
11th St NW
10th St NW
9th St NW
7th St NW
6th St NW
5th St NW
4th St NW
3rd St NW
Pennsylvania Ave NW
Constitution Ave NW
National Museum of African American History (2016)
National Museum of American History
National Museum of Natural History
National Gallery Sculpture Garden
National Gallery of Art West Building
National Gallery of Art East Building
Madison Dr NW
Washington Monument
Smithsonian Metro
Smithsonian Institution Building
Hirshhorn Museum
Jefferson Dr SW
start/finish
Freer Gallery of Art
Arthur M. Sackler Gallery
National Museum of African Art
Arts and Industries Building (2016)
National Air and Space Museum
National Museum of the American Indian
Independence Ave SW
14th St SW
12th St SW
7th St SW
6th St SW
4th St SW
3rd St SW
2nd St SW
C St SW
D St SW
E St SW
Tidal Basin
395
0 0.1 0.2 0.3 mile
0 0.1 0.2 0.3 kilometer

22 NATIONAL MALL EAST: MUSEUM MANIA

BOUNDARIES: **Madison Drive NW, Third Street SW, Maryland Avenue SW, and 17th Street NW**
DISTANCE: **About 3 miles**
DIFFICULTY: **Easy**
PARKING: **Extremely limited parking; public transportation recommended**
PUBLIC TRANSIT: **Smithsonian Metro station, 1200 Independence Avenue SW, and the $1 DC Circulator bus's National Mall route**

Millions of visitors. That's what you get when you cross "free" with some of the most educational, inspirational, and enjoyable museums on the planet. Sometimes it seems like all the roughly 28 million annual visitors pile into the 12 main museums flanking the grassy rectangle known as the National Mall all at once. But not to worry. Even during tourist season, museum hopping can be fun with a little planning. First, scout out the Smithsonian's and the National Gallery of Art's websites (si.edu and nga.gov) to choose the must-sees for your clan, including the current rotating exhibits, lectures, concerts, planetarium shows, and exclusive wingdings like kiddie sleepovers and the summer Folklife Festival. Then make a beeline to your favorites when the doors fling open. Even though museum admission is free, the cafés, gift shops, and Imax movies may seem a little pricey. But for just $19 a year, out-of-towners can join the Smithsonian to reap immediate benefits, including a 10% discount at some of its restaurants, stores, and theaters. The unique museum shops are almost as must-see as the collections. (The Smithsonian's collections include a whopping 142 million–plus objects. It's the world's largest museum complex, with 19 museums, a zoo, and multiple research centers.) At the start or end of "museum mile," zip to the top of the Washington Monument in just 70 seconds for a grand overview of America's beloved National Mall.

- **Start at the Smithsonian Metro Station's escalator exit on the National Mall. Turn right to reach Jefferson Drive SW and right again to head west. Follow it across 14th and 15th Streets to the Washington Monument. The 554-foot 7 11/32-inch monument, designed by architect Robert Mills to honor President George Washington, was the tallest building in the world when it was completed in 1884. This marble obelisk is now the tallest masonry structure in the world and the tallest structure in Washington, D.C., the National Park Service says. Awe-inspiring day and night views from its 500-foot-high observation deck and 490-foot-high mini museum are worth the wait in line. (The** monument reopened in May 2014 after nearly three years of construction to fix damages from a 5.8-magnitude earthquake in August 2011.) After the best view in town, with the monument to the rear, head east on Madison Drive toward museum row.

- Chartered in 2003, the National Museum of African American History and Culture, the first museum on the left, is slated to open in 2016. This bronze-clad museum is designed to "be a place where all Americans can learn about the richness and diversity of the African American experience, what it means to their lives and how it helped" shape the country, the museum says. Its iconic artifacts include a 1944 Tuskegee Airmen open cockpit biplane, Chuck Berry's 1973 red Cadillac convertible, and the orange velour jacket Marian Anderson wore during her 1939 performance at the Lincoln Memorial after the opera singer was barred from nearby DAR Constitution Hall.

- Next up is the National Museum of American History. Allow time to operate a cotton gin, daydream about Dorothy's size 5 ruby slippers from *The Wizard of Oz,* ogle the perpetually popular collection of first ladies' gowns, and soak in all the diversity found across this roughly 3.8-million-square-mile country we call home. Where else but in the nation's capital would objects as disparate as "The Star-Spangled Banner," Olympic medalist Apolo Ohno's shiny speed skates, Seinfeld's puffy shirt, Lewis and Clark's compass, and Julia Child's kitchen feel equally at home?

- Just next door, the National Museum of Natural History is spreading its great news: a nearly complete skeleton of dinosaur king *Tyrannosaurus rex* has arrived. The bad news: old *T. rex* can't entertain visitors until 2019, when the overhaul of its dino exhibit is complete. Meanwhile, the small exhibit on D.C.'s own dinosaur fossils is still open, and there are countless other exhibits to see—like the nearly 46-carat Hope Diamond showcased in the even more mesmerizing gallery of Geology, Gems, and Minerals. Visitors can also visit a live butterfly exhibit or stop by an insect zoo to watch tarantula feedings. Some scenes from *Night at the Museum: Battle of the Smithsonian* were filmed there. During the summer, kids ages 8 to 12 can enjoy sleepovers at the natural and American history museums.

- Next door is the National Gallery of Art's Sculpture Garden. The 6.1-acre garden showcases Claes Oldenburg's giant, old-fashioned *Typewriter Eraser;* an original Art Nouveau–style entrance to the Paris subway; and other modern sculptures. In the summer, free jazz concerts are held there. In the winter, the garden's tree-encircled fountain morphs into an outdoor ice-skating rink. Skaters can warm up with hot chocolate at the garden's Pavilion Café.

- After the garden, climb the steps into the West Building of the esteemed National Gallery of Art next door. The 1940 classical, stone edifice, with a rotunda modeled after the Pantheon, is where the museum stashes its world-class treasures, such as the sole painting in the Americas by Leonardo da Vinci. Thousands of other American and European masterpieces grace the public galleries or are stowed away for future exhibitions. This is the only private museum on the Mall. Andrew W. Mellon—financier; former Treasury Secretary; oil, steel, and aluminum tycoon; and one of the richest men in the country—donated the initial collection in 1937. In 2014, more family heirlooms joined the chorus after Rachel Lambert "Bunny" Mellon, the 103-year-old wife of Andrew's late son, Paul, died.

- Modern. Even though it was built in 1978, the East Building of the National Gallery of Art still screams "modern" inside and out. Architect I. M. Pei's design was inspired by the site's odd trapezoidal shape. The site "was sliced into two triangles," the architect's firm notes, one for the main exhibition space and one for offices "with a triangular atrium unifying the whole." The *AIA Guide to the Architecture of Washington, D.C.* calls his stone and glass design one of the country's finest "high modernist" works. Entering from the street, visitors step into the titanic skylighted atrium with an Alexander Calder mobile dangling overhead. They can also enter underground from the West Building on a moving sidewalk through a 200-foot-long twinkling

Claes Oldenburg's mammoth eraser

Mall Walkers (and Runners)

Look closely. Check out the folks ambling or running on the gravel paths and sidewalks at the National Mall. Some might be famous. President Bill Clinton ran there in his short shorts about three times a week even after a track was installed at the White House to ensure his safety. "He is a people person," Secret Service Agent Dan Emmett told *US News and World Report.* "His running was for meeting the public as much as it was for exercise." President Truman walked a mile or two daily, a biography says. Sometimes he walked around the Washington Monument. Virtually at all times he was decked out in a coat and tie while briskly marching at the Army's 120-steps-a-minute pace. Many celebrities have also sauntered, strolled, and sprinted by the National Mall, which is aptly nicknamed "America's Backyard." Heartthrob George Clooney ran along the Lincoln Memorial Reflecting Pool several times—in dress shoes—for the filming of the 2008 movie *Burn After Reading*. Some races also loop around the Mall, including the Marine Corps Marathon. Past finishers in this "People's Marathon" include Supreme Court Justice Clarence Thomas (3:11 in 1980), media mogul Oprah Winfrey (4:29 in 1994), second lady and college professor Jill Biden (4:30 in 1998), and Vice President Al Gore (4:54 in 1997).

light sculpture by Leo Villareal. Other East Building artists include Henri Matisse, Marc Chagall, Piet Mondrian, and Jackson Pollock.

- **After the East Building, continue east to Third Street NW and turn right. Walk south to Maryland Avenue SW and turn right into the National Museum of the American Indian. Like the East Building, this also occupies a trapezoidal site, and its design echoes its inner treasures. But it provides a proverbial yin to Pei's yang. East is angular; this is curvy and organic. East was created from a smooth, cold, pink limestone to match the West Building, while the American Indian Museum used rough, warm, buff-colored Kasota dolostone to resemble a wind-sculpted rock formation. It contains "one of the most extensive collections of Native American arts and artifacts in the world," the** museum says. Paintings, masks, and other artifacts are displayed in rotating exhibits. Its award-winning Mitsitam Café serves regional Native American dishes, such as cedar-planked salmon, traditional fry bread, and a fiddlehead fern salad. After exiting, stay in the courtyard and follow the building around to the left to reach Jefferson Drive SW.

- Next door is the two-block-long National Air and Space Museum, the most visited museum in the country if you count both its branches. This flagship museum, which opened in 1976, gained a sibling in 2003, the hangar-size Steven F. Udvar-Hazy Center about 30 miles away in Chantilly, Virginia. At both locations, even the most science-challenged will probably ooh and aah. Maybe the 1903 Wright Flyer, Amelia Earhart's Lockheed Vega, astronaut John Glenn's space suit, or another jewel from the 60,000-artifact collection will prompt the gaping jaws. Hands-on exhibits include ride simulators, including one where little tykes to great-grandmas can practice air-to-air combat in a F-4 Phantom II fighter jet. The main hall, always a jaw-dropper with history-making planes suspended overhead and space capsules, is getting a major makeover, courtesy of Boeing.

- Also spacelike is the cylindrical Hirshhorn Museum and Sculpture Garden next door. It's best known for its 19th and 20th century sculpture, including works by Rodin, Picasso, Matisse, and Calder. Its initial collection was donated by Joseph Herman Hirshhorn, a Latvian-born and Brooklyn-raised stock speculator and mining magnate.

- The Hirshhorn's other next-door neighbor is the Arts and Industries Building, the original home of the National Museum. The 1881 landmark will reopen in 2016 as a special-events venue.

- Next door is the venerable Smithsonian Institution Building, affectionately known as The Castle. While it hosts some exhibits, it's mainly known as the Smithsonian's information and administrative center, for its public café, and as the final home for the Institution's benefactor, James Smithson. The English scientist, who was born James Louis Macie, is entombed in a crypt on the first floor. He never visited the U.S. and the Smithsonian says the motive for his bequest remains a mystery. Since 1855, the Norman-style castle has anchored the Mall, when it sat alone on a spit of land isolated by a canal. Designed by architect James Renwick Jr., it was built with reddish-brown

Seneca sandstone from Maryland. The Castle is a garden complex ringed by the S. Dillon Ripley International Center, the National Museum of African Art, and the Smithsonian's twin Asian art museums: the Arthur M. Sackler Gallery and the Freer Gallery of Art. The Enid A. Haupt Garden behind the Castle explodes with cherries and magnolias each spring. Formal and informal gardens are scattered around the Smithsonian. Some feature a rainbow of native flowers to adorn the city, delight visitors, and nourish the butterflies and birds.

- Begun as a private entity in 1964, the National Museum of African Art coupled with the Smithsonian in 1979 and migrated to its present quarters in 1987. Its diverse collection "embraces the artistic expressions of Africa, from the ancient to contemporary times," the museum notes. As with its virtually matching counterpart museum across the courtyard (the Sackler), the bulk of this building is underground. Its collection includes textiles, masks, musical instruments, sculpture, and jewelry.

- The Arthur M. Sackler Gallery and Freer Gallery of Art, which are linked underground, are known for "some of the most important holdings of Asian art in the world," the museum says. The Sackler, whose modern abode opened in 1987 to house the art collection of New York psychiatrist, researcher, and publisher Arthur M. Sackler, features Xu Bing's *Monkeys Reaching for the Moon,* the "Perspectives" series of contemporary art from Asia, and South Asian sculpture, among other riches. The Freer will close for renovations from January 2016 to summer 2017. Cloaked in a 1923 Italianate palazzo, the Freer spotlights ancient Chinese bronzes and jades, Japanese Buddhist art, and other Asian art, along with 19th-century works by American James McNeill Whistler and his contemporaries. It's also renowned for its newly restored gold and blue Peacock Room, which the museum's founder, railroad-car manufacturer Charles Lang Freer, moved from London to his Detroit mansion in 1904.

- After visiting, with the museum behind you, walk west on Jefferson Drive SW and turn right to reach the Smithsonian Metro stop.

POINTS OF INTEREST

Smithsonian Metro Station National Mall exit near 1200 Independence Ave. SW, 202-637-7000, wmata.com/rail/station_detail.cfm?station_id=54

Washington Monument 2 15th St. NW, 202-426-6841, nps.gov/wamo/index.htm

National Museum of African American History and Culture 1400 Constitution Ave. NW, 202-633-1000, nmaahc.si.edu

National Museum of American History 14th Street NW and Constitution Avenue NW, 202-633-1000, americanhistory.si.edu

National Museum of Natural History 10th Street NW and Constitution Avenue NW, 202-633-1000, mnh.si.edu

National Gallery of Art, Sculpture Garden Ninth Street NW and Constitution Avenue NW, 202-633-1000, nga.gov/content/ngaweb/visit/maps-and-information/sculpture-garden.html

National Gallery of Art, West Building Sixth Street NW and Constitution Avenue NW, 202-633-1000, nga.gov/content/ngaweb.html

National Gallery of Art, East Building Fourth Street NW and Constitution Avenue NW, 202-633-1000, nga.gov/content/ngaweb.html

National Museum of the American Indian Fourth Street SW and Independence Avenue SW, 202-633-6644, nmai.si.edu/home

National Air and Space Museum Sixth Street SW and Independence Avenue SW, 202-633-2214, airandspace.si.edu

Hirshhorn Museum and Sculpture Garden Seventh Street SW and Independence Avenue SW, 202-633-4674, hirshhorn.si.edu/collection/home/#collection=home

Arts and Industries Building 900 Jefferson Dr. SW, 202-633-1000, si.edu/Museums/arts-and-industries-building

Smithsonian Institution Building (The Castle) 1000 Jefferson Dr. SW, 202-633-1000, si.edu/Museums/arts-and-industries-building

National Museum of African Art 950 Independence Ave. SW, 202-633-4600, africa.si.edu

Arthur M. Sackler Gallery 1050 Independence Ave. SW, 202-633-4880, asia.si.edu

Freer Gallery of Art Jefferson Drive SW and 12th Street SW, 202-633-4880, asia.si.edu

route summary

1. Start at the Smithsonian Metro Station's escalator exit on the National Mall.
2. At the top of the escalator, turn right to reach Jefferson Drive SW.
3. Turn right to head west on Jefferson Drive SW.
4. Follow Jefferson Drive SW across 14th and 15th Streets to reach the Washington Monument.
5. With the monument to the rear, walk east on Madison Drive NW.
6. Turn right onto Third Street NW.
7. Walk one block south on Third Street NW, which becomes Third Street SW.
8. Turn right onto Maryland Avenue SW and turn right into the National Museum of the American Indian.
9. After exiting the museum, stay in the courtyard and follow the building around to the left to reach Jefferson Drive SW.
10. Walk west on Jefferson Drive SW to visit all the museums on the left.
11. Turn right to reach the Smithsonian Metro stop.

CONNECTING THE WALKS

Walk 19 (Tidal Basin Cherries) also begins at the Smithsonian Metro. For Walk 15 (White House), at the Washington Monument, turn left onto 15th Street NW and cross Constitution Avenue NW to the White House. For Walk 23 (Capitol Hill), after the National Gallery of Art, continue straight along the Mall to the Capitol instead of turning right onto Third Street NW. For Walk 18 (Downtown: News Junkies East), at the National Museum of the American Indian, cross Independence Avenue SW to the Voice of America.

Washington Monument dominates the D.C. skyline.

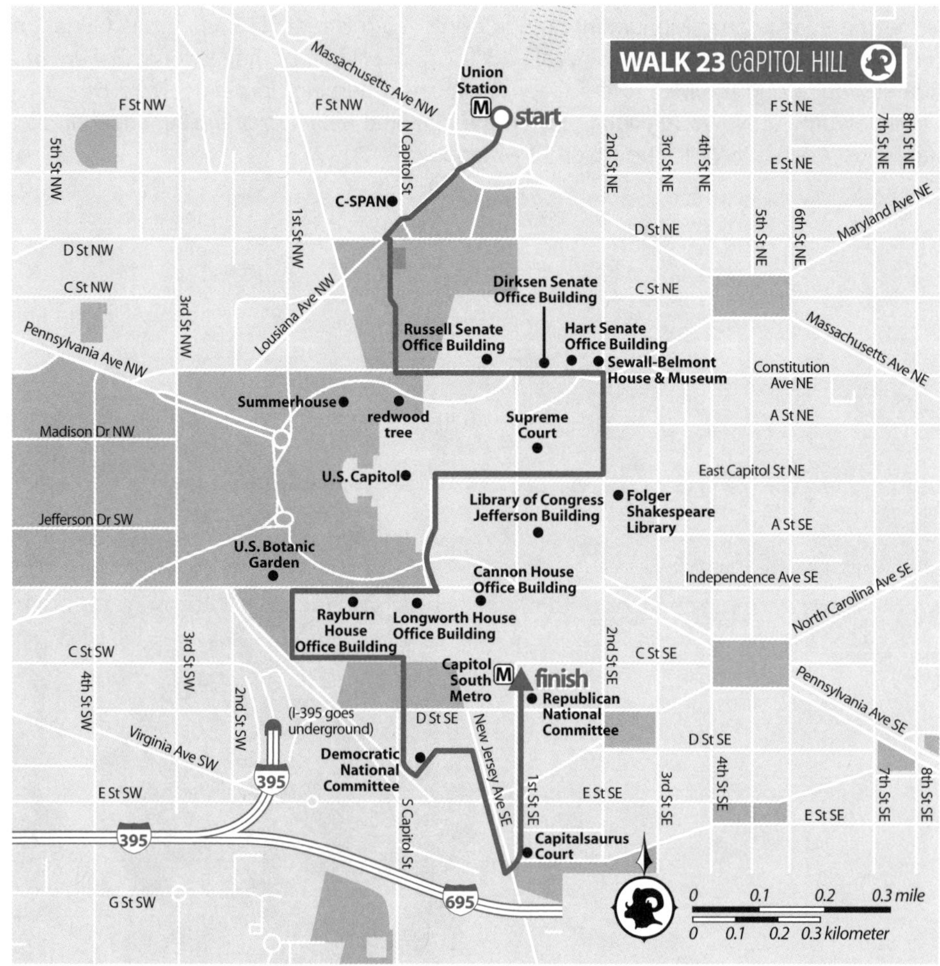
WALK 23 CAPITOL HILL
Union Station
start
Massachusetts Ave NW
F St NW
F St NW
5th St NW
N Capitol St
C-SPAN
1st St NW
D St NW
C St NW
3rd St NW
Lousiana Ave NW
Pennsylvania Ave NW
Madison Dr NW
Jefferson Dr SW
Summerhouse
redwood tree
U.S. Capitol
U.S. Botanic Garden
Russell Senate Office Building
Dirksen Senate Office Building
Hart Senate Office Building
Sewall-Belmont House & Museum
Supreme Court
Library of Congress Jefferson Building
Folger Shakespeare Library
Cannon House Office Building
Rayburn House Office Building
Longworth House Office Building
Capitol South Metro
finish
Republican National Committee
Democratic National Committee
Capitalsaurus Court
F St NE
E St NE
D St NE
C St NE
2nd St NE
3rd St NE
4th St NE
5th St NE
6th St NE
7th St NE
8th St NE
Maryland Ave NE
Massachusetts Ave NE
Constitution Ave NE
A St NE
East Capitol St NE
A St SE
Independence Ave SE
North Carolina Ave SE
C St SE
2nd St SE
Pennsylvania Ave SE
D St SE
E St SE
E St SE
3rd St SE
4th St SE
7th St SE
8th St SE
1st St SE
New Jersey Ave SE
D St SE
S Capitol St
C St SW
4th St SW
3rd St SW
2nd St SW
(I-395 goes underground)
Virginia Ave SW
E St SW
G St SW
395
395
695
0 0.1 0.2 0.3 mile
0 0.1 0.2 0.3 kilometer

23 Capitol Hill: Leaders, Laws, Landmarks, and a Dinosaur

BOUNDARIES: Massachusetts Avenue NE, Second Street NE, F Street SE, and First Street SW
DISTANCE: 2.6 miles
DIFFICULTY: Easy
PARKING: Limited street parking; public parking garage at Union Station; Metro recommended
PUBLIC TRANSIT: Union Station and Capitol South Metro

Washington, D.C., is America's Mecca. And Capitol Hill is at the bull's eye. Not only does democracy thrive there, but it's also drop-dead gorgeous. Even jaded Washingtonians seldom tire of its eye-candy icons: the stately white Capitol dome, the palatial Library of Congress, and the Supreme Court's classical "Temple of Justice." There's also much more to the Hill, such as the Democratic and Republican headquarters, walkable neighborhoods, a hidden grotto, redwood trees, and a dinosaur's home. Watch where you're walking. You might bump into your representative—or at least his or her aides.

- **Start at the main entrance of Union Station, 40 Massachusetts Avenue NE. Cross Columbus Circle NE to reach Louisiana Avenue NE. At North Capitol Street NW, the private nonprofit headquarters for C-SPAN (Cable-Satellite Public Affairs Network) is in an office building on the right. America's cable TV industry created C-SPAN in 1979 to provide gavel-to-gavel coverage of Congress.**

- **Cross D Street to follow the sidewalk along the reflecting pool in Senate Park, with its grand fountains and lawn leading straight toward the Capitol. Turn left on Constitution Avenue NE. The Senate's three venerable buildings are on the left. Even after 9/11 drastically changed life in Washington with closed roads and ramped-up security, the 100-member Senate still welcomes voters and other visitors. The outwardly staid Russell Senate Office Building harbors a marble rotunda worthy of a queen. It's also home to the newly renamed Kennedy Caucus Room, where the Watergate and other historic hearings occurred. The room's white marble walls, elaborate gilded ceiling, and 12 Corinthian columns make it one of the more impressive rooms in the city, the Senate says. Next door in the Dirksen Senate Office Building, visitors can dine in the Senate**

Cafeteria, which, in the spirit of beverage bipartisanship sells both Coke and Pepsi—unlike most restaurants. Around the corner, the (tax-free) Senate Gift Shop sells pewter baby rattles, Waterford crystal, Garnier-Thiebaut napkins, watches, T-shirts, and gobs of other unique loot emblazoned with the Senate seal. After Dirksen comes the Hart Senate Office Building, the most contemporary of the trio.

- Next door at Second Street and Constitution Avenue NE is the Sewall-Belmont House & Museum. This three-story brick home from the 1800s contains a library and exhibits documenting the National Woman's Party of 1917 and women's past and continuing struggles for equal rights.

- Turn right on Second Street NE and walk to East Capitol Street NE for the Folger Shakespeare Library on the left. Researchers can access the world's largest collection of Shakespeare materials there. The public can view exhibits and attend plays at its Folger Theatre. The Folger was founded by Henry Clay Folger, the former head of Standard Oil Company of New York, and his wife, Emily.

- Continue west on East Capitol Street for the Library of Congress's Thomas Jefferson Building on the left. It's the world's largest library, the world's largest law library, and it holds the world's largest collections of cartographic materials, comic books, and newspapers. Its rarities include a 15th-century Gutenberg Bible and a cuneiform tablet from 2040 B.C. Some of the treasures reside in the Jefferson building, which is sometimes called the "most beautiful building in Washington." The gilded rotunda of its Main Reading Room is unforgettable, along with the Great Hall, with its lavish mosaics, murals, and vaulted marble ceilings. The library was chartered to serve Congress in 1800, but the public can also tap some of its resources. The library sponsors a popular National Book Festival and hosts movies and other public events.

- Just across East Capitol Street NE is America's highest court. The Supreme Court invites visitors to tour its templelike home, eat in its café, spend a few bucks in its gift shop, and listen to oral arguments in potentially history-making cases. Architect Cass Gilbert designed the iconic white building, with its marble Corinthian columns. The newly renovated courthouse first opened in 1935.

- Walk across First Street SE to the U.S. Capitol, which may be partially covered by 1.1 million pounds of scaffolding. Construction began in 2014 to repair its crack-plagued, cast-iron dome. The Capitol's opulent 180-foot-high rotunda and other rooms are still accessible, especially the 580,000-square-foot underground Capitol Visitor Center, which opened in 2008. Construction of the Capitol began in 1793. It has been "built, burnt, rebuilt, extended, and restored" several times, says the Architect of the Capitol, whose more than 2,600 employees maintain these iconic federal landmarks on Capitol Hill. Tourists are welcome inside and outside. Some tours require reservations, and access to the Senate and House galleries requires passes from lawmakers' individual offices. The sprawling Capitol grounds were designed by Frederick Law Olmsted. His Summerhouse, a brick hexagon-shaped building, is practically hidden, tucked away on the West Front lawn by the north (Senate) side of the Capitol. Weary walkers can rest on its low stone benches and meditate on the grotto's waterfall. Nearby are historic trees, including a giant redwood, which typically just grows in the California mountains, and a dawn redwood. The giant was planted in 1966 by the Cherokee Indian Nation and replaced in 1969 after it died, says Melanie Choukas-Bradley in *City of Trees.*

- Exit the front of the Capitol and turn right on the sidewalk toward Independence Avenue, SE. Cross the street and turn right for the three main U.S. House of Representatives office buildings on the left. The first and the oldest is Cannon House Office Building, which was erected in 1908. Its rotunda and caucus room practically match those in the Russell Senate Office Building. Next is Longworth (1933) and then Rayburn (1965). Visitors can drop in on their representatives, grab some lunch in the buildings' cafés, and window-shop at the House Gift Shop in Longworth. They sell (tax-free) Tiffany sterling bracelets, blue and red aprons, and other mementos emblazoned with the House seal.

Classical Cannon House Office Building

D.C.'S STREET SYSTEM

Navigating D.C.'s roughly 1,500 miles of roads is easier if you understand its street system and its *many* quirks. It boils down to this: The U.S. Capitol occupies the center of a grid, with intersecting diagonals running through it.

GRID: Planner Pierre "Peter" Charles L'Enfant created the initial grid, which was divided into four quadrants (NW, NE, SE, and SW) beginning at the Capitol. The dividing lines are North, East, and South Capitol Streets, and the center of the National Mall on the west.

STREET NAMES: Numbered streets run north–south, lettered streets run east–west, and avenues (typically named for states) run diagonally.

Street numbers and letters increase moving away from the Capitol. W is the last lettered street. After that, although it's not consistent, generally east–west streets appear alphabetically, first with two syllables (Adams, Bryant, etc.), then three syllables (Allison, Buchanan, etc.), and then with plant names (Aspen, Butternut, etc.).

FINDING ADDRESSES: 1103 H St. NE: It runs east–west because it's a lettered street. It's northeast of the Capitol. 1103 is between 11th and 12th Streets. It's on the south side of the street because of its odd address.

730 21st St. NW: It runs north–south because it's a numbered street. It uses the same system as above, except 730 is between G and H Streets, the seventh and eighth letters of the alphabet. North of I Street is trickier because there's no J Street, so J isn't counted. So just remember that instead of counting as the 12th letter of the alphabet, L Street stands for 11 (they sound alike) and you won't get lost.

QUIRKS: I and Q Streets are sometimes written Eye and Que. There are no X, Y, or Z Streets because the original city didn't extend far enough to need those letters. There's no J Street by the regular lettered streets "to prevent confusion from the resemblance of I and J when written," said Alexander Hagner when he penned *Street Nomenclature of Washington City* in 1904. However, there is a Jay Street NE, by Gault Place NE and Hayes Street NE on the south side of the Anacostia River. Streets are most irregular on that bank of the river. Other aberrations occur for many reasons, including wholesale and individual street renaming over the years and in neighborhoods outside the original planned city.

D.C.'s Street Numbering System

Street numbering begins at the Capitol. Even-numbered addresses are on the left side of the street, and odd are on the right. Left or right depends on one's direction facing away from the Capitol, says the D.C. government's Master Address Repository Standards.Wikipedia (we really hate to admit) sums it up best:

QUADRANT	EAST–WEST STREETS	NORTH–SOUTH STREETS
NW	Odd numbers on NORTH side	Even numbers on WEST side
SW	Odd numbers on NORTH side	Even numbers on EAST side
SE	Odd numbers on SOUTH side	Even numbers on EAST side
NE	Odd numbers on SOUTH side	Even numbers on WEST side

- After the Rayburn House Office Building, the U.S. Botanic Garden's conservancy is catty-corner at First Street SW. Every inch of its greenery, glass, and stone seems to enchant and educate visitors. Formally founded in 1850, this "living plant museum" is actually three gardens: the restored 1933 Lord & Burnham greenhouse conservatory; the 3-acre National Garden abutting it; and Bartholdi Park, with its 30-foot-tall cast-iron fountain, across Independence Avenue SW. The glass conservatory is especially alluring in the winter, with the jungle of palm trees, fragrant orchids, and rainbow of exotic flowers that thrive it its blissfully hot home. The garden runs free tours and lectures year-round.

- Exit the garden, heading south on First Street SW. Turn left on C Street SW; turn right on South Capitol Street SE; and turn left on Ivy Street SE for the private headquarters of the Democratic National Committee on the left. This four-story, tan building has been the party's headquarters since 1984. Inside is the brown file cabinet that was broken into during the Watergate burglary at the DNC's former headquarters. After the DNC, continue east on Ivy Street SE and turn right onto New Jersey Avenue SE.

- Walk about a block and a half, and just before a bridge, turn left onto the short staircase leading down to the corner of First Street SE and F Street SE. In 2000, the D.C. government dubbed the street "Capitalsaurus Court" for the carnivorous dinosaur

whose vertebrae and bone fragments were unearthed there in 1898 during sewer construction. The fossils are displayed at the Smithsonian's National Museum of Natural History, along with a thighbone found at First and Channing Streets SW and other dinosaur fossils discovered in little-known "Dinosaur Alley," which runs from D.C. to Baltimore. After the dinosaur site, head north on First Street SE.

- **On the right, just after D Street SE, is the private headquarters of the Republican National Committee. This four-story, white brick building has been the party's headquarters since the 1960s. After the GOP, cross the street to the Metro station.**

POINTS OF INTEREST

Union Station 40 Massachusetts Ave. NE, 202-289-1908, unionstationdc.com

C-SPAN 400 N. Capitol St. NW, Suite 650; 202-737-3220; c-span.org

U.S. Senate 202-224-3121, senate.gov

Russell Senate Office Building Constitution Avenue NE and Delaware Avenue NE

Dirksen Senate Office Building Constitution Avenue NE and First Street NE

Hart Senate Office Building Constitution Avenue NE and Second Street NE

Sewall-Belmont House & Museum 144 Constitution Ave. NE, 202-546-1210, sewallbelmont.org

Folger Shakespeare Library 201 E. Capitol St. SE, 202-544-4600, folger.edu

Supreme Court of the United States 1 First St. NE, 202-479-3000, supremecourt.gov

Library of Congress's Thomas Jefferson Building 10 First St. SE, 202-707-8000, loc.gov

U.S. Capitol East Capitol St. NE and First St. SE, 202-224-3121 (switchboard) and 202-226-8000 (visitor center), visitthecapitol.gov

U.S. House of Representatives 202-224-3121, house.gov

Cannon House Office Building Independence Avenue SE and First Street SE

Longworth House Office Building Independence Avenue SE and South Capitol Street SE

Rayburn House Office Building Independence Avenue SW and First Street SW

U.S. Botanic Garden 100 Maryland Ave. SW, 202-225-8333, usbg.gov

Democratic National Committee 430 S. Capitol St. SE, 202-863-8000, democrats.org

Capitalsaurus Court First and F Streets SE, dccode.org/simple/sections/1-161.html

Republican National Committee 310 First St. SE, 202-863-8500, gop.com

Capitol South Metro 355 First St. SE, 202-637-7000, wmata.com/rail/station_detail.cfm?station_id=59

route summary

1. **Start at the main entrance of Union Station, 40 Massachusetts Avenue NE.**
2. **Cross Columbus Circle NE to walk southwest on Louisiana Avenue NE.**
3. **Cross D Street to reach the sidewalk in Senate Park.**
4. **Follow the sidewalk south along the reflecting pool to Constitution Avenue.**
5. **Turn left on Constitution Avenue NE.**
6. **Turn right on Second Street NE.**
7. **Turn right on East Capitol Street NE.**
8. **After exiting the front of the Capitol, turn right on the sidewalk to cross Independence Avenue SE.**
9. **Turn right to head west on Independence Avenue.**
10. **Turn left on First Street SW.**
11. **Turn left on C Street SW.**
12. **Turn right on South Capitol Street SE.**
13. **Turn left on Ivy Street SE.**
14. **Turn right on New Jersey Avenue SE.**
15. **After about a block and a half, just before a bridge, turn left onto the broad stairs leading down to the corner of First Street SE and F Street SE, otherwise known as Capitalsaurus Court.**
16. **Follow First Street SE north just past D Street SW to the Metro station on the left.**

connecting the walks

Walks 24 (NoMa and Union Market) and 25 (H Street NE) also begin at Union Station. Walk 22 (National Mall East) starts on the west side of the Capitol. For Walk 26 (Eastern Market to Barracks Row), continue south on Second Street SE and turn left on Pennsylvania Avenue SE.

U.S. Capitol

WALK 24 NoMa and Union Market
Penn St NE
Florida Ave NE
North Capitol St
O St NW
Bureau of Alcohol, Tobacco, Firearms and Explosives
4 St NE
Union Market (old)
Neal Pl NE
Union Market (new)
Morse St NE
N St NE
New York Ave NW
start
NoMa-Gallaudet Metro and the Metropolitan Branch Trail
Florida Ave NE
Gallaudet University
Patterson St NE
M St NE
Uline Arena
Abbey Pl NE
Orleans Pl NE
Pierce St NE
First St NE
Morton Pl NE
National Public Radio
L St NW
3rd St NE
4th St NE
5th St NE
6th St NE
L St NE
2nd St NE
West Virginia Ave NE
K St NW
K St NE
I St NE
I St NE
7th St NE
8th St NE
9th St NE
CNN
First St NE
North Capitol St
H St NW
H St NE
Government Printing Office Bookstore
G St NE
G St NW
Massachusetts Ave NW
National Postal Museum
Union Station
F St NW
F St NE
finish
2nd St NW
E St NW
0 0.1 0.2 0.3 mile
0 0.1 0.2 0.3 kilometer

24 NoMa and Union Market: Old Meets New

BOUNDARIES: Florida Avenue NE, Eighth Street NE, Massachusetts Avenue NE, and North Capitol Street NW
DISTANCE: 2.5 miles
DIFFICULTY: Easy
PARKING: Public parking lot at Union Station; limited metered parking and private lots near NoMa-Gallaudet Metro; free parking at Union Market
PUBLIC TRANSIT: NoMa-Gallaudet Metro station and Union Station

If an alien landed by North Capitol and L Streets NE in 1990 and again in 2015, it might not realize this was the same planet. That's how drastically this newly named "NoMa" neighborhood has changed. Once shunned as a dangerous and decaying outpost, now pricey high-rise apartments, hotels, and offices are sprouting up almost everywhere. NoMaBID—for "North of Massachusetts Avenue" and "business improvement district"—was created in 2007 to help keep priming the development pump in this 35-block area north of Union Station. It's roughly bordered by Massachusetts Avenue NE to R Street NE and North Capitol Street to Fourth Street NE. This public-private nonprofit seems determined to make the area lively for pedestrians even after the federal and private offices have closed for the night, by sponsoring outdoor movies, concerts, and more. Near its northeast boundary, the old and new Union Markets by Gallaudet University are the latest hot spots for foodies and other explorers. Shoppers can buy $300 Japanese kitchen knives and nibble chocolate-covered bacon in the new block-long retail market. At the well-worn wholesale warehouses, they can buy cows' feet, $5 "pashmina" shawls, and crates of cabbage. Stop by the old markets before their real-world grit and patina become completely "Disney-fied."

- **Start at the NoMa-Gallaudet Metro at Second and N Streets NE, which helped spur development when it opened in 2004. Unlike most Metrorail stations, this Red Line station was built with both public and private funds. When it debuted, *Washington Post* architectural columnist Roger K. Lewis said transformation of the area "stands a good chance of being substantially accomplished within the next 10 to 15 years." He was right.**

- **Across the street is the 2008 headquarters of the Bureau of Alcohol, Tobacco, Firearms and Explosives. One of two D.C. projects by architect Moshe Safdie, of Habitat '67 fame, it's designed to be ultrasecure yet open. On two sides, the public sees** a 21st-century version of a castle wall: a tall, partially open, bridgelike concrete "wall" that curves around two sides, creating a private interior courtyard. Inside is a 422,000-square-foot "blast-resistant fortress" of two eight-story buildings and a six-story crescent-shaped building, the contractor and architect say. It was the first federal building to follow the tough security standards instituted after 168 people were killed in the 1995 bombing of the Murrah Federal Building.

● Head north on Second Street NE and turn right on Florida Avenue NE. Walk under the train tracks and turn left on Fourth Street NE for the old and new Union Markets. The market area starts at Florida Avenue NE and runs to Penn Street NE, and from Sixth Street NE to just west of Fourth Street NE. This roughly 40-acre site has recently started to become gentrified.

The first part of the redevelopment is the new retail Union Market at Neal Place NE, which opened in late 2012. It's a block-long, open-plan warehouse with a huge new "Union Market" sign on top. About 40 trendy markets and eateries operate there, including the Rappahannock Oyster Co., named by *The Wall Street Journal* as one of the country's "outstanding oyster bars."

To the west are several rows of still largely independently owned wholesale warehouses, some grimy with graffiti and roll-down metal doors, typical of old working-class Washington. Many of the multicultural vendors welcome retail shoppers, but some only serve the trade. They sell the exotic and the commonplace: from skin off a cow's head, fufu flour, and oha leaves to T-shirts and 50-cent celery.

Two popular hangouts anchor the markets. To the south, A. Litteri, an Italian foodie's delight on Morse Street NE, has been in the grocery business since 1926. Now third-generation owner Michael DeFrancisci sells elusive Italian delicacies; hosts wine, vinegar, and olive oil tastings; and makes subs and salads in his compact and lovingly crammed shop. To the north on Penn Street NE is the new Angelika movie theater. Until it opens its planned eight-screen theatre, it's operating as a "popup" in a warehouse.

● With the new Union Market on the left, at Neal Place NE, cross Sixth Street NE into a side entrance for Gallaudet University. Gallaudet describes itself as "the world's only university with programs and services specifically designed to accommodate deaf and hard of hearing students." Chartered by Congress in 1864, its original campus was designed in 1866 by Calvert Vaux and Fredrick Law Olmsted, who created Central Park and the U.S. Capitol grounds. Chapel Hall, in contrasting-colored stone, and College Hall, with brick and brownstone, are worth a gander. Gallaudet invented the football huddle in the 1890s to hide their hand signals from their opponents.

- Turn right at the main exit onto Florida Avenue NE and turn left on M Street NE. On the left between Third Street NE and Delaware Avenue NE is the shell of the former Uline Arena, later known as the Washington Coliseum. Nearly forgotten, this barrel-vaulted building, which opened in 1941, was most famous as the venue for The Beatles' first U.S. concert in 1964 before just over 8,000 fans. Built as an ice-skating rink where hockey players battled and figure skater Sonja Henie once awed her fans, it was also home to the Washington Capitols basketball team and was the site where Malcolm X once spoke, Bob Dylan sang, and President Eisenhower partied at his 1957 inaugural festival. It's about to be reborn as part of a 244,000-square-foot office and retail development. Outdoor retailer REI (Recreational Equipment, Inc.) plans to open a 51,000-square-foot store there in 2016.

- Continue west on M Street NE. Turn left on First Street NE and then right on L Street NE. National Public Radio's new high-tech headquarters is on the right at North Capitol Street NE. This is where "All Things Considered" and other popular programs are produced. It's the epicenter for NPR's 34 domestic and international bureaus. NPR moved to this light-filled, seven-story building in 2013. The nonprofit organization, which began in 1970 and relies partially on federal funding, welcomes the public for free tours, which give it a chance to show off its two-story digital display walls, gift shop, and state-of-the-art newsroom and studios. The public can even rent one of the recording studios and other spaces for performances, meetings, and weddings. Tour-goers can check out the green roof. It's home to a honeybee hive with about 20,000 little-bitty worker bees—roughly 25 for each NPR employee.

- On the left is the CNN tower, reachable from First Street NE. Unlike its Atlanta headquarters, the Washington Bureau does not offer public tours.

- Turn left on North Capitol Street. Just past H Street on the right is the Government Printing Office's dignified brick headquarters and public bookstore. As the federal government's primary printer, GPO publishes the president's budget, Congressional documents, the Federal Register, and other books and pamphlets.

- Continue on North Capitol Street NE to Massachusetts Avenue NE. Turn left, make another left on First Street NE and another left into the Smithsonian's National Postal Museum, which opened in 1993. This "sleeper" occupies the lower levels of the City Post Office Building, a grand structure built in 1914 with marble floors, majestic columns, and old-fashioned bronze Post Office boxes and postal windows that Americans once took for granted in big cities. Some of its biggest draws are the handcuffs used to nab the Unabomber, the original anthrax-tainted letter sent to Vermont Sen. Patrick Leahy, and the plain manila envelope that jeweler Henry "Harry" Winston trusted to mail the famous Hope Diamond to the Smithsonian. Before leaving, check out the rare "Inverted Jenny," the country's most famous stamp error. "It's our *Mona Lisa,*" a museum worker proudly proclaimed.

- On the right is the always-impressive Union Station. One of the earliest Washington Nationals baseball teams played at a ballpark that straddled present-day Union Station and the Postal Museum. When the Nats played there from 1886 to 1889, it was called both Swampoodle Grounds and Capitol Park II, says author Paul Kelsey Williams.

POINTS OF INTEREST

NoMa-Gallaudet Metro and the Metropolitan Branch Trail Second and N Streets NE, 202-637-7000, wmata.com/rail/station_detail.cfm?station_id=108 and metbranchtrail.com

Bureau of Alcohol, Tobacco, Firearms and Explosives 99 New York Ave. NE, atf.gov

Union Market 1309 Fifth St. NE, 301-652-7400, unionmarketdc.com

Gallaudet University 800 Florida Ave. NE, 202-651-5000, gallaudet.edu

Uline Arena 1140 Third St. NE, 202-638-6300, douglasdevelopment.com/properties/the-coliseum

REI 1140 Third St. NE, rei.com

National Public Radio 1111 North Capitol St. NE, 202-513-2000, npr.org

CNN's Washington Bureau 820 First St. NE, 202-898-7900, cnn.com

Government Printing Office bookstore 710 N. Capitol St. NW, 202-512-0132, bookstore.gpo.gov

National Postal Museum 2 Massachusetts Ave. NE, 202-633-5555, postalmuseum.si.edu

Union Station 40 Massachusetts Ave. NE, 202-289-1908, unionstationdc.com

route summary

1. Start at the NoMa-Gallaudet Metro at Second and N Streets NE.
2. With the Metro to the rear, turn right to walk north on Second Street NE.
3. Turn right on Florida Avenue NE.
4. Turn left on Fourth Street NE.
5. Turn right on Morse Street NE.
6. Turn left on Sixth Street NE.
7. With Neal Place NE on the left, turn right into a side entrance for Gallaudet University.
8. Turn right at the second stop sign on Lincoln Circle.
9. Turn right at the main exit on Florida Avenue NE.
10. Turn right on Florida Avenue NE.
11. Turn left on M Street NE.
12. Turn left on First Street NE.
13. Turn right on L Street NE.
14. Turn left on North Capitol Street NE.
15. Turn left on Massachusetts Avenue NE.
16. Turn left at First Street NE for Union Station.

connecting the walks

Walks 23 (Capitol Hill) and 25 (H Street NE) also start at Union Station.

Union Market entices foodies.

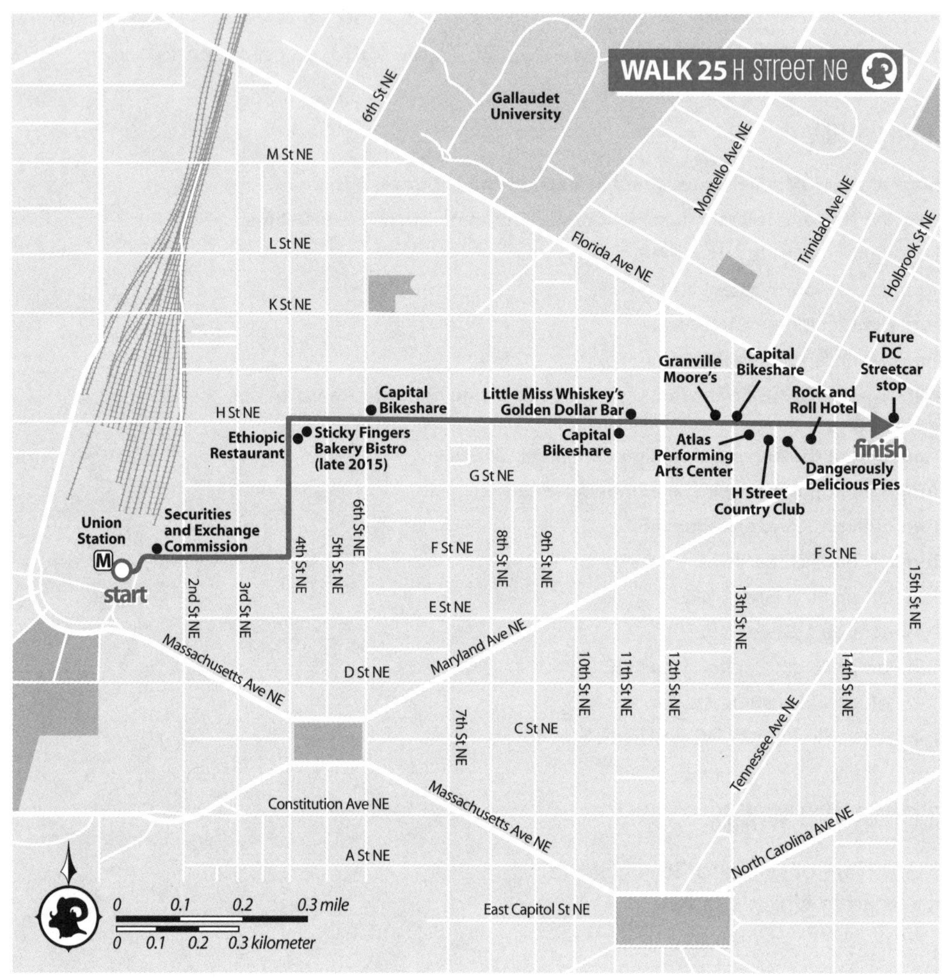
WALK 25 H Street NE
Gallaudet University
6th St NE
M St NE
L St NE
K St NE
H St NE
Florida Ave NE
Montello Ave NE
Trinidad Ave NE
Holbrook St NE
Granville Moore's
Capital Bikeshare
Future DC Streetcar stop
Rock and Roll Hotel
Little Miss Whiskey's Golden Dollar Bar
Capital Bikeshare
Sticky Fingers Bakery Bistro (late 2015)
Ethiopic Restaurant
Capital Bikeshare
Atlas Performing Arts Center
Dangerously Delicious Pies
H Street Country Club
finish
G St NE
Union Station
Securities and Exchange Commission
start
F St NE
E St NE
D St NE
C St NE
2nd St NE
3rd St NE
4th St NE
5th St NE
6th St NE
7th St NE
8th St NE
9th St NE
10th St NE
11th St NE
12th St NE
13th St NE
14th St NE
15th St NE
Maryland Ave NE
Massachusetts Ave NE
Tennessee Ave NE
Constitution Ave NE
A St NE
North Carolina Ave NE
East Capitol St NE
0 0.1 0.2 0.3 mile
0 0.1 0.2 0.3 kilometer

25 H Street NE: Eat, Drink, Dance, and Ride the Trolley

BOUNDARIES: H Street NE, 15th Street NE, Massachusetts Avenue, and First Street NE
DISTANCE: About 1.5 miles
DIFFICULTY: Easy
PARKING: Union Station public parking lot and limited metered and 2-hour street parking
PUBLIC TRANSIT: Union Station (Metro's Red Line, Amtrak, MARC, and VRE trains) is served by many buses. Capital Bikeshare rental stations (capitalbikeshare.com) are at Union Station, along H Street NE, and citywide.

After decades of decay and crime following race riots in 1968, H Street is hot again. Especially at night. More than two dozen bars, cafés, music venues, and other businesses have sprung up the past few years, many of them clustered between 11th and 14th Streets NE. Also called the Atlas District, this strip was named by *Forbes* magazine in 2014 as one of America's Best Hipster Neighborhoods. H Street's hot factor could spiral even higher after D.C.'s new delay-plagued streetcar line opens. It's scheduled for 2016. This inaugural leg of the city's first 21st-century streetcar runs on H Street NE from Union Station to Benning Road NE and Oklahoma Avenue NE. A trolley ran along the street from 1872 to 1949. After World War II, its heyday as the city's second busiest shopping district began to dim, and more residents fled to the suburbs. Now two of the biggest goals for the city and private developers are to make the corridor even more pedestrian friendly and to add more daylight draws—besides the lingering old-school fried-chicken takeouts and check-cashing stores.

- **Start at Union Station, 40 Massachusetts Avenue NE. It's a "three-fer": It's D.C.'s main transportation hub; it's a shopping and dining center (with dozens of destinations, including Neuhaus Belgian chocolates, Swedish fashion chain H&M, L'Occitane en Provence French toiletries, and a full floor of fast food); and it's historic eye candy. Architect Daniel H. Burnham patterned the monumental white granite building, which debuted in 1907, after the Baths of Caracalla. Its classical exterior and innards are equally impressive, with massive columns, arches galore, and marble planters. Repairs to the ornate vaulted ceiling damaged by the 2011 earthquake are expected to wrap up by 2016. Exit the front entrance and turn left to reach Columbus Circle NE.**

- Turn left on Columbus Circle NE and then turn right on F Street NE. On the left is the glass-clad Securities and Exchange Commission headquarters, which opened in 2003. This federal agency leases most of the three 10-story buildings in this complex dubbed Station Place. It's the only project in D.C. designed by Pritzker Architecture Prize Laureate Kevin Roche. After the SEC, continue on F Street NE and then turn left on Fourth Street NE past pastel and natural brick town houses.

- Ethiopic restaurant is on the right at Fourth and H Streets NE. This mom-and-pop eatery is a testament to D.C.'s new reputation as a foodie haven—after what seems like a lifetime of near drought. It's touted as one of *Washingtonian* magazine's top 100 restaurants in 2014.

- Practically next door, the award-winning Sticky Fingers Bakery Bistro is slated to open in 2015. Owner Doron Petersan started her first popular bakery in Columbia Heights in 2002. Her cupcakes snagged two wins on the Food Network's *Cupcake Wars.*

- Continue on H Street NE past mainly two- and three-story commercial buildings. On the left at Sixth Street NE (and at 11th and 13th Streets NE) is a Capital Bikeshare station. When Capital Bikeshare began in D.C., it was the first bike-sharing program in North America, the company says. It's owned by the D.C. government and other participating jurisdictions. An Oregon-based company operates it.

- Walk a little farther along H Street NE, where the buildings begin to gush with character. On the left is Little Miss Whiskey's Golden Dollar Bar in a two-story purple town house with a double-decker patio. Whiskey's is known for more than 70 craft beers and for a peach, tea, and vodka "slushie" called The Awesomeness. Other hits: weekend DJs, Kostume Karaoke, and a comedy night.

- On the same side of the street in a rustic row house is Granville Moore's. This "gastropub with a healthy Belgian fetish" is known for its mussels and fries. It routinely wins *City Paper*'s Best Mussels in D.C. award. The pub made its name in 2008 on the Food Network's *Throwdown with Bobby Flay,* when chef Teddy Folkman's mussels beat Flay's. It's named for the African American doctor who used to live there. Moore helped his needy neighbors by providing free or low-cost medical care.

- Continue on H Street NE to the epicenter of the neighborhood's rebirth: The Atlas Performing Arts Center on the right. Built as a whites-only movie theater in 1938, it closed in 1976. Fast-forward to 2001, when it was reborn as an arts center with plays, music, dance, films, and more. Its mission is to "bring people together through the arts to share and celebrate a range of artistic expressions and traditions." The Atlas, which gives the newly coined Atlas District its name, hosts D.C.'s eccentric Capital Fringe Festival each summer. The whole neighborhood acts as a stage during the H Street Festival each September.

- Next door, the H Street Country Club serves Mexican food and mojitos while customers play indoor mini-golf, Skee-Ball, and other games. *Washingtonian* magazine called the club a "boardwalk without a beach" when it named it one of the city's great bars in 2013. Its rooftop deck is open year-round.

- Also on the right side of the street is a whiff of heaven—from Dangerously Delicious Pies. The vegan bakery serves all types, from quiche to blueberry. Owner Rodney Henry made his mark as a finalist on *Food Network Star.*

- Practically next door is the Rock and Roll Hotel, which has plenty of live music but no hotel rooms. Its rooftop bar is open year-round. Before it opened in 2006, the building was a funeral home.

- When H Street bumps into Benning Road and Florida Avenue, turn around and walk back to the start, or—after it opens—hop aboard the red-and-gray streetcar to chug back along H Street to Union Station's parking garage.

Points of Interest

Union Station 40 Massachusetts Ave. NE, 202-289-1908, unionstationdc.com

Securities and Exchange Commission 100 F St. NE, 202-942-8088, sec.gov

Ethiopic 401 H St. NE, 202-675-2066, ethiopicrestaurant.com

Sticky Fingers Sweets & Eats 406 H St. NE, 202-299-9700, stickyfingersbakery.com

Capital Bikeshare Union Station and H Street NE at Third, Sixth, 11th, and 13th Streets NE, 877-430-2453, capitalbikeshare.com

Little Miss Whiskey's Golden Dollar Bar 1104 H St. NE, littlemisswhiskeys.com

Granville Moore's 1238 H St. NE, 202-399-2546, granvillemoores.com

Atlas Performing Arts Center 1333 H St. NE, 202-399-7993, atlasarts.org

H Street Country Club 1335 H St. NE, 202-399-4722, hstreetcountryclub.com

Dangerously Delicious Pies 1339 H St. NE, 202-398-7437, dangerouspiesdc.com

Rock and Roll Hotel 1353 H St. NE, 202-388-7625, rockandrollhoteldc.com

route summary

1. **Start at Union Station, 50 Massachusetts Avenue NE.**
2. **Exit the front entrance and turn left to reach Columbus Circle NE.**
3. **Turn left on Columbus Circle NE.**
4. **Turn right on F Street NE.**
5. **Turn left on Fourth Street NE.**
6. **Turn right on H Street NE.**
7. **At 15th Street NE, ride the DC Streetcar back to Union Station.**

CONNECTING THE WALKS

Walks 23 (Capitol Hill) and 24 (NoMa and Union Market) also start at Union Station.

Atlas Theater reigns over H Street, NE.

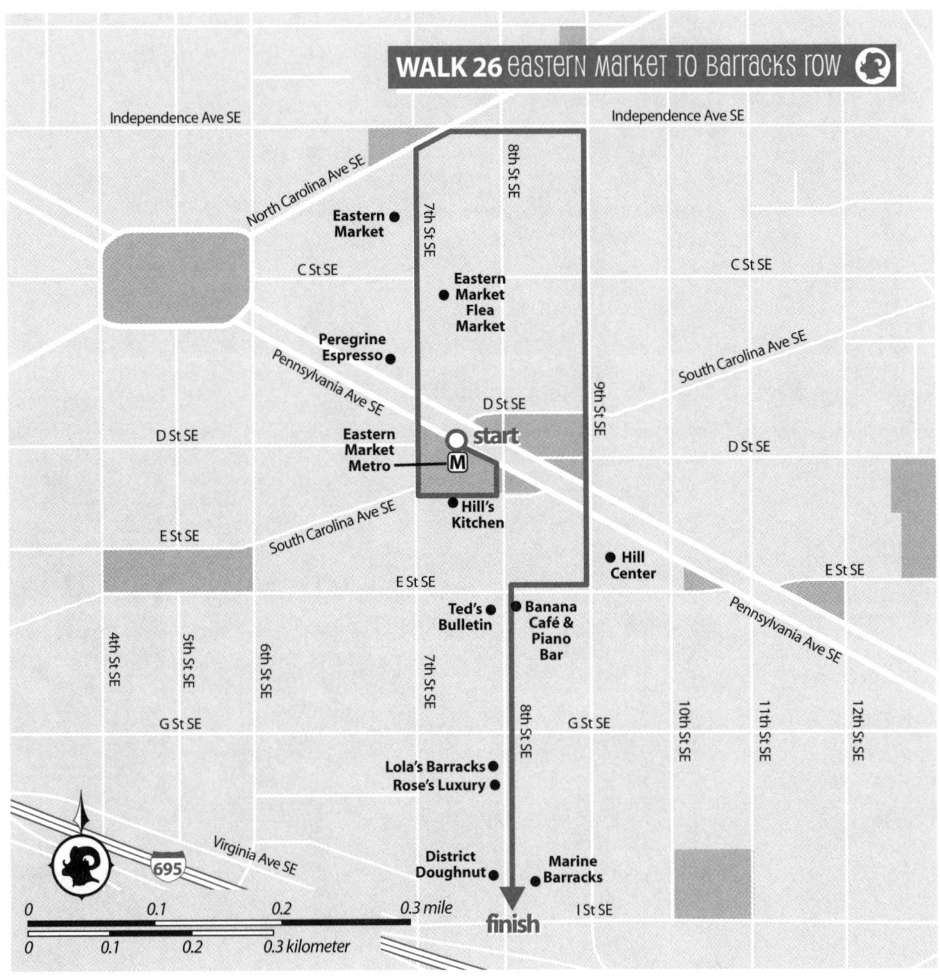
WALK 26 eastern market to barracks row
Independence Ave SE
Independence Ave SE
North Carolina Ave SE
Eastern Market
7th St SE
8th St SE
C St SE
C St SE
Eastern Market Flea Market
Peregrine Espresso
Pennsylvania Ave SE
South Carolina Ave SE
9th St SE
D St SE
D St SE
D St SE
start
Eastern Market Metro
M
Hill's Kitchen
South Carolina Ave SE
E St SE
Hill Center
E St SE
E St SE
Ted's Bulletin
Banana Café & Piano Bar
Pennsylvania Ave SE
4th St SE
5th St SE
6th St SE
7th St SE
8th St SE
G St SE
G St SE
10th St SE
11th St SE
12th St SE
Lola's Barracks
Rose's Luxury
Virginia Ave SE
695
District Doughnut
Marine Barracks
I St SE
finish
0
0.1
0.2
0.3 mile
0
0.1
0.2
0.3 kilometer

26 Eastern Market to Barracks Row: History and Hotties

BOUNDARIES: **Independence Avenue SE, Ninth Street SE, I Street SE, and Seventh Street SE**
DISTANCE: **1.25 miles**
DIFFICULTY: **Easy**
PARKING: **Limited street parking; Metro recommended**
PUBLIC TRANSIT: **Eastern Market Metro station is served by multiple buses. The DC Circulator bus runs along Eighth Street SE.**

Sandwiched between the historic Eastern Market and the storied Marine Barracks is a half mile of hotties, hot spots, and a few ho-hums. Hot bars, hot restaurants, hot mammas, and hot papas (including Hill staffers, lawmakers, and Marines) are all found in the storefront town houses flanking foot-friendly Barracks Row. As D.C.'s oldest commercial hub, this neighborhood east of the Capitol lost its luster from the 1940s to the 1990s, but now it's a magnet again. And it's still a "real" street, with a barber, dry cleaners, and more. That's the ho-hum part. Barracks Row bustles on workdays, but it awakens more on weekends and after the sun descends. Eastern Market has been a hot spot for decades. But it got way too hot when a fire destroyed part of it in 2007. That same year it played a stand-in for a Dutch market in the spy thriller movie *Body of Lies,* co-starring Leonardo DiCaprio. It was built in 1873 by German American architect Adolf Cluss, a pal of communist leader Karl Marx. At the southern end of Barracks Row, the Marine Corps Barracks was founded in 1801.

- **Start at the Eastern Market Metro, 701 Pennsylvania Avenue SE. With the Metro to the rear, turn right to walk southeast on Pennsylvania Avenue SE and turn right on Eighth Street SE.**

- **Turn right on D Street SE for Hill's Kitchen gourmet kitchenware in a town house on the left. Proprietor Leah Daniels lovingly commissions custom designs such as Capitol-shaped cutting boards. She also sells high-end copper cookware and low-cost (but high-joy) cookie cutters in the shapes of D.C. and states.**

- Turn right on Seventh Street SE. After crossing Pennsylvania Avenue SE, Peregrine Espresso is on the left. *Food & Wine* magazine named it one of the country's best coffee bars.

- Continue on Seventh Street SE for the outdoor Flea Market at Eastern Market on the right. On weekends, shoppers can find exotic goodies, such as Tibetan singing bowls and metal stars salvaged from Pennsylvanian barns, along with the more mundane, such as comic books.

- Across the street, vendors hawk food and other wares inside and outside Eastern Market. In the summer, it's a food fest, with awesome aromas from homemade pies, hefty heirloom tomatoes, and organic basil wafting through the air. Inside, some shops have been in business for decades, such as Bowers Fancy Dairy Products. Third-generation owner Michael Bowers says he carries about 350 cheeses from all over the world. Another mainstay is Market Lunch. Even frazzled Washingtonians cheerfully queue up to wolf down its famous blueberry buckwheat pancakes. The market's also a center for tango and pottery classes. After exiting on Seventh Street SE, continue north and turn right on North Carolina Avenue SE. Turn right on Independence Avenue and then right on Ninth Street SE.

- Follow the brick sidewalk on Ninth Street past town houses and tall trees to Pennsylvania Avenue SE. On the left is the stately Hill Center at the Old Naval Hospital in its gated garden. Originally a hospital built for the Civil War (but not completed until after its end in 1866), now it's a community culture center with art galleries, poetry, concerts, music lessons, cooking, and much more.

- Turn right on E Street SE and left on Eighth Street SE, otherwise known as Barracks Row. On the left is the festive Banana Café & Piano Bar. It serves Cuban, Puerto Rican, and Tex-Mex dishes downstairs and outside, with a serving of piano and karaoke at the upstairs bar.

- Across the street is Ted's Bulletin. This family-friendly restaurant is known for its comfort food, such as a homemade version of Pop-Tarts, milk shakes (with or without booze), and dozens of homespun suppers and sides. It's decorated with ornate bronze panels, marble cladding, and other treasures salvaged from the Art Deco–era convention hall at the Philadelphia Civic Center.

- Just south is Lola's Barracks Bar & Grill, which *Washingtonian* named one of D.C.'s best bars. Patrons can play pool and tabletop shuffleboard at this paneled bar or step out onto two small patios.

- Two doors down is the most prestigious commercial address on the Row: Rose's Luxury. Expect a wait for this restaurant, dubbed a "dining sensation" by *The Washington Post.* It only accepts reservations for its $125-per-person (minimum) rooftop table. Chef-owner Aaron Silverman named his "modern American" restaurant for his life-loving grandma, Rose.

- Near the end of the Row on the right is District Doughnut. It opened in 2014 after three years as a catering and special-order business. They sell caramel-apple streusel, cannoli, mocha crunch, and other concoctions.

- Across the street is the public entrance to the Marine Barracks, the Marines' oldest active post. President Thomas Jefferson trotted through the streets on horseback in 1801 to survey potential sites before choosing it, in part because it was near the Navy Yard and the Capitol, the Marine Corps history says. Its 23-room, Georgian-Federalist style Home of the Commandants, at the north end of the two-block-long walled compound, has housed every Marine commandant since 1806. The campus is also home base for the Marine Band, the official Marine Corps Color Guard, the Marine Corps Silent Drill Platoon, the Marine Drum and Bugle Corps, and the Marine Corps Body Bearers. From May through August, the public flocks there for the pomp and circumstance of the Marines' Tuesday sunset and Friday evening parades.

Eastern Market began in 1873.

L'Enfant: A Plan for Grandeur

Thanks, Peter. Thank you, master planner and Major Pierre "Peter" L'Enfant for your extraordinary vision, which helped morph a rural outpost into one of the prettiest and most prestigious cities on the planet.

It was a tough start. In 1791, L'Enfant created a majestic plan for the new city of Washington, which was a part of the original "10 miles square" territory chosen by President George Washington for the country's new capital. Washington chose L'Enfant after knowing him as an engineer in the American Revolutionary War. French émigré L'Enfant envisioned Washington as a grand, Baroque-style design with broad diagonal avenues, public parks, monuments, and vistas. Unfortunately, histories show he wasn't always the easiest fellow to get along with, so he was dismissed the following year. (One historian says he quit.) In his place, L'Enfant's colleague, Andrew Ellicott, drew the city's new map with a few alterations. Ellicott and Benjamin Banneker had completed the initial survey and boundary-stone laying for what would later become the District of Columbia. Decades came and went. By 1901, the capital wasn't progressing the way some leaders had hoped. So the Senate Park Commission (also called the McMillan Commission) was created.

Design legends Daniel Burnham, Frederick Law Olmsted Jr., Charles F. McKim, and

Points of Interest

Eastern Market Metro 701 Pennsylvania Ave. SE, 202-637-7000, wmata.com/rail/station_detail.cfm?station_id=60

Hill's Kitchen 713 D St. SE, 202-543-1997, hillskitchen.com

Peregrine Espresso 660 Pennsylvania Ave. SE, 202-629-4381, peregrineespresso.com

Eastern Market Flea Market Seventh and C Streets SE, 703-534-7612, easternmarket.net

Eastern Market 225 Seventh St. SE, 202-698-5253, easternmarket-dc.org

Hill Center at the Old Naval Hospital 921 Pennsylvania Ave. SE, 202-549-4172, hillcenterdc.org/home

L'Enfant: A Plan for Grandeur (continued)

Augustus St. Gaudens, who served on the committee, recommended magnifying and expanding L'Enfant's vision. In its 179-page report, they said the more they "studied the first plans of the Federal City, the more they became convinced that the greatest service they could perform would be done by carrying to a legitimate conclusion the comprehensive, intelligent, and yet simple and straightforward scheme devised by L'Enfant under the direction of Washington and Jefferson." The McMillan Plan they developed called for "opening up grand axial vistas on the Mall, defining its edges, building the great temples of government and culture that line its north and south sides, and generally reorienting the city of Washington around what is still known today as the "monumental core," writes *Washington Post* architectural critic Philip Kennicott.

Today, L'Enfant and his master plan are revered. But when he died in 1825 he was penniless and buried on a Maryland farm. In 1909, he was moved into a monumental marble tomb at Arlington National Cemetery. On his grave marker and almost everywhere, he is called by his stuffy French moniker, Pierre. But historian and author Kenneth R. Bowling says that since L'Enfant was 22 years old, he preferred using his Americanized name, Peter.

Banana Café & Piano Bar 500 Eighth St. SE, 202-543-5906, bananacafedc.com

Ted's Bulletin 505 Eighth St. SE, 202-544-8337, tedsbulletincapitolhill.com

Lola's Barracks Bar & Grill 711 Eighth St. SE, 202-547-5652, lolasgrilldc.com

Rose's Luxury 717 Eighth St. SE, 202-580-8889, rosesluxury.com

District Doughnut 749 Eighth St. SE, 202-350-0799, districtdoughnut.com

Marine Barracks Eighth and I Streets SE, 202-433-4173, barracks.marines.mil

route summary

1. Start at the Eastern Market Metro, 701 Pennsylvania Avenue SE.
2. With the Metro to the rear, turn right to walk southeast on Pennsylvania Avenue SE.
3. Turn right on Eighth Street SE.
4. Turn right on D Street SE.
5. Turn right on Seventh Street SE.
6. Turn right on North Carolina Avenue SE.
7. Turn right on Independence Avenue SE.
8. Turn right on Ninth Street SE.
9. Turn right on E Street SE.
10. Turn left on Eighth Street SE.

CONNECTING THE WALKS

For Walk 23 (Capitol Hill), walk northwest on Pennsylvania Avenue SE to Independence Avenue SE. For Walk 27 (Navy Yard), walk three blocks south on Eighth Street SE underneath the freeway to the Washington Navy Yard

Ted's Bulletin bakes a homemade version of Pop-Tarts.

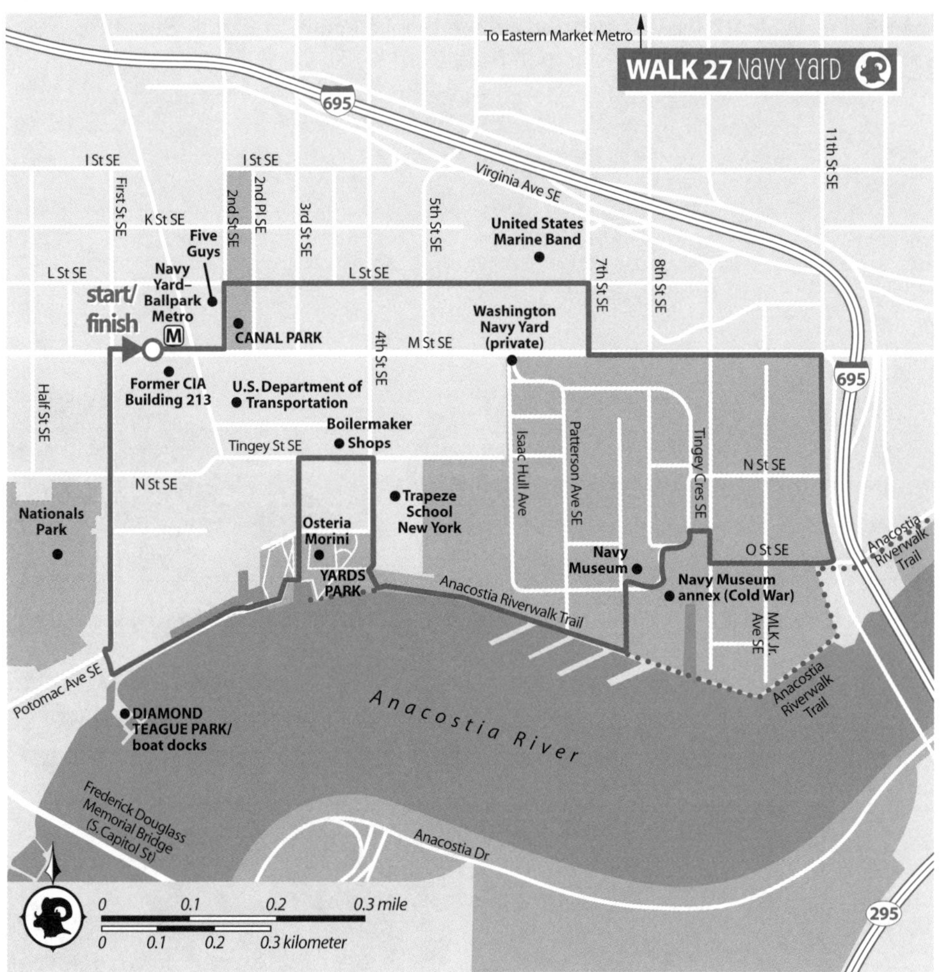

To Eastern Market Metro
WALK 27 Navy Yard
695
I St SE
I St SE
First St SE
2nd St SE
2nd Pl SE
3rd St SE
5th St SE
Virginia Ave SE
11th St SE
K St SE
Five Guys
United States Marine Band
L St SE
L St SE
7th St SE
8th St SE
Navy Yard–Ballpark Metro
M
start/ finish
CANAL PARK
Washington Navy Yard (private)
M St SE
4th St SE
695
Half St SE
Former CIA Building 213
U.S. Department of Transportation
Boilermaker Shops
Tingey St SE
Isaac Hull Ave
Patterson Ave SE
Tingey Cres SE
N St SE
N St SE
Nationals Park
Trapeze School New York
Osteria Morini
YARDS PARK
Navy Museum
O St SE
Navy Museum annex (Cold War)
Anacostia Riverwalk Trail
Anacostia Riverwalk Trail
MLK Jr. Ave SE
Anacostia Riverwalk Trail
Potomac Ave SE
DIAMOND TEAGUE PARK/ boat docks
Anacostia River
Frederick Douglass Memorial Bridge (S. Capitol St)
Anacostia Dr
0 0.1 0.2 0.3 mile
0 0.1 0.2 0.3 kilometer
295

27 Navy Yard: Baseball and Riverfront Escapades

BOUNDARIES: **L Street SE, 11th Street SE, the Anacostia Riverwalk Trail, and First Street SE**
DISTANCE: **2–2.75 miles (depending on which Navy Yard entrance is open)**
DIFFICULTY: **Easy**
PARKING: **Limited street parking. Private parking lots fill up during Nationals Park events. Metro recommended.**
PUBLIC TRANSIT: **Metro's Green Line and several Metrobuses stop at the Navy Yard-Ballpark Metro station. The DC Circulator bus runs along M Street to Union Station. Capital Bikeshare operates at the Metro and elsewhere.**

This resurrected neighborhood south of the Capitol is all about motion. Nats players sliding into home plate, tiny tots ice-skating outdoors, lovers strolling on a snazzy new waterfront trail, twenty-somethings swinging on a trapeze, the U.S. Department of Transportation (DOT), and diners rushing into the new cafés and bars that keep opening. And it just keeps getting livelier. The neighborhood has come a long way since the DOT unveiled its designer headquarters in 2006 and Nationals Park baseball stadium debuted in 2008. More high-rises have shot up, and many more folks are calling this once forlorn industrial waterfront their home. But many are *not* calling the neighborhood "Navy Yard" anymore, although Washington's Navy Yard has been the neighborhood anchor since it was founded in 1799 and its expansion in the late 1990s due to military base closings helped spark the neighborhood's rebirth. After focus groups and polling, the Capitol Riverfront Business Improvement District dubbed the entire northern Anacostia riverfront, from Second Street SW to 15th Street SE, the new Capitol Riverfront.

- **Start at the Navy Yard–Ballpark Metro Station at New Jersey Avenue SE and M Street SE. This Green Line station opened in 1991. Metro doesn't just sell fare cards. Its commercial vendor hawks a silver cuff bracelet embossed with a Metro map, a kiddie costume of a Metro track worker, and other goodies online.**

- **Directly across M Street from the Metro is where a "secret" Building 213 stood until 2014. It was the CIA's National Photographic Interpretation Center and then the National Geospatial Intelligence Agency, according to *The Washington Post.***

- Catty-corner from the Metro is the DOT's 2-million-square-foot headquarters designed by postmodernist Michael Graves. Two sides of the rusty orange, green, and ivory buildings feature a unique outdoor museum dubbed Transportation Walk.

- Walk east on M Street SE and turn left on Second Street SE. At the corner is the three-block-long Canal Park, which opened in 2012. Each winter it morphs into a figure-eight skating rink designed to mimic frozen European canals and the Washington City Canal, which ran there in the 1800s. The remainder of the year it's a family-friendly hangout, with native wildflowers, a pond, and a restaurant.

- Continue on M Street past office buildings to Five Guys on the left. This local success story began in 1986, when Jerry and Janie Murrell and the four Murrell brothers opened their first restaurant across the river in Arlington, Virginia. Now the red-and-white café sells fresh burgers and French fries in more than 1,000 locations. President Obama stopped by this branch in 2009. NBC taped him as he glad-handed patrons after ordering a cheeseburger and fries.

- Turn right on L Street SE and walk past new pastel town houses where the Capper/Carrollsburg public housing project once stood. The plight of the project's residents was featured in the regentrification documentary *Chocolate City.* On the left at Seventh Street SE is the handsome brick home of the United States Marine Band. It was founded in 1798 to perform for the president and the Marine Corps' commandant. The band also entertains its many fans in outdoor concerts on the National Mall and elsewhere. Its building is part barracks and part band space. The public can visit during its chamber museum series. "March King" John Philip Sousa directed the band in the 1880s.

- Turn right on Seventh Street SE to reach the Washington Navy Yard. Security tightened there in 2013 after a federal contractor killed 12 victims and wounded four inside the walled compound. When the main entrance is open, turn right on M Street SE and walk to the Sixth Street entrance on the left. When it's closed, turn left on M Street SE, walk to 11th Street SE, and turn right. The entrance for the U.S. Navy Museum is on the right at O Street SE. This former gun factory turned museum preserves historic treasures from wars, polar explorations, and other missions. The World War II memorabilia is the largest and most comprehensive exhibit, the museum says.

Visitors can peer through a submarine periscope, touch a torpedo, and stand guard atop a gun turret. They can also check out the most famous artifact: the bathyscaphe *Trieste.* That vessel set a world record by diving to the deepest part of the ocean for the first time in 1960. The Navy Yard, which is the oldest U.S. Navy shore facility, used to center around shipbuilding and munitions. Now it's mainly offices. It serves as the Navy's headquarters for the Naval Sea Systems and five other commands.

- Exit the Navy Yard and turn right onto the Anacostia Riverwalk Trail by the display ship *USS Barry,* which is sometimes open for tours. Begun in 2012, the asphalt and boardwalk trail will soon stretch 28 miles on both sides of the river, linking up to Bladensburg, Maryland. While walking along the river, you might hear an osprey—either the whir of a twin-rotored Osprey military helicopter or the whistling sound of a real live feathered osprey hawk.

- Follow the riverwalk until you see the Trapeze School New York's big white tent on the right. Turn right on the sidewalk that merges with Fourth Street SE. The school targets "thrill-seeker to fear-facer, athlete to couch potato, casual flyer to serious aerialist" with trampoline, acrobatics, and other classes.

- Turn left on Tingey Street SE. On the right is the Boilermaker Shops. Once a factory that manufactured heavy-duty boilers for Navy ships, this historic rehabbed building is now where Washingtonians gobble down South African–style chicken at Nando's Peri-Peri, check out walking and jogging gear at Pacers Running, and sip some suds at the Bluejacket microbrewery.

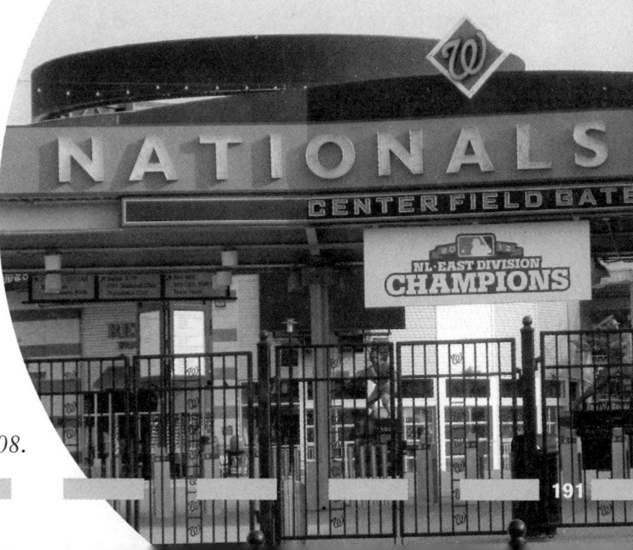

Nationals Park debuted in 2008.

- Continue on Tingey Street SE and then turn left onto Third Street SE. On the left is Osteria Morini. *Washington Post* food critic Tom Sietsema touted this Northern Italian restaurant as one of the best bets in the neighborhood. Its window wall faces an award-winning riverfront space called Yards Park. The two-level public park entices visitors with activities (concerts, yoga, movies, and more) and its interesting design (a playful pedestrian bridge that looks a little like a stretched-out Slinky toy, fountains, wavelike wooden benches, and other creative street furniture). The park is part of The Yards development, which was created by Cleveland-based Forest City. It took over the 44-acre Southeast Federal Center from the federal government in 2004. That center, the earliest development site outside the Navy Yard, was slated to become a new oasis for federal offices, but the DOT was the only cabinet-level agency to migrate there.

- Turn right to return to the riverwalk trail. Follow it to the metal gangplanks on the left. The Ballpark Boathouse rents canoes, kayaks, and paddleboards to explore the scenic (but polluted) Anacostia River Trail. A bit farther southwest, the Potomac Riverboat Company runs a "baseball boat" ferry to Nationals games. The park by the dock is home to the Earth Conservation Corps, a nonprofit that helps empower "endangered youth to reclaim the Anacostia River, their communities and their lives." It's called Diamond Teague Park for the 19-year-old honors student who was a "beloved member." He was shot in the head at his home just across the river in 2003. It's a sad reminder that D.C. can still be dangerous, although it's no longer the country's murder capital as it was in the 1990s. (There were 467 murders in 1993 and 105 in 2014.)

- Turn right on First Street SE toward Nationals Park on the left. This LEED-certified ballpark opened in 2008 as the home of the Washington Nationals. The present-day Nats began in 2005 as a reincarnation of the Montreal Expos. The first Washington Nationals team was founded in 1859, says James C. Roberts in *The Nationals Past Times.* When the boys of summer aren't playing, the stadium hosts rock concerts, the Kennedy Center's "Opera in the Outfield," and other performances. Continue on First Street SE and then turn right on M Street SE. The Metro is on the left.

POINTS OF INTEREST

Navy Yard–Ballpark Metro New Jersey Avenue SE and M Street SE, 202-637-7000 (schedules) and 877-410-8529 (DC Metro Gift Store), wmata.com/rail/station_detail.cfm?station_id=84 and dcmetrostore.com

Site of Former CIA Building 213 M Street SE, from First Street SE to New Jersey Avenue SE

U.S. Department of Transportation 1200 New Jersey Ave. SE, 202-366-4000, dot.gov

Canal Park 202 M St. SE, 202-465-7012, canalparkdc.org

Five Guys 1100 New Jersey Ave. SE, 202-863-0570, fiveguys.com

United States Marine Band Seventh and K Streets SE, 202-433-4011 (concert line), marineband.marines.mil

Washington Navy Yard's National Museum of the U.S. Navy Sixth and M Streets SE, 202-433-4882, history.navy.mil/branches/org8-1.htm

Anacostia Riverwalk Trail Anacostia River, anacostiawaterfront.org

Trapeze School New York Fourth and Tingey Streets SE, 410-459-6839, washingtondc.trapezeschool.com

Boilermaker Shops 300 Tingey St. SE, capitolriverfront.org/go/the-yards-boiler-maker-shop

Nando's Peri-Peri 300 Tingey St. SE, 202-554-1920, nandosperiperi.com

Pacers Running 300 Tingey St. SE, runpacers.com

Bluejacket 300 Tingey St. SE, 202-524-4862, bluejacketdc.com

Osteria Morini at Yards Park 301 Water St. SE, 202-484-0660, osteriamorini.com and yardspark.org

Docks at Diamond Teague Park First Street SE and Potomac Avenue SE

Ballpark Boathouse 202-337-9642, boatingindc.com

Potomac Riverboat Company 703-684-0580, potomacriverboatco.com/baseball-boat.php

Nationals Park 1500 S. Capitol St. SE, 202-640-7369 (tours) and 202-675-6287 (tickets), washington.nationals.mlb.com/was/ballpark

route summary

1. Start at the Metro Navy Yard-Ballpark Metro at New Jersey Avenue SE and M Street SE.
2. Turn left to walk north on Second Street SE.
3. Turn right on L Street SE.
4. Turn right on Seventh Street SE.
5. Turn left on M Street SE.
6. Turn right on 11th Street SE.
7. Turn right at O Street SE into the Navy Yard gate.
8. After the museum, ask to be escorted to the pedestrian gate onto the Anacostia Riverwalk Trail by the display ship *USS Barry.*
9. Turn right onto the riverwalk and follow it until you see the trapeze school on the right.
10. Turn right on the sidewalk that runs into Fourth Street SE.
11. Turn left on Tingey Street SE.
12. Turn left on Third Street SE.
13. Turn right to return to the riverwalk.
14. Turn right on First Street SE.
15. Turn right on M Street for the Metro on the left.

CONNECTING THE WALKS

For Walk 23 (Capitol Hill), catch the DC Circulator Bus on M Street SE between First and Eighth Streets SE to Union Station. For Walk 26 (Eastern Market to Barracks Row), walk east on M Street SE and turn left to walk north on Eighth Street SE.

Trapeze school thrills adventurers.

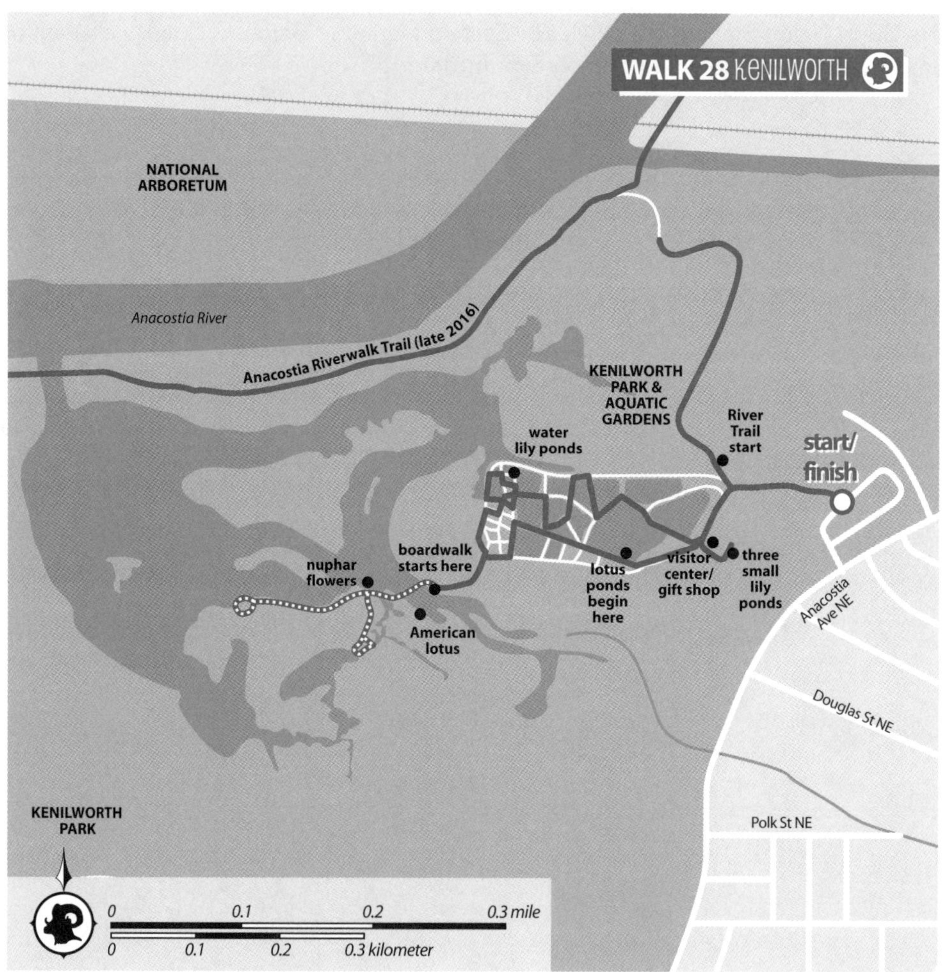
WALK 28 KENILWORTH
NATIONAL ARBORETUM
Anacostia River
Anacostia Riverwalk Trail (late 2016)
KENILWORTH PARK & AQUATIC GARDENS
River Trail start
start/ finish
water lily ponds
boardwalk starts here
nuphar flowers
American lotus
lotus ponds begin here
visitor center/ gift shop
three small lily ponds
Anacostia Ave NE
Douglas St NE
Polk St NE
KENILWORTH PARK
0 0.1 0.2 0.3 mile
0 0.1 0.2 0.3 kilometer

28 Kenilworth: Jaw-Dropping Giant Pink Lotuses

BOUNDARIES: Anacostia Avenue NE at Ponds Street NE
DISTANCE: 1–3 miles (roughly 1 mile for the closest lilies and lotuses)
DIFFICULTY: Moderate due to sometimes muddy dirt and grass trails
PARKING: Free parking
PUBLIC TRANSIT: Car preferred. Metro's Deanwood station (Orange Line) is about a half mile away. A Capital Bikeshare station is one block from the Metro at the Deanwood Recreation Center.

Washington's world-famous cherry blossoms seem downright drab next to the lesser-known, big and brazen lotus flowers at Kenilworth Park & Aquatic Gardens. Each summer these pink and white beauties—with flowers up to a whopping 10 inches in diameter—light up 2 to 3 acres of ponds. The flowers' stalks can reach 6 feet tall, and their umbrella-like leaves can stretch more than 2 feet wide. "Kenilworth is amazing. I've never seen anything like that in the United States," said Dr. James "Jim" Harbage of the renowned Longwood Gardens. Kenilworth is the largest public lotus garden in the nation, experts say. (Commercial grower Lilypons in Adamstown, Maryland, which welcomes the public, grows about 3 acres of lotuses, but Kenilworth's smaller scale and brighter colors create more intimate garden rooms.) Historically known for its water lilies, these days Kenilworth's jaw-dropping lotuses grab center stage. This former commercial aquatic garden was acquired by the federal government in 1938. As the only national park established to propagate and display water plants, Kenilworth grows more than 35 varieties of tropical and hardy water lilies and several varieties of lotuses. They thrive in 45 ponds and several display pools in the 8.5-acre historic aquatic garden ensconced in a 75-acre wetland. Lotuses have long been revered as a sacred symbol by Asian and Egyptian cultures. America's native lotuses, which have dwindled, currently lack clout in our country. Some of these native yellow lotuses and many other spring, summer, and fall wildflowers also grace the garden's formal ponds and wild habitats. Lotuses typically peak in early to mid-July, depending on the weather. Morning is the best time to visit. The lotuses open widest then, unfurling their flamboyant petals to reveal a green or yellow seedpod encircled with tiny nubs. Other reasons for going early are to catch a whiff of the flowers' subtle scent and to escape the steamiest heat. As with Washington's treasured cherry blossoms, photographs are encouraged, but picking or taking flowers, pods, or other property is a federal crime.

- Begin at the visitor center, just down a gravel trail from the parking lot. Originally the garden store, this small building showcases the garden's history, and it has a gift shop. Civil War veteran and Treasury Department employee Walter B. Shaw bought the land in 1879 and began running his commercial water lily garden full time in 1902. Shaw and his daughter, Helen Shaw Fowler, developed new varieties of water lilies at Shaw Gardens, as it was then known. She later expanded the business. By the 1920s and '30s, it was so popular as a commercial enterprise and a weekend destination that President Woodrow Wilson, President Calvin Coolidge, and their wives were frequent visitors, the park's history says. Copies of pioneer businesswoman Fowler's lotus paintings adorn several walls. The gift shop sells children's books, toy beavers, lotus postcards, and more. The center is busiest in mid-July when the park hosts its popular Lotus & Water Lily Festival.

- Exit the visitor center and turn left twice to reach the three rectangular ponds behind the building. The closest pond grows water lilies and soft-pink ancient lotuses. These lotuses, which typically bloom about two weeks before the others, were grown from centuries-old seeds unearthed in northern China. Hardy water lilies typically grow on the pond to the right. They start blooming in the spring when native wildflowers, such as yellow trout lilies, start poking through the ground nearby. The pond to the left usually hosts tropical water lilies and sometimes the world's largest water lily, the Victoria from the Amazon. At Kenilworth, its lily pad can stretch up to 7 feet wide. The Victoria blooms at night. It starts as a white flower and fades to pink by the time it closes in the morning, Kenilworth's gardener says. On cloudy days, early visitors can sometimes glimpse the bloom and smell its pineapplelike fragrance. The next day, the flower turns deep pink and drops off. New blooms appear throughout the summer.

- Return to the front of the visitor center. Facing away from it, turn left on the main path and then turn right onto the second-to-last trail. It runs between a small lotus pond on the left and a big lotus pond on the right. From this vantage point during the mid-July lotus peak, a sea of colossal pink-tinged flowers towers over the ponds and seems to glow in the sunlight. The spectacle lures painters, photographers, and other flower junkies to this out-of-the-way garden. The three biggest lotus ponds are planted with pink Egyptian lotuses, which are also known as Indian lotuses. One pond displays Empress lotuses, a white flower with pink tips. Another holds double-blooming pink lotuses. Two ponds grow deep-pink lotuses, the stars of the garden. Initial bloom

America's Own Lotuses

Lotuses don't just grow in the Far East. American lotuses—the biggest wildflowers in the nation—are scattered across at least 32 states in the eastern half of the country and in D.C. Once a valuable food for American Indians, now these native aquatic flowers are vilified in some states as invasive, even while they're being investigated as a vegetable, a medicine, and a pollution fighter. No one seems to dispute their beauty. American lotuses resemble their Asian counterparts, but they're smaller and their huge petals are yellow to yellowish-white. They grow about 3 feet tall, their flowers reach 10 inches wide, and their round leaves can stretch 2 feet in diameter. While many folks have never even seen them, an American lotus was touted as the country's largest flower on a 39-cent stamp in 2006. The multipetaled flower was part of the "America: Land of Superlatives" stamps, which featured 40 natural and man-made wonders. The stamp's description says it's "considered sacred by several American cultures and even said to have mystic powers." These succulent lotuses are known by multiple monikers, including their scientific name, *Nelumbo lutea,* and their common name, water chinquapin. Their starchy tubers can be cooked like potatoes, and their seeds can be roasted like nuts.

times for the waxy flowers largely depend on the water temperature. Air temperature and other weather conditions also affect them. Edging some of the ponds are native crimson-eyed mallow and swamp mallow, cousins of tropical hibiscus flowers. Their showy red or white flowers grow nearly as large as lotuses, but they aren't as tall.

- **Turn left when the trail passes the last lotus pond on the left (and before it runs straight into a small lily pond). Walk a few feet to a T-intersection and turn right. Then turn left onto the boardwalk. About 100 feet from the start where the guardrail begins, American lotuses grow across the small inlet to the left. The garden planted a couple of the yellow flowers here around 2009. Now there are roughly 50 plants, which peak around mid-August. A bit farther up the boardwalk on the right are ancient nuphar plants. Experts say this bright, compact yellow flower is probably the grandma of today's water lilies and lotuses. This is a good spot to watch birds, such** as green herons standing stick-still as they fish for dinner. Winter is also prime bird-watching time, when the park is ghostly quiet.

- At the end of the boardwalk, reverse direction to return to the ponds. Meander along any of the grassy walkways, which double as dikes, past lotus and water lily ponds, eventually steering back to the visitor center. Along the way, the ponds seem painted with hot-pink and white water lilies with rows of petals and perky yellow centers. Other plants pop out for their colorful blossoms or for the rainbow of insects and birds they attract. The buttonbush's white flower balls lure large yellow-and-black Eastern tiger swallowtail butterflies. Damselflies and dragonflies also flit nearby. These orange, blue, yellow, or green insects are photogenic with their lacy wings and bulging eyes. Crayon-yellow prothonotary warblers and bathed-in-blue indigo buntings also hang out in the garden.

- Back at the visitor center, while facing the building, turn left onto the main path; then turn left onto the farthest path, and turn right onto Kenilworth's own River Trail. Though most of it is closed due to construction of D.C.'s Anacostia Riverwalk Trail at the river's edge, here's a look at some of its goodies for when it reopens in late 2016. The dirt trail rambles roughly 0.7 mile past a marsh and a thicket of vines and trees to the river. As part of a community service event with former President Clinton in 2009, President Obama and First Lady Michelle Obama planted two trees along it. One survived. This is another spot to spy some of the park's five or more kinds of frogs, two kinds of toads, three kinds of snakes, five kinds of turtles, and several kinds of salamanders. On wet summer days, tiny frogs seem to frolic in the puddles on the path. In early spring, hundreds of pinky-toe-size spring peeper frogs begin their shrill chorus. At the end of the trail is the Anacostia River, home to otters, mink, and beavers. Even though the river is polluted, Kenilworth's marsh—one of the last tidal marshes on the river—is crucial as a wildlife habitat and for flood control. This area was once home to the Nacotchtank, an Algonquian-speaking American Indian tribe with male and female chiefs.

- At the end of the trail, turn around and return to the main path. Turn left there and then make the second left for the path to the parking lot.

POINTS OF INTEREST

Kenilworth Park & Aquatic Gardens 1550 Anacostia Ave. NE, 202-426-6905, nps.gov/keaq/index.htm

ROUTE SUMMARY

1. **Start at the parking lot.**
2. **Follow the gravel trail to the visitor center on the left.**
3. **Exit the visitor center and turn left twice for the three ponds behind the center.**
4. **Reverse direction and return to the front of the visitor center.**
5. **Facing away from the center, turn left onto the main path.**
6. **Turn right onto the second-to-last path, which runs between a small lotus pond on the left and a large lotus pond on the right.**
7. **When the trail passes the last lotus pond on the left (and before it runs straight into a small lily pond), turn left.**
8. **Walk a few feet to a T-intersection and turn right.**
9. **Turn left onto the boardwalk.**
10. **At the end of the boardwalk, reverse direction and return to the ponds.**
11. **Meander along the grassy paths back to the visitor center.**
12. **While facing the visitor center, turn left onto the main path.**
13. **Turn left onto the farthest path.**
14. **Turn right onto the dirt River Trail.**
15. **At the end of the River Trail (at the Anacostia River), turn around and return to the main path.**
16. **Turn left on the path.**
17. **Make the second left onto the gravel path toward the parking lot.**

Giant lotuses thrive at Kenilworth.

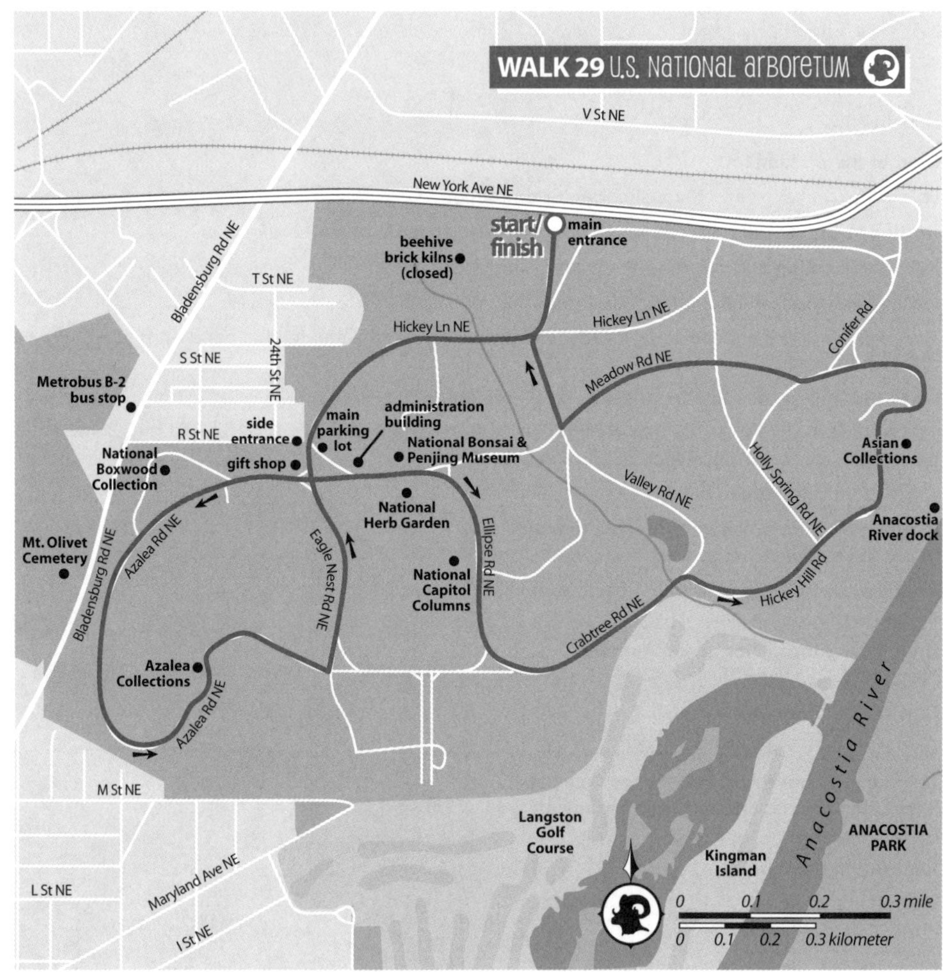
WALK 29 U.S. National Arboretum
V St NE
New York Ave NE
start/finish
main entrance
beehive brick kilns (closed)
Bladensburg Rd NE
T St NE
Hickey Ln NE
Hickey Ln NE
Conifer Rd
S St NE
24th St NE
Meadow Rd NE
Metrobus B-2 bus stop
main parking lot
administration building
side entrance
R St NE
National Bonsai & Penjing Museum
National Boxwood Collection
gift shop
Holly Spring Rd NE
Asian Collections
Valley Rd NE
National Herb Garden
Anacostia River dock
Azalea Rd NE
Eagle Nest Rd NE
Ellipse Rd NE
Mt. Olivet Cemetery
Hickey Hill Rd
National Capitol Columns
Bladensburg Rd NE
Crabtree Rd NE
Azalea Collections
Azalea Rd NE
Anacostia River
M St NE
Langston Golf Course
ANACOSTIA PARK
Kingman Island
L St NE
Maryland Ave NE
I St NE
0 0.1 0.2 0.3 mile
0 0.1 0.2 0.3 kilometer

29 U.S. National Arboretum: Flower Fireworks and Capitol Columns

BOUNDARIES: New York Avenue NE, just west of South Dakota Avenue NE, the Anacostia River, and Bladensburg Road NE
DISTANCE: 1–4 miles (along 9.5 miles of roads)
DIFFICULTY: Easy for short walk, moderate to strenuous to cover all 4 hilly miles
PARKING: Free parking
TRANSIT: Metrobus B2 stops on Bladensburg Road NE near the R Street NE side entrance.

Some of the sweetest-smelling flowers on the planet bloom at the U.S. National Arboretum—even in the winter. The arboretum is America's research arm for all kinds of dreamy plants, including glowing azaleas, delicate bonsai trees, and a snow-hardy palm. If that's not enough to draw a half million annual visitors to this otherwise dingy edge of the District, there's another lure: a grassy knoll studded with real U.S. Capitol Columns. There are 9.5 miles of walkers-welcome roads to explore and more pedestrian-only paths in the gardens themselves. To sample three of the hot spots (the columns, the National Herb Garden, and the National Bonsai & Penjing Museum), it's about a 1-mile round-trip loop from the main parking lot. With a mix of walking and driving (or cycling), visitors can hit every single garden, and not just the special ones highlighted in this 4-mile loop.

- **Start at the main entrance, 3501 New York Avenue NE. On the right, enclosed by a fence, are abandoned (and strictly off-limits) beehive brick kilns. They're the only survivors from more than 100 brickyards that operated in D.C. in the early 20th century. Today most of the region's brick hails from Virginia, Ohio, Pennsylvania, and the Carolinas, according to industry experts.**

- **Make the first right onto Hickey Lane. At Azalea Road, the main parking lot, the administration building, and the seasonal tram tour stop are on the left. On the right is a gift shop with free maps. Behind the shop is a hideaway patio with picnic tables and winter-blooming mahonia plants. These hollylike evergreens with spikes of tiny yellow flowers help nourish the somewhat rare visits by western rufous hummingbirds that overwinter around D.C. instead of migrating to Mexico. To find where these**

Walking Groups: Walk This Way

Washingtonians walk. A lot. And sometimes they do it in groups. Everyone can tag along on the following nonprofit groups' free or low-cost treks in D.C. and beyond. Although most of their year-round hikes follow dirt trails, occasionally they host urban treks on city sidewalks and paved paths. Their walks *inside* Washington, D.C., are typically free. Although it's not required, donations and memberships are welcome. (Check the clubs' websites to see how they rate hike difficulty and for their calendars.) Three groups also lead nature walks. Plus, the U.S. National Arboretum hosts a $22 full-moon hike in its own 446-acre garden. Those popular walks fill up in a D.C. minute. They might be even more popular in a few years. The Arboretum plans to build "the finest classical Chinese garden in North America" in collaboration with the Chinese government. The designs are complete; all they need is money.

GENERAL HIKES

Appalachian Mountain Club **amc-dc.org**

Capital Hiking Club **capitalhikingclub.org**

Center Hiking Club **centerhikingclub.org**

D.C. Metropolitan Hikers Meetup
meetup.com/hiking-162

MidAtlantic Hiking Group Meetup
meetup.com/Mid-Atlantic-Hiking-Group

Northern Virginia Hiking Club
meetup.com/NVHC-Hiking

Potomac Appalachian Trail Club **patc.net**

Sierra Club **sierrapotomac.org**

Wanderbirds **wanderbirds.org**

Washington DC Area Volksmarching Club
mdvolks.org/wdcavc/index.htm

NATURE HIKES

Audubon Naturalist Society
audubonnaturalist.org

Audubon Society of the District of Columbia
audubondc.org

U.S. National Arboretum **usna.usda.gov**

Washington, D.C., Chapter of the Maryland Native Plant Society
mdflora.org/chapters/washingtondc/dcchapter.html

and other plants grow in the garden, just tap ABE, the new Arboretum Botanical Explorer: usna.usda.gov/abe.

- Turn right on Azalea Road. Before it curves left, the musky scent from the boxwood gardens on the right often drifts over the road. Around the curve and across the street on the right is the stately Mt. Olivet Cemetery, where White House architect James Hoban and Lincoln assassination conspirator Mary Surratt are buried. Beyond that is a panoramic view downhill toward the Capitol.

- Back in the Arboretum, the hilly garden around the corner on the left comes alive like fireworks each April with about 10,000 pink, red, and purple Glenn Dale hybrid azaleas. The arboretum, which is part of the USDA's Agricultural Research Service, developed them in the 1940s to create more colorful, cold-hardy plants with bigger flowers. In 2010, the Arboretum planned to rip out thousands of these beloved plants, but protestors and a $1 million donation saved most of them. Arboretum scientists have developed at least 678 plants since Congress established it nine decades ago. Many flourish throughout the country.

- After the azaleas, make the first left onto Eagle Nest Road. Make the first right onto Meadow Road for The National Bonsai & Penjing Museum on the left and the National Herb Garden on the right.

- Slow down for the miniature masterworks at the bonsai museum. Amble through the Japanese, Chinese, and North American pavilions and the courtyard gardens to ponder the reverence for nature that produced such visual delights as a four-century-old white pine tree, big pink azalea flowers on pint-size plants, teensy orange maple leaves, and the sculptural beauty of leaf-bare trees. The indoor tropical conservatory features plants that the dinosaurs probably feasted on: palmlike cycads.

- Across the street is the country's largest herb garden. The formal elliptical garden features hundreds of herbs ranging from tapioca to teasel. They grow in individual plots around the edges of the ellipse, which is ringed by flowering crape myrtles and other trees. There's also a heritage rose garden, a knot garden, and two trellised garden rooms with a soothing view of a meadow and the National Capitol Columns.

- Either follow the sidewalk across the meadow to the columns or continue on Meadow Road and turn right on Ellipse Road. These 22 sandstone columns supported the East Portico of the U.S. Capitol from 1828 to 1958. When the Capitol was renovated, stronger marble columns replaced them. In the 1980s, preservationist Ethel Garrett helped rescue the roughly 34-foot-high columns from storage. These hand-carved Corinthian columns were dedicated in 1990.

- Continue on Ellipse Road, staying left at the fork to turn left on Crabtree Road. Make the first right onto Hickey Hill Road for the Asian Collections uphill on the right. Visitors don't have to wander far off-road to enjoy the splendor, but trekking down the sometimes steep gravel walkways pays off. The China Valley Trail leads to a dock on the Anacostia River. And the Asian gardens light up like a Monet masterpiece for much of the year. Colorful, cold-hardy camellias developed by the Arboretum bloom in midfall. Flowering witch hazels and Japanese apricot trees awaken in late winter, as do überfragrant wintersweet and sweetbox flowers. By spring, the rare Chinese dove tree and the flowering cherries are ablaze. During the hot and hazy months, there's a perennial parade of colors, from lime and avocado green to red berries and tangerine-colored lilies. And even though it can survive snow, the needle palm tree that has grown there since 1968 seems quite content when it's steamy hot.

- After the Asian Collections, continue on Hickey Hill Road and stay right at the fork, where it becomes Meadow Road. Take the second right onto Valley Road and follow it to the exit.

POINTS OF INTEREST

U.S. National Arboretum 3501 New York Ave. NE, 202-245-2726, usna.usda.gov

route summary

1. Start at the entrance at 3501 New York Avenue NE.
2. Make the first right onto Hickey Lane.
3. Turn right on Azalea Road.
4. Make the first left onto Eagle Nest Road.
5. Make the first right onto Meadow Road.
6. Make the first right onto Ellipse Road.
7. Stay left at the fork to turn left onto Crabtree Road.
8. Make the first right onto Hickey Hill Road.
9. After the Asian Collections, continue on Hickey Hill Road and stay right at the fork, where it becomes Meadow Road.
10. Take the second right onto Valley Road and follow it to the exit.

connecting the walks

For Walk 25 (H Street NE), ride Metrobus B-2 from R Street NE and Bladensburg Road NE to H Street NE and Florida Avenue NE.

Capitol columns adorn the U.S. National Arboretum.

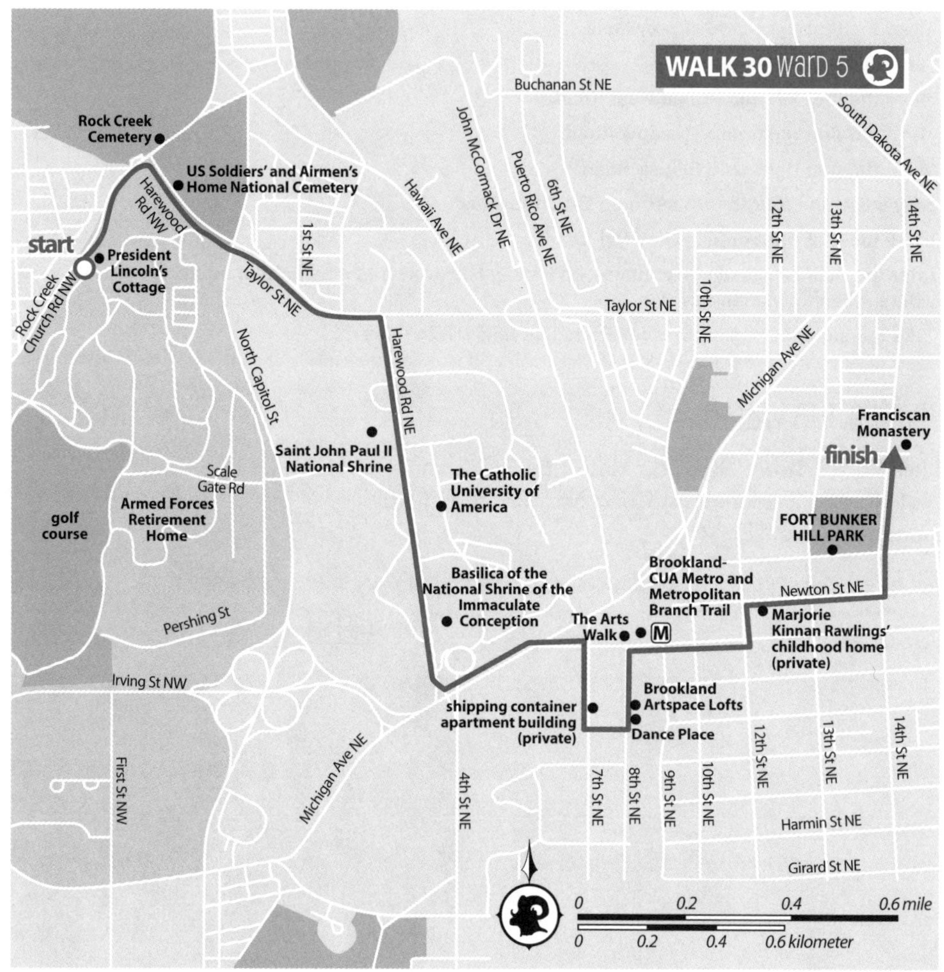

WALK 30 Ward 5
Buchanan St NE
South Dakota Ave NE
Rock Creek Cemetery
US Soldiers' and Airmen's Home National Cemetery
Harewood Rd NW
Hawaii Ave NE
John McCormack Dr NE
Puerto Rico Ave NE
6th St NE
12th St NE
13th St NE
14th St NE
start
President Lincoln's Cottage
Rock Creek Church Rd NW
1st St NE
Taylor St NE
10th St NE
Michigan Ave NE
North Capitol St
Harewood Rd NE
Saint John Paul II National Shrine
Franciscan Monastery
finish
Scale Gate Rd
The Catholic University of America
golf course
Armed Forces Retirement Home
FORT BUNKER HILL PARK
Brookland-CUA Metro and Metropolitan Branch Trail
Basilica of the National Shrine of the Immaculate Conception
Newton St NE
Pershing St
The Arts Walk
M
Marjorie Kinnan Rawlings' childhood home (private)
Irving St NW
Brookland Artspace Lofts
shipping container apartment building (private)
Dance Place
First St NW
4th St NE
7th St NE
8th St NE
9th St NE
Harmin St NE
Girard St NE
0 0.2 0.4 0.6 mile
0 0.2 0.4 0.6 kilometer

30 Ward 5: Lincoln's Cottage to Showy Shrines

BOUNDARIES: **Harewood Road NW, 14th Street NE, Kearney Street NE, and Rock Creek Church Road NW**

DISTANCE: **2.8 miles**

DIFFICULTY: **Moderate, slightly hilly**

PARKING: **Free 2-hour street parking at start and end; free on-site parking while visiting some attractions; 25 short-term metered spaces at the Brookland-CUA Metro station**

PUBLIC TRANSIT: **From the Brookland-CUA Metro station, Metrobus H8 runs to Lincoln's Cottage and Metrobus H6 runs to the Franciscan Monastery.**

It may be a scant 4 miles from the White House, but this largely verdant swathe of D.C. is spiritually distant from the hustle of downtown. It's a sanctuary. President Lincoln sought solace in this then-rural area (now known as the city's Ward 5 political district) during the bloodiest of all U.S. wars. Friars and other Catholics currently work and pray in some of the region's most exquisite religious shrines and gardens. Scholars find an oasis for education on The Catholic University's 180-acre campus. Soldiers, politicians, authors, and even a beloved political talk-show host found permanent peace in its historic cemeteries. Increasingly, its neighborhoods are providing livable respites for millennials and other transplants flooding the city. Yet this haven quickly connects to the rest of the city by subway and even a hiker-biker trail. President Lincoln typically commuted to the White House riding his gray horse or by horse-drawn carriage, Lincoln researchers say. His trot down the "Seventh Street Turnpike" (today's Georgia Avenue NW) and other roads took roughly 30 minutes, about the same time it takes by car in today's traffic.

- **Start at Lincoln's Cottage at Upshur Street NW and Rock Creek Church Road NW. Lincoln worked on his slave-freeing Emancipation Proclamation at this Carpenter Gothic–style home while he and his family dwelled there each summer. (He still commuted to the White House daily.) This 34-room "cottage" sits at the edge of the sprawling and otherwise off-limits parklike campus of the Armed Forces Retirement Home. Opened to the public in 2008, this cream-colored, stucco home with brown trim used to be federal property. Now the national monument is owned by the non-profit National Trust for Historic Preservation. Banker George W. Riggs built it in 1843** as his summer home. After exiting the main gate, turn right on Rock Creek Church Road NW.

- Turn left into Rock Creek Cemetery, D.C.'s oldest operating cemetery. The first church burial occurred in 1719, and the cemetery became public in 1840. It's the resting place for some of the city's "royalty," such as longtime *Meet the Press* TV show host Tim Russert, who was interred in the gardenlike burial ground in 2008. White House butler Eugene Allen, made famous in the 2013 movie *The Butler,* was buried beneath an oversize tombstone with a drawing of the White House in 2010. Other notables include Supreme Court Chief Justice Harlan Fiske Stone and Hope Diamond owner Evalyn Walsh McLean. One of the most famous graves belongs to author Henry Adams's wife, Marian "Clover" Hooper. Adams commissioned famous sculptor Augustus Saint-Gaudens to create a bronze statue of a shrouded, seated figure to honor his photographer wife after she killed herself by swallowing photo-developing chemicals. It's considered a masterpiece. Stop by the office for a hand-lettered map of the graveyard.

- Leaving behind the chiseled, gray, granite gravestones and extravagant mausoleums, cross Rock Creek Church Road NW to reach Harewood Road NW. On the left is the U.S. Soldiers' and Airmen's Home National Cemetery, with rows of about 14,000 stark white, narrow grave markers. President Lincoln personally watched many graves being dug there during the Civil War from his cottage.

- Follow Harewood Road to the Saint John Paul II National Shrine on the right. This Catholic think tank became a national shrine to the recently canonized pope in 2014. Architect Leo A. Daly designed the modern building with its small museum in 2000. Daly studied architecture across the street at The Catholic University of America (CUA).

- CUA graduated some more famous alumni, including actors Susan Sarandon and Jon Voight (Angelina Jolie's dad), former NBC anchor Brian Williams, and Costco co-founder Robert Graves, who died in 2014. Founded in 1887 by the U.S. Catholic bishops, CUA is the national university of the Catholic Church in the United States.

- Anchoring the southwest corner of CUA's private campus is the Basilica of the National Shrine of the Immaculate Conception, one of the largest churches in the world. This Romanesque-Byzantine–style shrine houses the "world's largest collection of contemporary ecclesiastical art," the church says. "Mary's Shrine," as it's sometimes called, was built from 1920 to 1924 to honor the Virgin Mary. With roughly 70 chapels and oratories, this palatial landmark was constructed of stone, brick, and tile. Many of its grandiose ceilings and walls sparkle with gold and brightly colored religious mosaics. When the organist plays, visitors can even feel the powerful music pulsating through the pews.

- With the basilica to the rear, turn left on Michigan Avenue NE along the edge of CUA's campus. Turn right onto Monroe Street NE past the first, extensive new development in the area in decades, with luxury apartments, art studios, a Busboys and Poets restaurant, and a 14,000-square-foot Barnes & Noble college bookstore.

- Turn right on Seventh Street NE for the (private) royal blue and gray steel-and-glass building on the left at 3307 Seventh Street NE. Travis Price Architects used 18 metal shipping containers to create the unusual four-unit apartment building with 24 bedrooms in 2014.

- Turn left on Kearny Street NE. When it dead-ends at Eighth Street NE, Dance Place and Brookland Artspace Lofts are directly across the still somewhat gritty street edging the railroad tracks. Dance Place, with its eye-catching (and musical) pink, blue, red, and green glass tower, offers dance classes and stages dance performances. Next door, the 41 apartments at the colorful Brookland Artspace Lofts opened in 2011 as affordable housing and studio space for artists.

- Turn left on Eighth Street and then right on Monroe Street NE. On the left is The Arts Walk, a showplace for local artists, next to the Brookland-CUA Metro and the Metropolitan Branch Trail, which connects D.C.'s Union Station to the Silver Spring, Maryland, Metro.

Civil War cemetery

- Turn left on 12th Street NE. After passing some mom-and-pop-type restaurants and stores, turn right on tree-lined Newton Street NE. On the right at 1221 Newton Street NE is the (private) red-trimmed Victorian house with a wraparound porch where author Marjorie Kinnan Rawlings lived. Rawlings grew up there with her mom, Ida, and her dad, Arthur Kinnan, an attorney for the U.S. Patent Office. She won a Pulitzer Prize for her 1938 classic *The Yearling.* The native Washingtonian was equally well known for *Cross Creek,* a nonfiction story of her life in the north Florida backwoods.

- Turn left on 14th Street NE. The overgrown Fort Bunker Hill Park on the left at Otis Street NE was built in 1861 as one of the circle forts protecting D.C. during the Civil War. Although NPS says little evidence remains of that seven-sided earthen fort, explorers can still find evidence of an amphitheater built in the 1930s by the Civilian Conservation Corps.

- Continue on 14th Street NE for the Franciscan Monastery of the Holy Land in America on the right. It's a "place like no other for architecture and garden lovers," says the D.C.-based American Society of Landscape Architects. Religious pilgrims are drawn to the replicas of famous Holy Land shrines, such as the newly reopened Grotto of Gethsemane and the Hagia Sofia–inspired church. Everyone seems to drool over the intricate columns and Roman arches of the cloister walk, its formal and sunken gardens, and more spring and summer flowers than the Garden of Eden. Out of sight are the friars' quarters behind the church, along with beehives and a greenhouse. Also hidden is a "hermitage," a rentable "place of quiet retreat" at this 40-acre hilltop hideaway for one person to stay and experience solitude and peace.

POINTS OF INTEREST

President Lincoln's Cottage Upshur Street NW and Rock Creek Church Road NW, 202-829-0436, lincolncottage.org

Rock Creek Cemetery Rock Creek Church Road NW and Webster Street NW, 202-726-2080, rockcreekparish.org/cemetery

US Soldiers' and Airmen's Home National Cemetery 21 Harewood Rd. NW, 877-907-8585, nps.gov

Saint John Paul II National Shrine 3900 Harewood Rd. NE, 202-635-5400, jp2shrine.org/jp/en/about/index.html

The Catholic University of America 620 Michigan Ave. NE, 202-319-5000, cua.edu

Basilica of the National Shrine of the Immaculate Conception 400 Michigan Ave. NE, 202-526-8300, nationalshrine.com

(Private) shipping container apartment building 3307 Seventh St. NE

Dance Place 3225 Eighth St. NE, 202-269-1600, danceplace.org

Brookland Artspace Lofts 3305 Eighth St. NE, 301-927-3586, artspace.org/our-places/brookland-artspace-lofts

Brookland-CUA Metro and Metropolitan Branch Trail 801 Michigan Ave. NE, 202-637-7000, wmata.com/rail/station_detail.cfm?station_id=27 and metbranchtrail.com

(Private) childhood home of Marjorie Kinnan Rawlings 1221 Newton St. NE, brooklandbridge.com/2118/brookland-history-lives-marjorie-kinnan-rawlings-house

Fort Bunker Hill Park 14th Street NE and Perry Street NE, 202-895-6070, nps.gov/cwdw/historyculture/fort-bunker-hill.htm

Franciscan Monastery of the Holy Land in America 1400 Quincy St. NE, 202-526-6800, myfranciscan.org

route summary

1. Start at President Lincoln's Cottage inside the Armed Forces Retirement Home on Rock Creek Church Road NW at Upshur Street NW.
2. Turn right on Rock Creek Church Road NW.
3. Turn right on Harewood Road NW (which briefly becomes Fort Drive NE and Taylor Street NE).
4. Turn left on Michigan Avenue NE.
5. Turn right onto Seventh Street NE.
6. Turn left on Kearny Street NE.
7. Turn left on Eighth Street NE.
8. Turn right on Monroe Street NE.
9. Turn left on 12th Street NE.
10. Turn right on Newton Street NE.
11. Turn left on 14th Street NE.

Appendix 1: Walks by Theme

Eating, Drinking, and Nightlife

Friendship Heights (Walk 1)
Forest Hills to Tenleytown (Walk 2)
National Zoo to National Cathedral (Walk 3)
Georgetown (Walks 5, 6, and 7)
Adams Morgan (Walk 9)
U Street (Walk 10)
Dupont Circle (Walk 12)
Potomac River Panorama and Watergates (Walk 13)
White House (Walk 15)
Downtown: News Junkies (Walks 16 and 18)
Penn Quarter–Chinatown (Walk 17)
Southwest Waterfront (Walk 21)
Capitol Hill (Walk 23)
NoMa and Union Market (Walk 24)
H Street NE (Walk 25)
Eastern Market to Barracks Row (Walk 26)
Navy Yard (Walk 27)

Embassies and Ambassadors' Residences

Forest Hills to Tenleytown (Walk 2)
National Zoo to National Cathedral (Walk 3)
Foxhall and Beyond (Walk 4)
Embassy Row (Walk 8)
16th Street NW (Walk 11)
Dupont Circle (Walk 12)
Potomac River Panorama and Watergates (Walk 13)
Downtown: News Junkies East (Walk 18)

Museums, Monuments, and Memorials

Friendship Heights (Walk 1)
Foxhall and Beyond (Walk 4)
Embassy Row (Walk 8)
U Street (Walk 10)
Dupont Circle (Walk 12)
National Mall West (Walk 14)
White House (Walk 15)
Downtown: News Junkies (Walks 16 and 18)
Penn Quarter–Chinatown (Walk 17)
Tidal Basin Cherries (Walk 19)
Columbia Island (Walk 20)
Southwest Waterfront (Walk 21)
National Mall East (Walk 22)
Capitol Hill (Walk 23)
Ward 5 (Walk 30)

Parks, Gardens, and Nature

Friendship Heights (Walk 1)
Forest Hills to Tenleytown (Walk 2)
National Zoo to National Cathedral (Walk 3)

Georgetown (Walks 5, 6, and 7)
Embassy Row (Walk 8)
Adams Morgan (Walk 9)
16th Street NW (Walk 11)
Potomac River Panorama and Watergates (Walk 13)
National Mall West (Walk 14)
Downtown: News Junkies (Walks 16 and 18)
Tidal Basin Cherries (Walk 19)
Columbia Island (Walk 20)
Southwest Waterfront (Walk 21)
National Mall East (Walk 22)
Capitol Hill (Walk 23)
Navy Yard (Walk 27)
Kenilworth (Walk 28)
U.S. National Arboretum (Walk 29)
Ward 5 (Walk 30)

SCIENCE

Forest Hills to Tenleytown (Walk 2)
National Zoo to National Cathedral (Walk 3)
Foxhall and Beyond (Walk 4)
Georgetown (Walks 5, 6, and 7)
Embassy Row (Walk 8)
Adams Morgan (Walk 9)
16th Street NW (Walk 11)
National Mall West (Walk 14)
Penn Quarter–Chinatown (Walk 17)
National Mall East (Walk 22)
Capitol Hill (Walk 23)
U.S. National Arboretum (Walk 29)

SHOPPING

Friendship Heights (Walk 1)
Georgetown (Walks 5, 6, and 7)
Adams Morgan (Walk 9)
U Street (Walk 10)
Dupont Circle (Walk 12)
Downtown: News Junkies (Walks 16 and 18)
Penn Quarter–Chinatown (Walk 17)
National Mall East (Walk 22)
NoMa and Union Market (Walk 24)
Eastern Market to Barracks Row (Walk 26)

SPIES

Friendship Heights (Walk 1)
Forest Hills to Tenleytown (Walk 2)
Georgetown (Walks 5, 6, and 7)
Embassy Row (Walk 8)
National Mall West (Walk 14)
Penn Quarter–Chinatown (Walk 17)
Navy Yard (Walk 27)

Appendix 2: POINTS OF INTEREST

ASSOCIATIONS AND OTHER GROUPS

American Institute of Architects and the Octagon 1735 New York Ave. NW, 800-AIA-3837, aia.org (Walk 15)

American Red Cross headquarters 430 17th St. NW, tours@redcross.org (Walk 15)

District Architecture Center (American Institute of Architects, D.C. chapter) 421 Seventh St. NW, 202-347-9403, aiadac.com (Walk 17)

IBM's birthplace (Canal Square Building) 1054 31st St. NW, www-03.ibm.com/ibm/history/exhibits/vintage/vintage_4506VV2027.html (Walk 7)

Motion Picture Association of America 1600 I St. NW, 202-293-1966, mpaa.org (Walk 15)

National Society of the Daughters of the American Revolution 1776 D St. NW, 202-628-1776, dar.org (Walk 14)

United States Institute of Peace 2301 Constitution Ave. NW, 202-457-1700, usip.org (Walk 14)

Volta Laboratory and Bureau (now the Alexander Graham Bell Association for the Deaf and Hard of Hearing) 1537 35th St. NW, 202-337-5220, listeningandspokenlanguage.org (Walk 5)

CEMETERIES

Oak Hill Cemetery 3001 R St. NW, 202-337-2835, nps.gov/nr/travel/wash/dc9.htm (Walk 5)

Rock Creek Cemetery Rock Creek Church Road NW and Webster Street NW, 202-726-2080, rockcreekparish.org/cemetery (Walk 30)

U.S. Soldiers' and Airmen's Home National Cemetery 21 Harewood Road NW, 877-907-8585, nps.gov (Walk 30)

CLUBS

City Tavern Club 3206 M St. NW, 202-337-8770, citytavernclubdc.org (Walk 6)

The Congressional Club 2001 New Hampshire Ave. NW, 202-332-1155, thecongressionalclub.com (Walk 11)

Cosmos Club 2121 Massachusetts Ave. NW, 202-387-7783, cosmosclub.org (Walk 8)

International Order of the Eastern Star headquarters 1618 New Hampshire Ave. NW, 202-667-4737, oesdistrictofcolumbia.org (Walk 12)

Metropolitan Club 1700 H St. NW, 202-835-2500, metroclub.com (Walk 15)

Scottish Rite of Freemasonry, Supreme Council 33°, Southern Jurisdiction headquarters 1733 16th St. NW, 202-232-3579, scottishrite.org (Walk 11)

Scottish Rite of Freemasonry, District of Columbia chapter 2800 16th St. NW, 202-232-8155, dcsr.org (Walk 11)

Sulgrave Club 1801 Massachusetts Ave. NW, 202-462-5800, sulgraveclub.org (Walk 12)

Eating, Drinking, and Nightlife

Banana Café & Piano Bar 500 Eighth St. SE, 202-543-5906, bananacafedc.com (Walk 26)

Ben's Chili Bowl 1213 U St. NW, 202-667-0909, benschilibowl.com (Walk 10)

Black Cat 1811 14th St. NW, 202-667-4490, blackcatdc.com (Walk 10)

Bluejacket 300 Tingey St. SE, 202-524-4862, bluejacketdc.com (Walk 27)

Blues Alley 1073 Wisconsin Ave. NW, 202-337-4141, bluesalley.com (Walk 6)

Bohemian Caverns 2001 11th St. NW, 202-299-0800, bohemiancaverns.com (Walk 10)

Buck's Fishing & Camping 5031 Connecticut Ave. NW, 202-364-0777, bucksfishingandcamping.com (Walk 2)

Busboys and Poets 2021 14th St. NW, 202-387-7638, busboysandpoets.com (Walk 10)

Cashion's Eat Place 1819 Columbia Rd. NW, 202-797-1819, cashionseatplace.com (Walk 9)

C.F. Folks 1225 19th St. NW, 202-293-0162, cffolks.com (Walk 12)

Dangerously Delicious Pies 1339 H St. NE, 202-398-7437, dangerouspiesdc.com (Walk 25)

District Doughnut 749 Eighth St. SE, 202-350-0799, districtdoughnut.com (Walk 26)

Ethiopic Restaurant 401 H St. NE, 202-675-2066, ethiopicrestaurant.com (Walk 25)

Five Guys Burgers and Fries 1100 New Jersey Ave. SE, 202-863-0570, fiveguys.com (Walk 27)

Five Guys Burgers and Fries (formerly Au Pied de Cochon) 1335 Wisconsin Ave. NW, 202-337-0400, fiveguys.com (Walk 6)

Jack Rose Dining Saloon 2007 18th St. NW, 202-588-7388, jackrosediningsaloon.com (Walk 9)

The Gangplank Marina 600 Water St. SW, 202-554-5000, gangplank.com (Walk 21)

- **Cantina Marina** 202-554-8396, cantinamarina.com
- ***Odyssey* cruises** 866-306-2469, odysseycruises.com/Washington-dc
- ***Spirit* Cruises** 866-404-8439,
- ***USS* Sequoia Presidential Yacht** 202-337-7300, sequoiayacht.com

Georgetown Cupcake 3301 M St. NW, 202-333-8448, georgetowncupcake.com (Walk 6)

Granville Moore's 1238 H St. NE, 202-399-2546, granvillemoores.com (Walk 25)

H Street Country Club bar 1335 H St. NE, 202-399-4722, hstreetcountryclub.com (Walk 25)

Iron Gate 1734 N St. NW, 202-524-5202, irongaterestaurantdc.com (Walk 12)

Kramerbooks & Afterwords Cafe & Grill 1517 Connecticut Ave. NW, 202-387-1400, kramers.com (Walk 12)

Lebanese Taverna 2641 Connecticut Ave. NW, 202-265-8681, lebanesetaverna.com (Walk 3)

Little Miss Whiskey's Golden Dollar Bar 1104 H St. NE, littlemisswhiskeys.com (Walk 25)

Lola's Barracks Bar & Grill 711 Eighth St. SE, 202-547-5652, lolasgrilldc.com (Walk 26)

Madam's Organ 2461 18th St. NW, 202-667-5370, madamsorgan.com (Walk 9)

Martin's Tavern 1264 Wisconsin Ave. NW, 202-333-7370, martinstavern.com (Walk 6)

Mintwood Place 1813 Columbia Rd. NW, 202-234-6732, mintwoodplace.com (Walk 9)

Nando's Peri-Peri 300 Tingey St. SE, 202-554-1920, nandosperiperi.com (Walk 27)

Nightclub 9:30 815 V St. NW, 202-265-0930, 930.com (Walk 10)

Osteria Morini at Yards Park 301 Water St. SE, 202-484-0660, osteriamorini.com and yardspark.org (Walk 27)

Peregrine Espresso 660 Pennsylvania Ave. SE, 202-629-4381, peregrineespresso.com (Walk 26)

Perry's 1811 Columbia Road NW, 202-234-6218, perrysadamsmorgan.com (Walk 9)

Rock & Roll Hotel 1353 H St. NE, 202-388-7625, rockandrollhoteldc.com (Walk 25)

Rose's Luxury 717 Eighth St. SE, 202-580-8889, rosesluxury.com (Walk 26)

Seafood markets 1100 Maine Ave. SW (Walk 21)

Sticky Fingers Sweets & Eats (opens late 2015) 406 H St. NE, 202-299-9700, stickyfingersbakery.com (Walk 25)

Sweetgreen 1512 Connecticut Ave. NW, 202-387-9338, sweetgreen.com (Walk 12)

Ted's Bulletin 505 Eighth St. SE, 202-544-8337, tedsbulletincapitolhill.com (Walk 26)

U Street Music Hall 1115 U St. NW, 202-588-1889, ustreetmusichall.com (Walk 10)

The Washington Harbour and Georgetown Waterfront Park restaurants 3000 and 3050 K St. NW, 202-295-5007, thewashingtonharbour.com (Walk 13)

The Wharf 690 Water St. SW, info@swdcwaterfront.com, thewharfdc.com (Walk 21)

educational

Alice Deal Middle School 3815 Fort Dr. NW, 202-939-2010, alicedeal.org (Walk 2)

American University 4400 Massachusetts Ave. NW, 202-885-1000, american.edu (Walk 4)

DC Public Library, Georgetown branch 3260 R St. NW, 202-727-0232, dclibrary.org/georgetown (Walk 5)

DC Public Library, Martin Luther King Jr. Memorial (main) branch 901 G St. NW, 202-727-0321, dclibrary.org/mlk (Walk 17)

DC Public Library, Tenley-Friendship branch 4450 Wisconsin Ave. NW, 202-727-1488, dclibrary.org/tenley (Walk 2)

Gallaudet University 800 Florida Ave. NE, 202-651-5000, gallaudet.edu (Walk 24)

George Washington University (Mount Vernon Campus) Foxhall Road NW and Whitehaven Parkway NW, 202-994-1000, gwu.edu/mount-vernon-campus (Walk 4)

Georgetown University Reservoir Road NW to Prospect Street NW (main entrance: 3700 O St. NW), 202-687-0100, georgetown.edu (Walk 4)

Georgetown University: Joseph Mark Lauinger Memorial Library 37 and N Streets NW, 202-687-7607, library.georgetown.edu/libraries/lauinger (Walk 6)

Historical Society of Washington, D.C. 801 K St. NW, 202-249-3955, dchistory.org (Walk 17)

Howard University 2041 Georgia Ave. NW, 202-865-6100, howard.edu (Walk 10)

Library of Congress's Thomas Jefferson Building 10 First St. SE, 202-707-8000, loc.gov (Walk 23)

Government

Bureau of Alcohol, Tobacco, Firearms and Explosives 99 New York Ave. NE, atf.gov (Walk 24)

Bureau of Engraving and Printing 14 and C Streets SW, 202-874-2330, moneyfactory.gov/home.html (Walk 19)

Central Intelligence Agency's former "Building 213" M Street SE from First Street SE to New Jersey Avenue SE (Walk 27)

Central Intelligence Agency's former headquarters At the United States Department of State annex, 23 and D Streets NW, 202-647-4000, state.gov (Walk 14)

Federal Bureau of Investigation 935 Pennsylvania Ave. NW, 202-324-3000, fbi.gov (Walk 18)

Federal Communications Commission 445 12th St. SW, 888-225-5322, fcc.gov (Walk 21)

Federal Reserve 20th Street NW and Constitution Avenue NW, 202-452-3324, federalreserve.gov (Walk 14)

Federal Trade Commission 600 Pennsylvania Ave. NW, 202-326-2222, ftc.gov (Walk 18)

Fort Lesley J. McNair P Street SW and Third Avenue SW, www.jbmhh.army.mil/web/jbmhh/AboutJBMHH/FortMcNairHistory.html (Walk 21)

General Services Administration 1800 F St. NW, gsa.gov (Walk 15)

Government Printing Office bookstore 710 North Capitol St. NW, 202-512-0132, bookstore.gpo.gov (Walk 24)

Marine Barracks Eighth and I Streets SE, 202-433-4173, www.barracks.marines.mil (Walk 26)

Securities and Exchange Commission 100 F St. NE, 202-942-8088, sec.gov (Walk 25)

Supreme Court of the United States 1 First St. NE, 202-479-3000, supremecourt.gov (Walk 23)

United States Botanic Garden 100 Maryland Ave. SW, 202-225-8333, usbg.gov (Walk 23)

United States Capitol East Capitol St. NE and First St. SE, 202-224-3121 (switchboard), 202-226-8000 (visitor center), visitthecapitol.gov (Walk 23)

United States Department of Agriculture Wing 2, C Street SW west of 12th Street SW, 202-488-7279, www.dm.usda.gov/oo/cafemenu.htm (Walk 19)

United States Department of Homeland Security 3801 Nebraska Ave. NW, 202-282-8000, dhs.gov (Walk 4)

United States Department of Interior 1849 C St. NW, 202-208-3100, doi.gov/index.cfm (Walk 14)

United States Department of Justice 950 Pennsylvania Ave. NW, 202-514-2000, justice.gov (Walk 18)

United States Department of State 2201 C St. NW, 202-647-4000, state.gov (Walk 14)

United States Department of the Treasury 15th Street NW and Hamilton Place NW, treasury.gov (Walk 15)

United States Department of Transportation 1200 New Jersey Ave. SE, 202-366-4000, dot.gov (Walk 27)

United States House of Representatives 202-224-3121, house.gov (Walk 23)

- **Cannon House Office Building** Independence Avenue SE and First Street SE
- **Longworth House Office Building** Independence Avenue SE and South Capitol Street SE
- **Rayburn House Office Building** Independence Avenue SW and First Street SW

United States Immigration and Customs Enforcement 500 12th St. SW, ice.gov (Walk 21)

United States Marine Band Seventh and K Sts. SE, 202-433-4011, www.marineband.marines.mil (Walk 27)

United States Mint 801 Ninth St. NW, 800-USA-MINT, usmint.gov (Walk 17)

United States Naval Observatory and vice president's private residence 3450 Massachusetts Ave. NW, 202-762-1467, www.usno.navy.mil/USNO (Walk 8)

United States Senate 202-224-3121, senate.gov (Walk 23)

Russell Senate Office Building Constitution Avenue NE and Delaware Avenue NE

Dirksen Senate Office Building Constitution Avenue NE and First Street NE

Hart Senate Office Building Constitution Avenue NE and Second Street NE

Washington, D.C., government offices 1100 and 1101 Fourth St. SW, dc.gov (Walk 21)

White House 1600 Pennsylvania Ave. NW, 202-456-1111 (public comment line), 202-456-1414 (switchboard), whitehouse.gov (Walk 15)

Hotels

Four Seasons hotel 2800 Pennsylvania Ave. NW, 202-342-0444, fourseasons.com/washington (Walk 7)

The Hay-Adams 800 16th St. NW, 202-638-6600, hayadams.com (Walk 15)

Hotel Tabard Inn 1739 N St. NW, 202-785-1277, tabardinn.com (Walk 12)

The Jefferson 1200 16th St. NW, 202-448-2300, jeffersondc.com (Walk 16)

Mandarin Oriental 1330 Maryland Ave. SW, 202-554-8588, mandarinoriental.com (Walk 21)

Mayflower Renaissance Washington, DC 1127 Connecticut Ave. NW, 202-347-3000, marriott.com (Walk 16)

Omni Shoreham Hotel 2500 Calvert St. NW, 202-234-0700, omnihotels.com (Walk 3)

Trump International Hotel (Old Post Office Pavilion) 1100 Pennsylvania Ave. NW, 855-878-6700, trumphotelcollection.com/washington-dc (Walk 18)

W Washington D.C. hotel 515 15th St. NW, 202-661-2400, wwashingtondc.com (Walk 15)

Washington Hilton 1919 Connecticut Ave. NW, 202-483-3000, thewashingtonhilton.com (Walk 9)

Washington Marriott Wardman Park Hotel 2660 Woodley Rd. NW, 202-328-2000, marriott.com/hotels/travel/wasdt-washington-marriott-wardman-park (Walk 3)

Wardman Tower Southwest corner of Connecticut Ave. NW and Woodley Rd. NW, wardmantowerdc.com

Watergate Complex 2600 Virginia Ave. NW, watergateeast.com/watergateMall.html (Walk 13)

The Westin Washington, D.C. City Center 1400 M St. NW, 202-429-1700, westinwashingtondccitycenter.com (Walk 16)

The Willard 1401 Pennsylvania Ave. NW, 202-628-9100, washington.intercontinental.com (Walk 15)

International

Angola, Embassy of 2100–2108 16th St. NW, 202-785-1156, angola.org (Walk 11)

Australia, Embassy of 1601 Massachusetts Ave. NW, 202-797-3000, usa.embassy.gov.au (Walk 11)

Belgium, private residence of the ambassador 2300 Foxhall Rd. NW, 202-333-6900 (embassy), countries.diplomatie.belgium.be/en/united_states (Walk 4)

British Embassy 3100 Massachusetts Ave. NW, 202-588-6500, gov.uk/government/world/organisations/british-embassy-washington (Walk 8)

Canada, Embassy of 501 Pennsylvania Ave. NW, 202-682-1740, can-am.gc.ca/washington (Walk 18)

Congo, Embassy of the Republic of 1720 16th St. NW, 202-726-5500, ambacongo-us.org (Walk 11)

Cuba, Embassy of 2630 16 St. NW, 202-797-8518, cubadiplomatica.cu/sicw/EN/Home.aspx (Walk 11)

Denmark, Embassy of 3200 Whitehaven St. NW, 202-234-4300, usa.um.dk (Walk 8)

El Salvador, Embassy of 1400 16th St. NW, 202-595-7500, elsalvador.org (Walk 11)

Equatorial Guinea Embassy 2020 16th St. NW, 202-518-5700, egembassydc.com (Walk 11)

Finland, Embassy of 3301 Massachusetts Ave. NW, 202-298-5800, finland.org (Walk 8)

France, Embassy of 4101 Reservoir Rd. NW, 202-944-6000, ambafrance-us.org (Walk 4)

France, private residence of the ambassador 2221 Kalorama Road NW, 202-944-6000, ambafrance-us.org (Walk 8)

Germany, Embassy and private residence of the ambassador 1800 Foxhall Road NW, 202-298-4000, germany.info/embassy (Walk 4)

Goethe-Institut 812 Seventh St. NW, 202-289-1200, goethe.de/ins/us/was/uun/enindex.htm (Walk 17)

Indonesia, Embassy of the Republic of 2020 Massachusetts Ave. NW, 202-775-5200, embassyofindonesia.org (Walk 8)

Inter-American Defense Board 2600 16th St. NW, 202-939-6041, iadb.jid.org (Walk 11)

Italy, Embassy of 3000 Whitehaven St. NW, 202-612-4400, www.ambwashingtondc.esteri.it/Ambasciata_Washington (Walk 8)

Japan, Embassy of 2520 Massachusetts Ave. NW, 202-238-6700, www.us.emb-japan.go.jp/english/html (Walk 8)

Japan, private residence of the ambassador 4000 Nebraska Ave. NW, 202-238-6900 (Japan Information Center), www.us.emb-japan.go.jp/jicc/index.html (Walk 4)

Kazakhstan, Embassy of the Republic of 1401 16th St. NW, 202-232-5488, kazakhembus.com (Walk 11)

Lithuania, Embassy of the Republic of 2622 16th St. NW, 202-234-5860, usa.mfa.lt/usa/en (Walk 11)

Meridian International Center 1630 Crescent Place NW, 202-667-6800, meridian.org (Walk 11)

Mexican Cultural Institute 2829 16th St. NW, 202-728-1628, instituteofmexicodc.org (Walk 11)

Organization of American States 17th Street and Constitution Avenue NW, 202-370-5000, oas.org/en/about/our_locations.asp (Walk 14)

Peru, private residence of ambassador 3001 Garrison St. NW, 202-833-9860 (embassy), embassyofperu.org/residence (Walk 2)

Poland, Embassy of the Republic of 2640 16th St. NW, 202-499-1700, polandembassy.org (Walk 11)

Russian Federation, Embassy of the 2650 Wisconsin Ave. NW, 202-298-5700, russianembassy.org (Walk 8)

Russian Federation, private residence of the ambassador 1125 16th St. NW, 202-298-5700, russianembassy.org (Walk 16)

Spain, private residence of the ambassador 2350 Foxhall Road NW, 202-452-0100 (embassy), spainemb.org (Walk 4)

Switzerland, Embassy of 2900 Cathedral Ave. NW, 202-745-7900, www.eda.admin.ch/washington (Walk 3)

Sweden, Embassy of 2900 K St. NW, 202-467-2600, houseofsweden.com/en/House-Of-Sweden (Walk 13)

Sweden, private residence of the ambassador 3900 Nebraska Ave. NW, 202-467-2600 (embassy), swedenabroad.com (Walk 4)

The World Bank 1818 H St. NW, 202-473-1000, worldbank.org (Walk 15)

Monuments and Memorials

African American Civil War Memorial & Museum 1925 Vermont Ave. NW, 202-667-2667, afroamcivilwar.org (Walk 10)

Bust of William O. Douglas Chesapeake & Ohio Canal between Thomas Jefferson and 30 Sts. NW, 301-767-3714, nps.gov/choh/planyourvisit/georgetownvisitorcenter.htm (Walk 7)

DC War Memorial North side of Independence Ave. SW between the World II Memorial and the Lincoln Memorial, 202-426-6841, nps.gov/nama/planyourvisit/dc-war-memorial.htm (Walk 14)

Franklin Delano Roosevelt Memorial 400 West Basin Dr. SW, 202-426-6841, nps.gov/frde (Walk 19)

John Ericsson National Memorial 23rd St. and Ohio Dr. SW, 202-426-6841, nps.gov/joer (Walk 20)

George Mason Memorial Ohio and East Basin Drives SW, 202-426-6841, nps.gov/gemm (Walk 20)

Korean War Veterans Memorial North side of Independence Ave. SW between the DC War Memorial and the Lincoln Memorial, 202-426-6841, nps.gov/kowa (Walk 14)

Lincoln Memorial and reflecting pool 23rd St. NW between Constitution Ave. NW and Independence Ave. SW, 202-426-6841, nps.gov/nama/planyourvisit/lincoln-memorial-reflecting-pool.htm (Walk 14)

Lyndon Baines Johnson Memorial Grove Columbia Island, 202-289-2500, nps.gov/lyba (Walk 20)

Martin Luther King Jr. Memorial 1850 West Basin Dr. SW, 202-426-6841, nps.gov/mlkm (Walk 19)

National Law Enforcement Memorial E St. between Fourth and Fifth Sts. NW, 202-737-3400, nleomf.org/memorial (Walk 17)

Navy and Marine Memorial Mount Vernon Trail northwest of the 14th Street bridge, 703-289-2500, nps.gov/gwmp/planyourvisit/brochures.htm (Walk 20)

Thomas Jefferson Memorial East Basin Dr. SW at Ohio Dr. SW, 202-426-6841, nps.gov/thje (Walk 19)

***Titanic* Memorial** Alongside the Washington Channel at the sidewalk leading to P St. SW (Walk 21)

The United States Navy Memorial 701 Pennsylvania Ave. NW, 202-737-2300, navymemorial.org (Walk 18)

Vietnam Veterans Memorial and Vietnam Women's Memorial 22nd St. and Constitution Ave. NW, 202-426-6841, nps.gov/vive (Walk 14)

Washington Monument 2 15th St. NW, 202-426-6841, nps.gov/wamo (Walk 22)

World War II Memorial 17th St. SW between Constitution Ave. NW and Independence Ave. SW, 202-426-6841, nps.gov/nwwm (Walk 14)

MUSEUMS AND GALLERIES

Arthur M. Sackler Gallery 1050 Independence Ave. SW, 202-633-4880, asia.si.edu (Walk 22)

Arts and Industries Building (reopening 2016) 900 Jefferson Dr. SW, 202-633-1000, si.edu/Museums/arts-and-industries-building (Walk 22)

Brookland Artspace Lofts 3305 Eighth St. NE, 301-927-3586, artspace.org/our-places/brookland-artspace-lofts (Walk 30)

Christian Heurich House Museum 1307 New Hampshire Ave. NW, 202-429-1894, heurichhouse.org (Walk 12)

Corcoran Gallery of Art 500 17th St. NW, 202-639-1700, corcoran.org (Walk 15)

Dance Place 3225 Eighth St. NE, 202-269-1600, danceplace.org (Walk 30)

Decatur House 1610 H St. NW, 202-842-0917, whitehousehistory.org/decatur-house (Walk 15)

District of Columbia Arts Center 2438 18th St. NW, 202-462-7833, dcartscenter.org (Walk 9)

Donald W. Reynolds Center for American Art and Portraiture Eighth and F Sts. NW, 202-633-7970, americanart.si.edu (Walk 17)

Dumbarton Oaks Research Library and Collection 1703 32nd St. NW, 202-339-6401, doaks.org (Walk 5)

Folger Shakespeare Library 201 E. Capitol St. SE, 202-544-4600, folger.edu (Walk 23)

Freer Gallery of Art Jefferson Dr. SW and 12th St. SW, 202-633-4880, asia.si.edu (Walk 22)

Hill Center at the Old Naval Hospital 921 Pennsylvania Ave. SE, 202-549-4172, hillcenterdc.org/home (Walk 26)

Hirshhorn Museum and Sculpture Garden Seventh St. SW and Independence Ave. SW, 202-633-4674, hirshhorn.si.edu (Walk 22)

International Spy Museum 800 F St. NW, 202-393-7798, spymuseum.org (Walk 17)

The Kreeger Museum 2401 Foxhall Rd. NW, 202-337-3050, kreegermuseum.org (Walk 4)

Madame Tussauds 1001 F St. NW, 866-823-9565, madametussauds.com/washington (Walk 18)

National Archives and Records Administration 700 Pennsylvania Ave. NW, 202-357-5000, archives.gov (Walk 18)

National Building Museum 401 F St. NW, 202-272-2448, nbm.org (Walk 17)

National Gallery of Art, East Building Fourth St. NW and Constitution Ave. NW, 202-633-1000, nga.gov (Walk 22)

National Gallery of Art, West Building Sixth St. NW and Constitution Ave. NW, 202-633-1000, nga.gov (Walk 22)

National Gallery of Art, Sculpture Garden Ninth St. NW and Constitution Ave. NW, 202-633-1000, nga.gov (Walk 22)

National Museum of African American History and Culture (opens 2016) 1400 Constitution Ave. NW, 202-633-1000, nmaahc.si.edu (Walk 22)

National Museum of African Art 950 Independence Ave. SW, 202-633-4600, africa.si.edu (Walk 22)

National Museum of American History 14th St. NW and Constitution Ave. NW, 202-633-1000, americanhistory.si.edu (Walk 22)

National Museum of the American Indian Fourth St. SW and Independence Ave. SW, 202-633-6644, nmai.si.edu (Walk 22)

National Museum of Women in the Arts 1250 New York Ave. NW, 202-783-5000, nmwa.org (Walk 16)

National Postal Museum 2 Massachusetts Ave. NE, 202-633-5555, postalmuseum.si.edu (Walk 24)

Newseum 500 Pennsylvania Ave. NW, 202-292-6100, newseum.org (Walk 18)

The Old Stone House 3051 M St. NW, 202-895-6070, nps.gov/olst (Walk 7)

The Phillips Collection 1600 21st St. NW, 202-387-2151, phillipscollection.org (Walk 8)

President Lincoln's Cottage Upshur St. NW and Rock Creek Church Rd. NW, 202-829-0436, lincolncottage.org (Walk 30)

The President Woodrow Wilson House 2340 S St. NW, 202-387-4062, woodrowwilsonhouse.org (Walk 8)

Renwick Gallery of the Smithsonian American Art Museum 1661 Pennsylvania Ave. NW, 202-633-7970, americanart.si.edu/renwick (Walk 15)

Sewall-Belmont House & Museum 144 Constitution Ave. NE, 202-546-1210, sewallbelmont.org (Walk 23)

Smithsonian Institution Building (The Castle) 1000 Jefferson Dr. SW, 202-633-1000, si.edu (Walk 22)

The Society of the Cincinnati headquarters and museum 2118 Massachusetts Ave. NW, 202-785-2040, societyofthecincinnati.org (Walk 8)

Tudor Place Historic House & Garden 1644 31st St. NW, 202-965-0400, tudorplace.org (Walk 5)

United States Holocaust Memorial Museum 100 Raoul Wallenberg Place SW, 202-488-0400, ushmm.org (Walk 19)

Washington Navy Yard's National Museum of the US Navy Sixth and M Sts. SE, 202-433-4882, history.navy.mil/museums/NationalMuseum/org8-1.htm (Walk 27)

News Media

ABC News 1717 DeSales St. NW, 212-456-7777, abcnews.go.com (Walk 16)

Bloomberg News 1399 New York Ave. NW, 212-318-2000, bloomberg.com (Walk 16)

Boston Globe 1130 Connecticut Ave. NW, 888-694-5623, bostonglobe.com (Walk 16)

CNN 820 First St. NE, 202-898-7900, cnn.com (Walk 24)

Corporation for Public Broadcasting 401 Ninth St. NW, 202-879-9600, cpb.org (Walk 18)

C-SPAN 400 N. Capitol St. NW, Suite 650, 202-737-3220, c-span.org (Walk 23)

Hearst News Service 700 12th St. NW, 212-649-2000, hearst.com (Walk 16)

The McClatchy Company 700 12th St. NW, 916-321-1855, mcclatchydc.com (Walk 16)

National Press Club 529 14th St. NW, 202-662-7500, press.org (Walk 18)

National Public Radio (NPR) 1111 N. Capitol St. NE, 202-513-2000, npr.org (Walk 24)

NBC4 Washington and NBC News 4001 Nebraska Ave. NW, 202-885-4000, nbcwashington.com (Walk 4)

New York Times 1627 Eye St. NW, 888-698-6397, nytimes.com (Walk 16)

Reuters News Agency 1333 H St. NW, 646-223-4000, reuters.com (Walk 16)

Voice of America 330 Independence Ave. SW, 202-203-4990 (tours), voanews.com (Walk 18)

Wall Street Journal 1025 Connecticut Ave. NW, 800-568-7625, wsj.com (Walk 16)

***Washington Post* (future)** 1301 K St. NW, 202-334-6000, washingtonpost.com (Walk 16)

***Washington Post* (until 2016)** 1150 15th St. NW, 202-334-6000, washingtonpost.com (Walk 16)

Parks, Gardens, and Nature

Anacostia Riverwalk Trail Anacostia River, anacostiawaterfront.org (Walk 27)

Canal Park 202 M St. SE, 202-465-7012, canalparkdc.org (Walk 27)

East Potomac Park cherry trees Ohio Dr. SW, 202-426-6841, nps.gov/cherry (Walks 19 and 20)

Fort Bayard Western Ave. NW and River Rd. NW, nps.gov/cwdw/historyculture/fort-bayard.htm (Walk 1)

Fort Bunker Hill Park 14th St. NE and Perry St. NE, 202-895-6070, nps.gov/cwdw/historyculture/fort-bunker-hill.htm (Walk 30)

Fort Reno Park Chesapeake St. NW and Nebraska Ave. NW, 202-895-6000, nps.gov/cwdw/historyculture/fort-reno.htm (Walk 2)

Glover-Archbold Trail Reservoir Rd. NW at 44th St. NW, 202-895-6000, nps.gov/rocr (Walk 4)

Japanese stone lantern Independence Ave. SW at the Tidal Basin southwest of 17th St. SW, 202-426-6841, nps.gov/cherry and nationalcherryblossomfestival.org (Walk 19)

Kenilworth Park and Aquatic Gardens 1550 Anacostia Ave. NE, 202-426-6905, nps.gov/keaq (Walk 28)

Lady Bird Johnson Park Columbia Island, 703-289-2500, nps.gov/gwmp/planyourvisit/ladybirdjohnsonpark.htm (Walk 20)

Lafayette Park and President's Park H St. NW to Pennsylvania Ave. NW and Madison Place NW to Jackson Place NW, 202-208-1631, nps.gov/whho (Walk 15)

Lockkeeper's House 17th St. and Constitution Ave. NW, 202-426-6841, nps.gov/nr/travel/wash/dc34.htm (Walk 14)

McPherson Square 13th to 14th Sts. NW between I and K Sts. NW (Walk 16)

Meridian Hill Park 16th St. NW to 15th St. NW and W St. NW to Euclid St. NW, 202-895-6070, nps.gov/mehi (Walk 11)

Mount Vernon Trail Along the Potomac River from Key Bridge in Arlington, Virginia, to Mount Vernon, Virginia, 703-289-2500, nps.gov/pohe/planyourvisit/nova-hike-3.htm (Walk 13)

Potomac riverfront walkway From Washington Harbour complex to Key Bridge, 202-895-6070, georgetownwaterfrontpark.org (Walk 13)

Smithsonian National Zoological Park 3001 Connecticut Ave. NW, 202-633-4888, nationalzoo.si.edu (Walk 3)

Theodore Roosevelt Island George Washington Memorial Parkway, south of Key Bridge on west side of the Potomac River, 703-289-2500, nps.gov/this (Walk 13)

Tregaron Conservancy Klingle Rd. NW and Cortland Place NW, tregaronconservancy.org (Walk 3)

U.S. National Arboretum 3501 New York Ave. NE, 202-245-2726, usna.usda.gov (Walk 29)

Wesley Heights Trail (National Park Service) Foxhall Rd. NW at Edmunds St. NW, 202-895-6000, nps.gov/rocr (Walk 4)

West Potomac Park Polo Grounds Ohio Dr. SW, 202-426-6841, nps.gov/nacc (Walk 20)

Political Parties, Polls, and Think Tanks

American Enterprise Institute 1789 Massachusetts Ave. NW, 202-862-5800, aei.org (Walk 12)

Brookings Institution 1775 Massachusetts Ave NW, 202-797-6000, brookings.edu (Walk 12)

Democratic National Committee 430 South Capitol St. SE, 202-863-8000, democrats.org (Walk 23)

Gallup corporation 901 F St. NW, 202-715-3030, gallup.com (Walk 17)

Republican National Committee 310 First St. SE, 202-863-8500, gop.com (Walk 23)

Woman's National Democratic Club in The Whittemore House 1526 New Hampshire Ave. NW, 202-232-7363, democraticwoman.org (Walk 12)

Religious

All Souls Church Unitarian 1500 Harvard St. NW, 202-332-5266, all-souls.org (Walk 11)

Basilica of the National Shrine of the Immaculate Conception 400 Michigan Ave. NE, 202-526-8300, nationalshrine.com (Walk 30)

The Catholic University of America 620 Michigan Ave. NE, 202-319-5000, cua.edu (Walk 30)

Christ Church Georgetown 31 and O Sts. NW, 202-333-6677, christchurchgeorgetown.org (Walk 7)

Franciscan Monastery of the Holy Land in America 1400 Quincy St. NE, 202-526-6800, myfranciscan.org (Walk 30)

The Islamic Center 2551 Massachusetts Ave. NW, 202-332-8343, islamiccenterdc.com (Walk 8)

Mt. Zion United Methodist Church 1334 29th St. NW, 202-234-0148, mtzionumcdc.org (Walk 7)

National Baptist Memorial Church 1501 Columbia Rd. NW, 202-265-1410, nbmchurchdc.org (Walk 11)

Saint John Paul II National Shrine 3900 Harewood Rd. NE, 202-635-5400, jp2shrine.org (Walk 30)

St. John's Church 1525 H St. NW, 202-347-8766, stjohns-dc.org (Walk 15)

St. John's Episcopal Church 3240 O St. NW, 202-338-1796, stjohnsgeorgetown.org (Walk 6)

Washington DC Jewish Community Center 1529 16th St. NW, 202-518-9400, washingtondcjcc.org (Walk 11)

Washington Family (Unification) Church 1610 Columbia Rd. NW, 202-462-5700, unification.net/ucdc (Walk 11)

Washington National Cathedral 3101 Wisconsin Ave. NW, 202-537-6200, nationalcathedral.org (Walk 3)

Science

Capitalsaurus Court First and F Sts. SE, dccode.org/simple/sections/1-161.html (Walk 23)

Carnegie Institution for Science 5241 Broad Branch Rd. NW, 202-387-6400, carnegiescience.edu (Walk 2)

Carnegie Institution for Science 1530 P St. NW, 202-387-8092, carnegiescience.edu (Walk 11)

Geological fault NW side of Adams Mill Rd. NW at Clydesdale Place NW, nationalzoo.si.edu/AboutUs/History/beneathitall.cfm (Walk 9)

National Academy of Sciences 525 E St. NW, 202-334-1201, koshland-science-museum.org (Walk 17)

National Academy of Sciences headquarters and the Einstein Memorial 2101 Constitution Ave. NW, 202-334-2000, nasonline.org (Walk 14)

National Air and Space Museum Sixth St. SW and Independence Ave. SW, 202-633-2214, airandspace.si.edu (Walk 22)

National Geographic 1145 17th St. NW, 202-857-7588, nationalgeographic.com (Walk 16)

National Museum of Natural History 10th St. NW and Constitution Ave. NW, 202-633-1000, mnh.si.edu (Walk 22)

SHOPPING

The Brass Knob Architectural Antiques 2311 18th St. NW, 202-332-3370, thebrassknob.com (Walk 9)

Crooked Beat Records 2116 18th St. NW, 202-483-2328, crookedbeat.com (Walk 9)

Eastern Market 225 Seventh St. SE, 202-698-5253, easternmarket-dc.org (Walk 26)

Eastern Market Flea Market Seventh and C Sts. SE, 703-534-7612, easternmarket.net (Walk 26)

Fleet Feet Sports 1841 Columbia Rd. NW, 202-387-3888, fleetfeetdc.com (Walk 9)

Hill's Kitchen 713 D St. SE, 202-543-1997, hillskitchen.com (Walk 26)

Mazza Gallerie 5300 Wisconsin Ave. NW, 202-966-6114, mazzagallerie.com (Walk 1)

Pacers Running 300 Tingey St. SE, runpacers.com (Walk 27)

Politics and Prose 5015 Connecticut Ave. NW, 202-364-1919, politics-prose.com (Walk 2)

REI (opens 2016) 1140 Third St. NE, rei.com (Walk 24)

Shopping centers 5333 and 5335 Wisconsin Ave. NW (Walk 1)

Toro Mata 2410 18th St. NW, 202-232-3890, toromata.com (Walk 9)

Union Market 1309 Fifth St. NE, 301-652-7400, unionmarketdc.com (Walk 24)

World Bank InfoShop 701 18th St. NW, 202-458-4500, worldbank.org/infoshop (Walk 15)

SPORTS AND RECREATION

Ballpark Boathouse 202-337-9642, boatingindc.com (Walk 27)

Columbia Island Marina George Washington Memorial Parkway, 202-347-0173, columbiaisland.com (Walk 20)

Docks at Diamond Teague Park First St. SE and Potomac Ave. SE (Walk 27)

East Potomac Tennis Center 1090 Ohio Dr. SW, 202-554-5962, eastpotomactennis.com (Walk 19)

Nationals Park stadium 1500 S. Capitol St. SE, 202-640-7369 (tours), 202-675-6287 (tickets), washington.nationals.mlb.com/was/ballpark (Walk 27)

Potomac Riverboat Company 703-684-0580, potomacriverboatco.com (Walk 27)

Thompson Boat Center 2900 Virginia Ave. NW, 202-333-9543, thompsonboatcenter.com (Walk 13)

Trapeze School New York Fourth and Tingey Sts. SE, 410-459-6839, washingtondc.trapezeschool.com (Walk 27)

Verizon Center 601 F St. NW, 202-628-3200, verizoncenter.monumentalnetwork.com (Walk 17)

Structures

Arlington Memorial Bridge Ohio Dr. SW at Lincoln Memorial and George Washington Memorial Pkwy. just east of Arlington Memorial Cemetery to the Lincoln Memorial, nps.gov/nr/travel/wash/dc69.htm (Walk 13)

Exorcist Steps 36th St. NW, between M and Prospect Sts. NW, maps.georgetown.edu/exorciststeps (Walk 6)

Francis Scott Key Bridge and park M and 35th Sts. NW, nps.gov/olst/planyourvisit/keypark.htm (Walk 13)

Friendship Arch H and Seventh Sts. NW (Walk 17)

Pedestrian bridge to the Pentagon Columbia Island (Walk 20)

Washington, D.C., Boundary Stone NW6 Boundary Park Neighborhood Conservation Area, 5000 Western Ave., Chevy Chase, MD, boundarystones.org/view.php?stone=NW6 (Walk 1)

Watergate Steps Ohio Dr. SW between the American Legion Bridge and Rock Creek and Potomac Parkway NW, nps.gov/linc/parkmgmt/upload/LIME_CLR_Chap4_(14).pdf (Walk 13)

Zero Milestone on the Ellipse By the South Lawn of the White House, fhwa.dot.gov/infrastructure/zero.cfm (Walk 15)

Theaters

Arena Stage 1101 Sixth St. SW, 202-554-9066, arenastage.org (Walk 21)

Atlas Performing Arts Center 1333 H St. NE, 202-399-7993, atlasarts.org (Walk 25)

Ford's Theatre 511 10th St. NW, 202-347-4833, fordstheatre.org (Walk 18)

The Howard Theatre 620 T St. NW, 202-803-2899, thehowardtheatre.com (Walk 10)

The Kennedy Center 2700 F St. NW, 202-467-4600, kennedy-center.org (Walk 13)

Lincoln Theater 1215 U St. NW, 202-888-0050, thelincolndc.com (Walk 10)

National Theatre 1321 Pennsylvania Ave. NW, 202-628-6161, nationaltheatre.org (Walk 18)

Shakespeare Theatre Company 610 F St. NW, 202-547-1122, shakespearetheatre.org (Walk 17)

Shakespeare Theatre Company 450 Seventh St. NW, 202-547-1122, shakespearetheatre.org (Walk 17)

The Source Theatre 1835 14th St. NW, 202-315-1305, culturaldc.org (Walk 10)

Warner Theatre 513 13th St. NW, 202-783-4000, warnertheatredc.com (Walk 18)

Woolly Mammoth Theatre Company 641 D St. NW, 202-393-3939, woollymammoth.net (Walk 17)

Transit

Capital Bikeshare H Street NE at 3rd, 6th, 11th, and 13th Sts. NE and Union Station, 877-430-2453, capitalbikeshare.com (Walk 25 and citywide)

Union Station 40 Massachusetts Ave. NE, 202-289-1908, unionstationdc.com

Washington Metropolitan Area Transit Authority 202-637-7000, wmata.com (Walks 23, 24, and 25)

Visitor Information

Destination DC 901 Seventh St. NW, 202-789-7000, washington.org (Walk 17)

U Street Visitor Center 1211 U St. NW, culturaltourismdc.org (Walk 10)

White House Visitor Center 1450 Pennsylvania Ave. NW, 202-208-1631, nps.gov/whho (Walk 15)

Appendix 3: Further Reading

Books

Applewhite, E.J. ***Washington Itself.*** Lanham, MD: Madison Books, 1993. Insider's guide to classic D.C.

Berman, Richard L. and Deborah Gerhard. ***Natural Washington.*** McLean, VA: EPM Publications, 1994. Parks and other natural attractions in D.C., MD, VA, and WV.

Choukas-Bradley, Melanie. ***City of Trees: The Complete Field Guide to the Trees of Washington, D.C.*** Charlottesville and London: University of Virginia Press, 2008. Types of trees in D.C. and where to find them.

Fleming, Cristol, Marion Blois Lobstein, and Barbara Tufty. ***Finding Wildflowers in the Washington-Baltimore Area.*** Baltimore: The Johns Hopkins University Press, 1995. Where to find wildflowers in the DMV.

Kessler, Pamela. ***Undercover Washington.*** Sterling, Virginia: Capital Books, 2005. Famous spies who lived, worked, and loved in the District.

Means, John. ***Roadside Geology of Maryland, Delaware, and Washington, D.C.*** Missoula, Montana: Mountain Press Publishing Company, 2010. Guide to local geology.

Moeller, Martin G. Jr. ***AIA Guide to the Architecture of Washington, D.C.*** Baltimore: The Johns Hopkins University Press, 2012. Key buildings in the nation's capital.

Protopappas, John J. and Judith Meany, eds. ***Washington on Foot.*** Washington, DC: Smithsonian Books, 2012. Architecture-focused walking tours of Washington, D.C.; Old Town Alexandria, VA; and Takoma Park, MD. (Published with the National Capital Area Chapter American Planning Association.)

Schneider Smith, Kathryn, ed. ***Washington at Home: An Illustrated History of Neighborhoods in the Nation's Capital.*** Baltimore: The Johns Hopkins University Press, 2010. Historical look at D.C.'s neighborhoods.

Scott, Pamela and Antoinette J. Lee. ***Buildings of the District of Columbia.*** New York and Oxford: Oxford University Press, 1993. Society of Architectural Historians' guide to D.C. and its architecture.

Villegas, Benjamin. ***Embassy Residences in Washington, D.C.*** Bogota: VillegasAsociados, 2003. Illustrated guide to the residences of Washington's ambassadors.

Wilds, Claudia. ***Finding Birds in the National Capital Area.*** Washington, DC: Smithsonian Institution Press, 1992. When, where, and how to find the more than 350 species of birds in D.C. and itssuburbs.

Youth, Howard. ***Field Guide to the Natural World of Washington, D.C.*** Baltimore: The Johns Hopkins University Press, 2014. Washington's wildlife and parks.

Websites

Cultural Tourism, DC
culturaltourismdc.org
Neighborhood heritage trail guides, Passport DC embassy tour, and much more.

Destination, DC
washington.org
Washington's official tourism association.

Federal Government
usa.gov
Citizen-oriented links to the White House, Congress, and agencies.

Historical Society of Washington, D.C.
dchistory.org
Nonprofit, member-based educational and research group.

National Park Service, Washington, D.C.
nps.gov/state/dc

Smithsonian Institution
si.edu
Museums, membership, events, research centers, and more.

Washington City Paper
washingtoncitypaper.com
Alternative weekly newspaper.

Washington, D.C. city government (official site)
dc.gov

Washington Post
washingtonpost.com
D.C.'s Pulitzer-prize winning daily newspaper of record.

Washingtonian
washingtonian.com
Monthly magazine

INDEX

K

L

M

Q

R

S

about the author

Barbara J. Saffir felt like a full-fledged Washingtonian the first time she chose to put a call from the White House on hold to take another call. She has been exploring D.C.'s urban treasures and its softer side for the *Washington Post*, other publications, and herself for three decades. That involved chasing a White House limo through a courthouse garage; strapping herself in a two-seater, wooden World War II airplane; interviewing politicos and bureaucrats; and unearthing gems from government offices, archives, and libraries. All the while she was biking, hiking, running, and paddling through the District's streets, parks, trails, and rivers. As a former reporter, political researcher, architecture critic, and nature photographer, she has always adored sharing adventures and discoveries that inspire people to say, "Wow!"